FAITH AND FREEDOM

Challenges in Contemporary Theology

Series Editors: Gareth Jones and Lewis Ayres
Canterbury Christ Church University College, UK and Emory University, US

Challenges in Contemporary Theology is a series aimed at producing clear orientations in, and research on, areas of "challenge" in contemporary theology. These carefully co-ordinated books engage traditional theological concerns with mainstreams in modern thought and culture that challenge those concerns. The "challenges" implied are to be understood in two senses: those presented by society to contemporary theology, and those posed by theology to society.

Published

Forthcoming

FAITH AND FREEDOM
An Interfaith Perspective

David Burrell

Blackwell
Publishing

© 2004 by David Burrell

BLACKWELL PUBLISHING
350 Main Street, Malden, MA 02148-5020, USA
108 Cowley Road, Oxford OX4 1JF, UK
550 Swanston Street, Carlton, Victoria 3053, Australia

The right of David Burrell to be identified as the Author of this Work has been asserted in accordance with the UK Copyright, Designs, and Patents Act 1988.

First published 2004 by Blackwell Publishing Ltd

Library of Congress Cataloging-in-Publication Data

Burrell, David B.
    Faith and freedom : an interfaith perspective / David Burrell.
        p.   cm. — (Challenges in contemporary theology)
    Includes bibliographical references and index.
    ISBN 1-4051-2170-X (hardcover : alk. paper) — ISBN 1-4051-2171-8 (pbk. : alk. paper)
    1. Philosophical theology.   2. Creation–Comparative studies.
3. Liberty–Religious aspects–Comparative studies.   I. Title.
II. Series.

    BT55.B87 2004
    231—dc22

                                                    2004003094

A catalogue record for this title is available from the British Library.

Set in 10.5 on 12.5 pt Bembo
by SNP Best-set Typesetter Ltd., Hong Kong
Printed and bound in the United Kingdom
by TJ International Ltd, Padstow, Cornwall

The publisher's policy is to use permanent paper from mills that operate a sustainable forestry policy, and which has been manufactured from pulp processed using acid-free and elementary chlorine-free practices. Furthermore, the publisher ensures that the text paper and cover board used have met acceptable environmental accreditation standards.

For further information on
Blackwell Publishing, visit our website:
www.blackwellpublishing.com

CONTENTS

PREFACE

I have become increasingly convinced that human freedom is one of the least understood features of our existence, and that largely because it has been (especially in a capitalist culture) unduly limited to choosing. In fact, it seems that the major decisions of our lives have a kind of inevitability about them. A corollary of restricting freedom to choosing is a valuation of *choice* for its own sake, with little or no attention to its *telos*. My conviction is that this distortion of our views on human freedom, while congenial to and perhaps contributory to a capitalist culture, has its roots in the imperative of modernity to remove a free creator from the scene, and with that drastic elision, any hope of recovering that metaphysical perspective on freedom associated with ancient philosophy – Platonic, Aristotelian, Stoic, or Plotinian. It was these frameworks which Augustine and Aquinas employed to characterize human freedom, as did Maimonides and al-Ghazali. What has replaced them is a theory of freedom dubbed "libertarian," which identifies *freedom* with *autonomy*, so defined as to demand that a free agent parallel a creator *ex nihilo*, thereby making of free action an act initiated totally by the self, and so vulnerable to countless counter-examples of "external influence."

Alternatively, classical views of freedom see it as a response to the gift of being, whereby persons are drawn to return what they have received; ideally, even returning everything to the One from whom they have received everything. Such a view is inherently teleological, yet includes choosing as an integral part since the means to this inbuilt end cannot be determined antecedently. The fact that the orientation to an end is inbuilt has been offensive to moderns, and hence their concoction of a "libertarian" freedom. I hope, through these chapters taken cumulatively, to replace that theory with a far more robust account of human freedom which, while requiring a heftier metaphysical commitment, remains more phenomenologically accurate than the modernist theory it seeks to supplant.

Jews, Christians, and Muslims can ground the classical view of freedom in the free creation of the universe, buttressing our inbuilt orientation to the good as a return to the one from whom all comes as gift. Distinctively free human initiative then becomes a response to the call of existence, whereby through discrete actions one seeks to return everything to the One from whom they have received everything. Such a view of freedom will require, however, that we say something coherent about this grounding "fact" of free creation, and do so in such a say that the admittedly ineffable relation of creatures to creator does not entail competition. My Abrahamic guides – al-Ghazali, Moses Maimonides, and Thomas Aquinas – each developed ways of tracing that interaction, and we shall see how they involve an understanding of the creator adequately distinct from a creation which cannot *be* separate from it. The Prologue will set the scene for a journey which will make various attempts to articulate this grounding relation.

Decades of inquiry gather sweet debts of gratitude to those who have helped one along. Yet they are so densely interlocking that I shall limit myself to three mentors, then noting coworkers who have brought this edition to its completion. Years in Rome from 1956 to 1960 brought me in contact with Bernard Lonergan, S.J., whose mode of inquiry has shaped my own in subterranean ways. He was wont to divide the world into those who quest after truth and those who need certitude, and that pregnant divider has continued to steer my inquiry into intercultural and interfaith explorations. Later, in Jerusalem and Cairo, Marcel Dubois, O.P. and Georges Anawati, O.P. have guided me into the complementary domains of Jewish and of Islamic philosophical theology. Beyond these three, interlocutors young and old, from Notre Dame to Bangladesh and places in between (like Cambridge and Utrecht), have prodded me to reflect again and again on these recondite issues, often witnessing to a proper way to continue when one felt quite unable to say anything.

Most recently, Lewis Ayres and Rebecca Harkin solicited this endeavor by an offer to publish, while Steven Schweitzer and Kristin Brantman Colberg have contributed mightily to bringing it to completion. The inadequacies remain my own, but that simply allows us all room to continue to quest after the truth of these hidden things.

ACKNOWLEDGMENTS

With the exception of the Prologue, all the essays in this volume have appeared in other settings, and have been included here with minor revisions. Where the copyright lies with the earlier publisher, I am grateful for permission to reproduce the material here. Publication details are:

"Distinguishing God from the World," in Brian Davies, O.P., ed., *Language, Meaning and God: Essays in Honour of Herbert McCabe, O.P.* (London: Geoffrey Chapman, 1987), pp. 75–91.

"The Unknowability of God in al-Ghazali," in *Religious Studies* 23 (1987), pp. 171–82.

"Why not Pursue the Metaphor of Artisan and View God's Knowledge as Practical?," in Lenn E. Goodman, ed., *Neoplatonism and Jewish Thought* (Albany NY: State University of New York Press, 1992), pp. 207–16.

"Maimonides, Aquinas and Gersonides on Providence and Evil," in *Religious Studies* 20 (1984), pp. 335–51.

"Aquinas' Debt to Maimonides," in Ruth Link-Salinger et al., eds, *A Straight Path: Studies in Medieval Philosophy and Culture* (Washington DC: Catholic University of America Press, 1989), pp. 37–48.

"Creation and 'Actualism': The Dialectical Dimension of Philosophical Theology," in *Medieval Philosophy and Theology* 4 (1994), pp. 25–41.

"Aquinas and Scotus: Contrary Patterns for Philosophical Theology," in Bruce D. Marshall, ed., *Theology and Dialogue: Essays in Honor of George Lindbeck* (Notre Dame IN: University of Notre Dame Press, 1990), pp. 105–30.

"From Analogy of 'Being' to the Analogy of Being," in Thomas Hibbs and John O'Callaghan, eds, *Recovering Nature: Essays in natural philosophy, ethics and metaphysics in honor of Ralph McInerny* (Notre Dame IN: University of Notre Dame Press, 1999).

"The Challenge to Medieval Christian Philosophy: Relating Creator to Creatures," in John Inglis, ed., *Medieval Philosophy and the Classical Tradition in Islam, Judaism, and Christianity* (Richmond: Curzon, 2002).

"Freedom and Creation in the Abrahamic Traditions," in *International Philosophical Quarterly* 40 (2000), pp. 161–71.

"Al-Ghazali on Created Freedom," in *American Catholic Philosophical Quarterly* 73 (1999), pp. 135–57.

"Creation, Will and Knowledge in Aquinas and Duns Scotus," in *Pragmatik I* (Hamburg: Felix Meiner, 1986), pp. 246–57.

"God, Religious Pluralism, and Dialogic Encounter," in Rebecca Chopp and Mark Lewis Taylor, eds, *Reconstructing Christian Theology* (Minneapolis: Fortress, 1994), pp. 49–78.

"The Christian Distinction Celebrated and Expanded," in John Drummond and James Hart, eds, *The Truthful and the Good* (Dordrecht: Kluwer Academic Publishers, 1996), pp. 191–206.

"Incarnation and Creation: The Hidden Dimension," in *Modern Theology* 12 (1996), pp. 211–20.

"Assessing Statements of Faith: Augustine and Etty Hillesum," in Gregory D. Pritchard, ed., *Hermeneutics, Religious Pluralism, and Truth* (Wake Forest, NC: Wake Forest University Press, 1989), pp. 35–50.

A Note on Sources

The advantage of standard references is that readers can use any edition. Yet those references may need explanation.

For Plato, the standard numerical reference is to the Stephanus edition; for Aristotle, to the Becker edition. These numbers will be found alongside the page in any edition.

For Augustine, *Confessions* 5.26 = book 5, paragraph 26.

For Moses Maimonides, references to *The Guide of the Perplexed*, trans. Schlomo Pines (Chicago: University of Chicago Press, 1963), 1.5: book 1, chapter 5.

For Aquinas, references to the *Summa Theologiae* will be abbreviated ST 1.2.4.5 for part 1, question 2, article 4, response to objection 5 (if the last be relevant). Translations are from the Blackfriars edition (London: Eyre & Spottiswoode, 1964). References to *Summa Contra Gentiles* 3.2: book 3, chapter 2; *Questiones Disputatae de Veritate* will be noted as *de Ver.* 3.2.6: question 3, article 2, response to objection 6 (if last be relevant); *Questiones Disputatae de Malo* will be noted as *de Malo* 2.3: question 2, article 1, response to objection 3 (if relevant). Aquinas' commentaries on

Aristotle will be referenced as follows: on the *Metaphysics*: *In Metaphysica* 2.3 for chapter [*lectio*] 3 of his commentary on Book 2; on Aristotle's *On Interpretaton*: *In peri hermenias* 2.4 for chapter [*lectio*] 4 of his commentary on Book 2.

References to John Duns Scotus will adopt a format similar to that of Aquinas, with the parts spelled out: *Ordinatio*,1, d. 2, q. 1, a. 2 ad.2 = part 1, distinction 2, question 1, article 2, response to objection 2. *Ordinatio*, ed. Carl Balic (Vatican City, 1954–) may be abbreviated "*Ord.*"

PROLOGUE: CREATION
AND WONDER

Understanding, Aristotle reminds us, begins in wonder. Yet were that quest to reach its goal, wonder would cease, much as travelers can stop moving when they reach their destination. For Aristotle, understanding seeks explanation, and the sign that we have one consists in being able to identify the four causes germane to any thing or event. Finding the material, moving, formal and final causes will answer why something is what it is or happens the way it happens. We may not be very successful in finding all these causes; in fact, Aristotle himself often had to concede falling short of a proper explanation, yet the ideal stands. In fact, Aristotle's account of proper explanation offers a brilliant way of adapting Plato's central goal of knowledge to the changing world we experience. Plato, however, was less sanguine about achieving knowledge; indeed, his many inconclusive dialogues attest the way in which a seeker's quest never ends. If what Plato deems to be philosophical inquiry were to come to term, the animating *eros* would dissipate – as Aristotle's scheme appropriately acknowledges. Plato has a way of finessing the despair attendant upon unending inquiry, however, by having recourse to myth to signal harmony obtaining between inquirers and their objectives. Aristotle would of course profess to be true to Socrates in eschewing myth as unequal to the task of explaining the universe, yet the price he pays for this is to limit explanation to things or events within the universe. Indeed, the order of the universe itself – the objective correlate of our persistent wonder – apparently admits of no explanation. The prime mover accounts for its characteristic activity of change, but nothing accounts for the amazing order among the kinds of things inherently ordered to their proper goals. Where Plato had recourse to myth, Aristotle was mute. In short, he left his successors with a clear view of what explanation could be, yet an impossible dream of reaching it.

It was left to Plotinus (205–70) to attempt an account of the universe with its order, yet by his time a fresh proposal had entered the scene –

not as an explanation, but as a revelation. Philo had taken the book of Genesis to recast it in philosophic terms, thereby preparing the way for others to show how this revelation of a free creator would assure that inquiries which began in wonder would peak in wonder as well. It would require a millennium to effect that transition, as the path wound through thickets of Neoplatonic commentary, including philosophical adaptations made by thinkers presenting both Jewish and Christian reflections on the book of Genesis, soon to be joined by Islamic voices as well. In fact, it could be argued that the Qur'an provided the needed impetus for Jews and Christians to face up to the metaphysical implications of Genesis, since Judaism in its rabbinic phase, as well as Christianity in its Christological struggle, both tended to take creation for granted, as each focused on covenant or incarnation, respectively. For the revelation of the Qur'an eschews a particular covenant as well as the need for humankind's redemption in a way so dramatic as Jesus' death and resurrection, to say nothing of its proto-Trinitarian implications. As a result, everything must turn on creation, as the Qur'an will characteristically parry objections to bodily resurrection with references to the One "who says 'be' and it is,"[1] while reminding skeptics regarding free creation that this same God promises to reconstitute decayed corpses on "that day."[2] Never catering to a need for extrinsic proof, the Qur'an encourages seekers to adopt this startling revelation as their salvation. Yet the encounter with Hellenic philosophy, and notably Plotinus, demanded some elucidation of creation, much as that same philosophical tradition had helped Christians to clarify the ontological status of Jesus a few centuries earlier.

Indeed, by the twelfth century, a Jewish thinker of Mosaic stature, Moses Maimonides (1135–1204), immersed in the culture of the Islamicate, adapted the stringent criticisms his Muslim predecessor, al-Ghazali (1058–1111), had made of Islamic "philosophers," to defend the free creation of the universe by one God, in the face of alternatives inspired by Plotinus. (Indeed, as we shall see, Plotinus at once blocked and inspired the efforts of thinkers of the three Abrahamic faiths to articulate their respective revelations.) Thomas Aquinas (1225–74) adopted the signal philosophical work of the one whom he called "Rabbi Moses," *The Guide of the Perplexed*, to advance his project of expounding Christian revelation by using the philosophies of Aristotle and Plato which he encountered through the writings of Ibn Sina [Avicenna] (980–1037). Thus, the task of articulating the free creation of the universe, and thereby showing how

---

[1] Qu'ran 2.111.
[2] Qu'ran 50.38–9.

human inquiry begun in wonder can peak there as well, became the fruit of an unwitting but immensely fruitful collaboration among Jewish, Christian, and Muslim scholars, on the strength of initiatives taken by Islamic thinkers.[3] The earliest of these attempts to articulate the Qur'anic teaching on free creation was clearly modeled on Plotinus' image of *emanation*, yet adapted in a way that constrained that "overflowing" to the necessary parameters of logical deduction schemes. Al-Farabi's (875–930) logical model for Plotinus' metaphor effectively removed freedom from the creator, and so incurred the fierce critique of another Muslim, al-Ghazali, showing that internal criticism was never absent from these traditions. Aquinas encountered this trenchant discussion of these recondite issues in reading Maimonides' work, indicating how beholden was his treatment of free creation to Muslim and Jewish predecessors. Indeed, this early medieval interchange among paradigmatic thinkers of the three Abrahamic faiths has impelled us to mine all three traditions in our search for the ground of a responsive freedom, despite the fact that the Qur'an lacks an extended narrative and merely nods to the "seven day" account, contenting itself with reiterating the compelling phrase: "God says 'be' and it is." Yet free creation has been even more central to Islamic theology than to Jewish or Christian reflection, so recent attempts to develop its significance in those traditions can be bolstered from the side of Islam.[4]

Yet even though Moses Maimonides found al-Ghazali's critique of the "necessary emanation" scheme for creation extremely useful in underscoring the freedom of the One to create, Aquinas would need further intellectual strategies to carry out his endeavor to articulate more positively the relation of that One to creatures. A spontaneous way to pose the question would be to ask: "how does God create?" Yet the advantage of Plotinus' pregnant metaphor of "overflowing" is to remove that singular activity from any Aristotelian account of happenings in the universe. Indeed, Aquinas had profited from al-Ghazali's critique of Ibn Sina, as he had learned it through Moses Maimonides, to the point where he refused to picture creation as an orderly logic-like progression from "the First" (as al-Farabi always characterized the creator). He objected primarily, of course, to the logical necessity that model presumed, but Aquinas also

---

[3] See my *Knowing the Unknowable God* (Notre Dame IN: University of Notre Dame Press, 1986) and *Freedom and Creation in Three Traditions* (Notre Dame IN: University of Notre Dame Press, 1993).

[4] See my *Original Peace: Restoring God's Creations* (with Elena Malits, C.S.C.) (New York: Paulist, 1997); John Levenson: *Creation and the Persistence of Evil* (New York: Harper and Row, 1988).

chafed at the need for intermediaries to effect the activity, as logical deduction must progress via a chain of premises. Insisting that creation-from-nothing could hardly involve any *change*, in Aristotle's sense, would also entail that no Aristotelian scheme (fashioned precisely to account for change) could serve to articulate this faith-assertion. Aristotle, after all, had eschewed accounting for the origin of all things, and Aquinas may have seen why: his four causes could not be stretched that far. So another intellectual strategy would be required to articulate the revelation of Genesis in Hellenic philosophical terms. At this point, after having removed any hint of necessity or mediation in creating, Aquinas turns to Plotinus' metaphor, now set free from the accompanying model of logical deduction, and offers a lapidary formula for *creation*: "the emanation of the whole of being from the universal cause of being [God]."[5] But how to characterize this "universal cause of being" when none of Aristotle's causes can do the job?

Here Aquinas makes an explicit turn to the Neoplatonic tradition, providing an extended commentary on the work known in Latin as the *Liber de causis*, which was in effect a translation of an Islamic adaptation of Proclus, the *Kitab al-khair mahd*, or "the Book of Pure Good."[6] Aquinas recognized its true origin, which may have helped him to make allowance (as we shall see) for its characteristic Neoplatonic idiom, which he in turn adapted to his purposes. Such an adaptation of Neoplatonic texts to Islamic use is also evident in the so-called "Theology of Aristotle," which adapted several of Plotinus' *Enneads* to harmonize the difference between Plato and Aristotle, so as to offer a single "philosophy" more appropriate to articulating a revealed creation.[7] What interests us, however, is the way in which Aquinas himself adapted the Islamic text, presented to him in Latin translation, to try to articulate a "cause of being." Again, if Aristotelian strategies tailored to intramundane explanations – the celebrated "four causes" – were not up to this task, how might this Neoplatonic account help? Recall that Aquinas had no apparent difficulty adopting the idiom of Plotinus – *emanation* – in his mature formula for creation. The strategy which the *Liber de causis* offered him was a description of that

[5] *Summa Theologiae* (= ST) 1.45.5.1.
[6] For an overview, see Cristina D'Ancona Costa, *La Casa della Sapienze* (Milano: Guerini, 1996), and also my "Aquinas's Appropriation of *Liber de causis* to Articulate the Creator as Cause-of-Being," in *Contemplating Aquinas*, eds Laurence Paul Hemming and Susan Frank Parsons (Oxford: Blackwell, 2003), pp. 55–74.
[7] See Peter Adamson, *The Arabic Plotinus: A Philosophical Study of the "Theology of Aristotle"* (London: Duckworth, 2003).

emanation in which the One first created *being* [*esse* = "to-be"], and through this *being* everything else that is. On the face of it, however, this strategy veers towards a stage-wise "process" of emanation which Aquinas had explicitly denied, insisting that creatures must come forth immediately from God, since there can be no change, no process, in creating.[8]

So Aquinas' strategy is to adopt another Platonic principle, and one which Aristotle had criticized as a "mere metaphor," *participation*, along with his own unique way of identifying "the One" as that One whose essence is identified with its very "to-be" [*esse*]. So creation becomes that act whereby the One whose essence is to-be makes everything else to-be by participating in being. *Participation* remains a metaphor, so this account cannot serve as an explanation in any ordinary sense, yet the assertion of revelation regarding the free creation of the universe is presented in an acceptable philosophical idiom. We remain bereft of any satisfactory idea of what creating is like, of course, but that was inevitable since we already knew that the "the emanation of the whole of being from the universal cause of being" could not be accounted for in terms tailored to any mundane process. So it is hardly surprising that a "cause of being" will transcend Aristotelian categories, and thereby invite the use of metaphors to serve a role not unlike the myths which Plato employed to conclude otherwise inconclusive inquiries. For like those myths, these metaphors invite us to an intelligibility beyond the standard parameters of explanation, so reminding us that *creation* is, after all, a properly theological notion. Yet determined as he was to show how *theologia* could be a form of knowing, paradigmatically exhibited in Aristotle's explanatory scheme of four causes, Aquinas will also offer us a way to move from that idiom to the one needed to articulate a "cause of being."

The way is embodied in his celebrated "five ways" of "proving" that God exists, located at the beginning of his *Summa Theologiae*, just after he has clarified how this "theological" inquiry can be construed as one leading to "knowledge." Many students have been treated to these "arguments" only to find out that they "do not work," so we need to clear the air regarding what they do and do not purport to do. Aquinas explicitly notes that they are not intended as "proofs" in the sense of demonstrations (or deductions), but are rather presented as a form of what Charles Sanders Peirce will call "abductions": if things were to be construed in this way, then what we see would follow. (It turns out that most of our scientific "explanations" also proceed in this hypothetical

---

[8]   ST 45.2.2.

fashion.) Nor are they intended as "foundational" for the entire enterprise of *theologia*, as Aquinas perceives it; the preceding question had already established that this peculiar form of inquiry involves knowing-by-faith, and so is rooted in the "knowledge only the blessed can have" who share the vision of God![9] So what role do they play, located as they are so near the outset of his inquiry into "God as the source and goal of all things?"[10] They are offered as "proofs" (as in an automotive "proving ground") to "test" the limits of any purportedly total explanation of the universe itself. If none of these can achieve their goal, then we must undertake the enterprise of *theologia*, even though it cannot be "explanatory" in the paradigmatic sense established by Aristotle, for it emerges at the very point where total explanations give out.[11]

Let us focus on the "third way," from the "directness of things to a goal," which exposes how the leading presumption of Aristotle's universe – that each proper kind of thing has its specific goal – itself stands in need of an explanation. Yet Aquinas respects the fact that Aristotle offered none, apparently aware that his conceptual strategies would not have allowed him to do so. Indeed, only "what we call 'God'" will be able to account for the fact that each kind of thing displays a proper finality, for whatever displays intellect yet is not endowed with intellect must have been so endowed by an intelligent first cause. But such an account cannot be proffered as an explanation in any ordinary sense, for the cause will not emerge as the culmination of a chain of reasoning, but will have to be postulated as a unique cause transcending any causal chain we know: "what we call 'God.'" So the way is opened to considering the origin of the universe, but only upon realizing that any set of this-worldly strategies will not be up to the task. Considering the origin of the universe itself will have to move us beyond the universe: a move which will involve us in metaphorical strategies inspired by a revelation that begs for philosophical articulation. Yet the poetic, narrative, or paranetic mode of that revelation suggests that our attempts to articulate free creation will outstrip categories constructed for explaining things or events within the universe. But is not *metaphysics* – the study of "being *qua* being" – the supreme branch of philosophy designed to carry us beyond the universe to give an account of its origin?

---

[9]   ST 1.2.
[10] ST 2.Prol.
[11] See Nicholas Lash, "Ideology, metaphor and analogy," in *Philosophical Frontiers of Christian Theology: Essays presented to D. M. MacKinnon*, eds Brian Hebblethwaite and Stewart Sutherland (Cambridge: Cambridge University Press, 1982), pp. 68–94.

Responding to that query will introduce us to an arena contested between those who presume that a philosophical account can bridge the gap between creator and creatures (a position dubbed "onto-theology"), and those who insist that the best even metaphysics can do is to call attention to that "ontological difference" in such a way as to offer a "negative" articulation of it.[12] While one can find "Thomists" on both sides of this divide, it is my contention that it best illustrates what separates Aquinas himself from John Duns Scotus. To understand what is at stake, recall the strategies Aquinas used to appropriate the *Liber de causis* to his purposes of articulating a "cause of being." The Neoplatonic structure of the book had the universe emanating from the One in an ordered way which followed the Porphyrean tree of logic, moving from the most general to the most specific: from being to inanimate to rational creatures. While it may seem unlikely to most that these logical categories could in any way be generative, the scheme also requires that *being* name the most general category of all, as though something first had to be a thing before it could be a kind of thing. But to make such a stipulation serves to remind us of Aristotle's stricture against treating *being* as a univocal term. It simply makes no sense to ask how many beings are in the room; whatever-is must be as a kind of thing. That there can be no things that are simply beings – or "bare particulars" in more contemporary jargon – underscores the metaphysical fault lines operative here. So Aquinas proceeds to interpret the *Liber's* insistence that "*being* is the first of created things" with his own insistence that every kind of thing that exists does so by participating in the being of God in an orderly fashion which distributes things according to their kind, as in Genesis.

Now the "ontological difference" between created things and their source is expressed by another Platonic strategy: distinguishing what exists in itself from what exists by participation. Used by Plato to distinguish forms from things named after them but subject to generation and corruption, the presence of a creator elicits a yet more radical "distinction": between the One whose essence is simply to-be, and everything which it brings into existence, whether those things be subject to generation and corruption or not. *Contingency* then means not only what could be otherwise, but what might not be at all. To celebrate this "distinction," as Robert Sokolowski dubs it, is to see how Aquinas' identification of God as the One whose essence is to-be effectively brings him into alignment

[12]   See Robert Sokolowski, *The God of Faith and Reason* (Washington DC: Catholic University of America Press, 1990); Jean-Luc Marion, "Saint Thomas d'Aquin et l'onto-théologie," in *Revue Thomiste* 95 (1995), pp. 31–66.

with Plotinus, whose One is said to be "beyond being." For by making
the demarcation where he does, Aquinas disallows any talk of God as
though it were an item in the universe – even a necessary one. So we are
forbidden to think of *being* as a category spanning the uncreated and the
created; indeed as a category at all. As Aquinas puts it, "God is not contained within the genus of *substance*."[13] And when asked whether creatures "resemble" their creator, he finesses the ordinary sense of the
question by stating that "things resemble the source of their existence by
possessing existence [*esse*],"[14] but of course the "One who is" does not
"possess existence," and the metaphysical tools he has assembled make it
clear that *esse* cannot be a feature of things, so "resemblance" can hardly
mean what we normally take it to mean. In other words, he might just
as well have answered "no," but then he would have been unable to articulate any connection between creatures and creator – a position he criticized "Rabbi Moses" for taking.[15] Yet astute readers might wonder what
really separates these two, since the *resemblance* which Aquinas asserts is
not a recognizable one. It turns out that what makes the difference is a
vigorously analogical notion of *being*, which the Rambam [= Rabbi Moses
ben Maimon] could not comprehend.[16]

Yet a vigorous sense of the analogical structure of discourse about *being*
is the semantic counterpart to "the distinction" of creatures from the
creator – a realization which led the late Josef Pieper, a most astute contemporary interpreter of Aquinas, to remark that "creation is the hidden
element in the philosophy of St. Thomas."[17] Where Duns Scotus will
identify God as the infinite being, Aquinas will employ the metaphysical
tools at his disposal – notably the distinction between *essence* and *esse* – to
identify God as the one whose essence is simply to-be. Notice that Scotus'
formula demands that something called "being" embrace both finite creatures and infinite creator, and will then require a separate argument to
show that this "infinite being" is indeed the creator; whereas Aquinas'
formula offers a direct metaphysical articulation of the revelation of a
creator. For the characteristic activity of the One whose essence is to-be
can only be to bring other things to participate in being. Indeed,

---

[13] ST 1.3.5.1.
[14] ST 1.4.3.
[15] ST 1.13.2.
[16] For a careful treatment, see Alexander Broadie, "Maimonides and Aquinas on the
Names of God," in *Religious Studies* 23 (1987), 157–70.
[17] Josef Pieper, "The Negative Element in the Philosophy of St. Thomas," in *Silence of
St. Thomas* (New York: Pantheon, 1957), pp. 47–67.

whatever activity we can predicate of God must be in the form of creating – unless, that is, we would be privy to a form of activity "within"
divinity itself, which Christians enjoy in the revelation of God in Jesus.
The upshot of these apparently recondite reflections is that any attempt
to articulate the creating activity of God, with the subsequent relation of
creatures to their creator, must surpass ordinary ways of expression. So
attempts to do so will invariably invoke poetry and art, for while *participation* remains a metaphor, metaphors can be elaborated by yet further
metaphors, and often better by nonverbal forms of expression. As Aquinas
taught us by his efforts to enrich and transform Aristotle's paradigm for
knowing [*scientia*] to include knowing-by-faith, there are indeed "more
things in heaven and earth than are found in philosophy" as he (or we)
have received it.

For introducing a free creator into Hellenic philosophy demands that
we learn how to speak of the One from whom all things freely flow, yet
not as an item in the universe – even an "infinite" such item. For this
One is indeed "beyond being" as we know beings. So our relation to this
One who speaks the universe – "God says 'be' and it is" – cannot be on
a par with our relation to any other thing. This crucial corollary of the
"distinction" enshrined in Aquinas' analogical semantics has remained
unappreciated in the west, though we find it expressed eloquently in
Meister Eckhart's arresting paradoxes.[18] A recent set of reflections on
Aquinas in relation to the Hindu sage, Shankara, offers that quality of
"mutual illumination" which intercultural perspectives can often bring to
formulations which have become too familiar. Sara Grant's 1989 Teape
lectures, subtitled "Confessions of a Non-Dualist Christian," offer a
narrative of the journey of this Religious of the Sacred Heart to India
and her subsequent life of study and prayer in the context of a Hindu–
Christian ashram in Pune.[19] Pondering the manner in which Aquinas characterizes creation in things as a *relation* to their source, she observes how
malleable is this maverick Aristotelian category of *relation*: this relation (of
creatures to their creator) can hardly be assimilated to the relations among
creatures themselves, lest we fail to distinguish the creator from creatures.
Her prolonged study of Shankara, with the subtle language he introduces
of "nonduality," helps her to see what many commentators on Aquinas
have missed: the way his insistence that the *esse* of creatures is an *esse-ad-*

[18]   For a reliable guide, see Bernard McGinn, *The Mystical Thought of Meister Eckhart* (New
York: Crossroad, 2001).
[19]   Bradley Malkovsky (ed.), *Toward an Alternative Theology* (Notre Dame IN: University of
Notre Dame Press, 2002).

creatorem (their to-be is to-be-towards-the-creator) utterly transforms Aristotle's world, where the hallmark of *substance* is to "exist in itself." Yet
ironically enough, the reason we may miss the transformation that Aquinas
makes of Aristotle is that the relation is so *sui generis* that it does not alienate the creature from itself. Since God cannot be "other" in the sense in
which other things are other, and God remains the very source of anything's being, anything's to-be [*esse*] is at once a participation in the very
being of God and "more intimate to things than anything else."[20]

So we begin to see why a proper articulation of the mystery of creation undergirds any robust account of human freedom, as well as any
attempt to articulate our intentional relations to our creator, any "spiritual" discourse. For if Jews, Christians, or Muslims end up praying to
"someone else" in addressing their praise and thanksgiving to God, they
are misdirecting attention which should be focused on the One who is
the very source of their being. Only by carefully distinguishing this One
from all other things can we properly relate to that same One, for if we
think God must be separate from us, then we must be separate from God.
That is the self-defeating notion of "autonomy" concocted by a modernity which felt it had to renounce a creator, so that anyone who employs
such outmoded categories cannot help but misconstrue the God whom
they wish to elaborate.[21] For once we appreciate how radical is our act of
faith in a free creator, then it becomes clear that we cannot *be* separate
from God. Yet we will fail to understand that corollary of free creation,
perhaps even mistake it for "pantheism," if we have not seen how the
unique character of the *relation* called "creation" also demands that we
learn how to think the creator *not* as an item in the universe, but as its
One free creator! That mode of thinking, which Kathryn Tanner dubs
"non-constrastive," will also demand that we appreciate how to employ
language analogously.[22] For this reason, a foray into metaphysics will
require poetic sensibility as well, since all analogous speech – whether used
of divinity or used to evaluate human situations, as in ethical discourse –
will invariably display a touch of metaphor.[23] So we are brought, via these
extended reflections, to the threshold of poetry and art as we attempt to
attune our minds and hearts to the wonder of creation.

---

[20] ST 1.8.1. For a discussion of *participation* consult Rudi teVelde's *Participation and Substantiality in Thomas Aquinas* (Leiden: Brill, 1995).
[21] See my "Creation, Metaphysics, and Ethics," in *Faith and Philosophy* 18 (2001), pp.
204–21.
[22] Kathryn Tanner, *God and Creation in Christian Theology* (Oxford: Blackwell, 1988).
[23] See my *Analogy and Philosophical Language* (New Haven CT: Yale University Press,
1973).

Part I

CREATOR/CREATION RELATION

Chapter 1

DISTINGUISHING GOD FROM THE WORLD

Two features which have shaped philosophical considerations of divinity in Jewish, Christian, and Muslim worlds since the beginnings of such reflection – God's simpleness and God's eternity – have recently been subject to severe questioning. An entire theological movement (so-called "process theology") has developed to offer an alternative construction of divinity, while an increasing number of philosophers of religion simply proceed as though these features (which are "formal features") no longer constrained discourse about divinity.[1] While the arguments which theologians offer for rejecting the "classical doctrine" differ somewhat in perspective from those which philosophers offer for avoiding the "Anselmian conception" of divinity, there is significant overlap between the two groups.[2]

I shall focus here on the forms of argument philosophers normally adduce for eschewing divine eternity and simpleness, and I shall try to show how alternative routes inevitably jeopardize the cardinal teaching of Jewish, Christian, and Muslim traditions, that of creation. (I have already shown [see note 1 below] how theological alternatives in fact replace creation with a far weaker notion of *creativity* borrowed from Whitehead; I shall merely state here that the tendency which some forms of Christianity have of virtually eclipsing creation by redemption can only weaken the import of redemption itself.) The direction of my constructive argument, then, shows how philosophical theology must answer not only to criteria

[1] On "formal features," see my *Aquinas: God and Action* (Notre Dame IN: University of Notre Dame Press, 1979), pp. 14–17, where I acknowledge my indebtedness to Eddy Zemach.

[2] Schubert Ogden refers to "classical theism," following Charles Hartshorne, while Tom Morris speaks of "the Anselmian conception": "The God of Abraham, Isaac, and Anselm," in *Faith and Philosophy* 1 (1984), pp. 177–87.

of consistency but also do justice to practices and beliefs shared in living religious traditions, much as philosophers of science construct models of explanation with a keen eye to laboratory practice. The reference to three distinct "monotheistic" traditions is meant to offer converging and mutually corroborative testimony, as shall be seen, and not to propose a syncretic common faith.[3]

Philosophers have come to be persuaded that it is impossible to link an eternal God with temporal events (here their arguments often overlap with those brought forward by "process theologians"), and that the very notion of divine simplicity is freighted with incoherence. Yet the arguments which have persuaded so many of them display little understanding of the roots of the notions being disputed as they were elaborated in the service of the three traditions referred to above. Those dealing with divine eternity invariably settle for its abstract component – *timelessness* – without asking themselves whether that dimension captures the traditional sense of *eternity*.[4] Two articles by Norman Kretzmann and Eleanore Stump (on "Eternity" and "Absolute Simplicity") can be extremely useful in confronting this current myopia. Each offers constructive ways of recovering the tradition and responding to certain consequences of the traditional notions which many have judged should invalidate them.[5] While indebted to their treatment, I propose to undergird a wider endeavor to understand the central role played by *simpleness* and *eternity* in doing philosophical theology, by showing how these formal features secure "the distinction" of God from the world.[6]

Without a clear philosophical means of distinguishing God from the world, the tendency of all discourse about divinity is to deliver a God

[3] "Monotheism" is of course an abstraction, though useful in identifying a family of faiths; on the proprieties of speaking of a "common faith," see my review of Wilfrid Cantwell Smith's recent publications: "Faith and Religious Convictions: Studies in Comparative Epistemology," in *Journal of Religion* 63 (1983), pp. 64–73.

[4] A common starting point for philosophers is Nelson Pike's *God and Timelessness* (London: Routledge & Kegan Paul, 1970), which presumes the identification: see my "God's Eternity," in *Faith and Philosophy* 1 (1984), pp. 389–405. Characteristic arguments against the notion of divine simplicity can be found in Alvin Plantinga, *Does God Have a Nature?* (Milwaukee: Marquette University Press, 1980). I prefer "simpleness" to "simplicity" for rhetorical reasons: see *Summa Theologiae* (= ST), vol. 2: *Existence and Nature of God*, trans. Timothy McDermott, O.P. (London: Eyre and Spottiswoode, 1964).

[5] Norman Kretzmann and Eleanore Stump, "Eternity," in *Journal of Philosophy* 78 (1981), pp. 429–58; "Absolute Simplicity," in *Faith and Philosophy* 2 (1985), pp. 353–82.

[6] For "the distinction," see Robert Sokolowski, *The God of Faith and Reason* (Notre Dame IN: University of Notre Dame Press, 1983/Washington, DC: Catholic University of America Press, 1995).

who is the "biggest thing around." That such is the upshot of much
current philosophy of religion cannot be doubted; that it stems from overlooking the crucial role of these "formal features" is the burden of this
article. The wary will note that talking about a God distinct from the
world will inevitably involve one in analogical forms of speech, yet the
aversion many philosophers show to this dimension of our discourse can
only reflect an oversight of recent explorations of this domain.[7] It may also
be the case that this aversion stems from an overpowering concern for
clear-cut meaning which issues in treatments of God in which little care
is taken to do justice to the notion of God as "the creator of heaven and
earth." If this be the case, the current surge of interest in philosophy of
religion may ill-serve religion, since (adapting an observation of Aquinas)
misleading conceptions of matters divine on the part of believers can only
subject the faith to ridicule.[8] Lest my own efforts seem overly pretentious,
I am not promising an adequate response to the objections raised to God's
eternity and simpleness. I am trying to make the case for grappling
with those objections more honestly and directly, after the manner of
Kretzmann and Stump, in an effort to capture the role these formal
features play in philosophical theology. For disregarding or overlooking
their role risks failing to speak of God at all.

Inner Connection of Eternity with Simpleness

I have consistently referred to *simpleness* and *eternity* as "formal features"
of divinity, thereby marking them off from attributes or characteristics. It
is like determining whether to treat light as particles or waves, after which
one may ask about the velocity of the particles or the length of the waves;
or whether to adopt an "event" or a "substance" ontology. Formal features concern our manner of locating the subject for characterization, and
hence belong to a stage prior to considering attributes as such – a stage
which will in part determine which attributes are relevant and certainly
how they are to be attributed to the subject in question. (Or if one
remains wedded to an undiscriminating use of "property," these would be
ur-properties.) The order of Aquinas' treatment in the *Summa Theologiae*

---

[7]   See James Ross, *Portraying Analogy* (Cambridge: Cambridge University Press, 1981);
Patrick Sherry, "Analogy Reviewed," in *Philosophy* 51 (1976), pp. 337–45; "Analogy Today,"
ibid., pp. 431–46.
[8]   Most notable are treatments of divine knowledge which proceed, quite innocent of the
creator/creature relation, to presume God to be an omniscient onlooker.

clearly distinguishes those features the psalmist attributes to God from these formal ones, thereby making a semantic and ontological distinction among what many would indiscriminately call "divine attributes".[9] It is my contention, moreover, that it is the formal features which secure the proper distinction of God from the world, thus determining the kind of being (so to speak) said to be just and merciful, and hence establishing critical modifications in those attributes. This complex assertion will be unraveled as we proceed. In short, God's simpleness and God's eternity are part of what assures us we are talking about divinity.

How so? Aquinas' treatment is illustrative here, the more so as one realizes how much he is resuming developments in Muslim and Jewish philosophical theology which preceded him.[10] The first step is to articulate a nominal definition of God suitable to all three traditions: "beginning and end of all things and of rational creatures especially."[11] While this formula would be compatible with an emanationist view like Avicenna's, Aquinas will develop it in an unmistakably creationist manner, following Maimonides.[12] A first step in that direction is to note an immediate consequence of the formula itself: the One who begins and is the end of all things is *not* one of those things. Or as Aquinas put it, "God does not belong to the genus of substance."[13] God is not one of the items in the world of which God is the origin. Avicenna expressed this distinction in terms of *necessary* and *possible* beings, where the First alone exists "by its essence" (and is hence *necessary*) while everything else – *possible* in itself – derives its existence from the First.[14] Aquinas prefers to mark the distinction by separating what is utterly without composition (or "simple") from everything else, which is *composed* of essence and *esse* (or existence). The idea for such a division came to him from Avicenna, but his development of it assures a clear creation perspective by insisting that the "proper effect" of the simple One is the to-be (*esse*) of the cosmos. So the formal feature of divine simpleness is intended to distinguish God from every-

---

[9]   See my *Aquinas* (note 1), chapter 2, and Mark Jordan, "Names of God and the Being of Names," in *Existence and Nature of God*, ed. Alfred J. Freddoso (Notre Dame IN: University of Notre Dame Press, 1983), pp. 161–90.

[10]   See my *Knowing the Unknowable God* (Notre Dame IN: University of Notre Dame Press, 1986).

[11]   ST 1.2. intro.

[12]   The crucial difference between these perspectives is of course the gratuity of the universe; hence Josef Pieper insists that creation is "the hidden element in the philosophy of Aquinas," see: *Philosophia Negativa* (Munich: Kösel, 1953).

[13]   ST 1.3.5.1.

[14]   *al-Shifa: al-Ilahiyyat* I, eds G. C. Anawati and S. Zayad (Cairo, 1960), chapter 8, section 4 (p. 346, line 11).

thing else – God's creation. That is, divine simpleness assures God's distinction from "all things" as well as providing the ground for asserting the gratuity of creation.

What then can *simpleness* mean? And why must one say that God is simple? To reply to the second question first: because we have no other way of assuring ourselves that we are talking about the One from whom all things come. What distinguishes divinity from all that is not divine, in such a way as to be able to characterize that One as the source of all the rest, must have to do with the *nature* of the subject in question and not simply its *attributes*. It will not do to inquire into God's knowing, willing, or moral character without first asking what sort of thing it is to which we are attributing knowledge and will and moral character. The price one pays for adopting such a short-cut is uncritically to presume similarities between God and humans, as in the opener: "assuming God to be a person. . . ."[15] Or one presumes a univocal understanding of powers (or properties) like knowing and willing, as though the world consisted of such properties, shared by God and creatures according to more or less. Both presumptions can be found in current philosophy of religion, presumably embodying a fear that admitting analogical discourse leaves us conceptually at sea. Yet a vague notion of similarity, coupled with strategic avowals of difference (at least in degree) hardly represents a critical approach to the central issue: the distinction of God (creator) from the world (creation).

How does *simpleness* secure that distinction? To answer this question we must articulate what *simpleness* means. I have noted that Aquinas' elaboration of divine simpleness replaced a distinction which Avicenna had drawn across the field of being (all that is) between that which is necessary in itself and that which is possible in itself (and made necessary – in another sense – by another). What is "necessary in itself" is so because it exists "by its essence" (*bi-thatihi*). Aware as he was of the many senses of the term "necessary," Aquinas eschewed using that term as the primary one distinguishing God from all that is not God, preferring to articulate Avicenna's distinction in terms borrowed from him as well: essence and existence (*esse*).[16] What gives divinity the necessity peculiar to it is the formal fact that God's nature is nothing other than its own existence: to

---

[15] This statement is particularly ambiguous from within the Christian tradition, which has appropriated the term "person" to express divine triunity. That our discourse about, as well as our address to, God is *personal* cannot be gainsaid; yet asserting God to be a *person* begs a number of critical questions.

[16] For the story of that borrowing and subsequent transformation on the part of Aquinas. see Armand Maurer, *On Being and Essence*, second revised edition (Toronto: Pontifical

be divine is (simply) to-be. That is what *simpleness* means for Aquinas, at any rate, who uses it principally and essentially (*primo et per se*) of God alone.[17] There is no doubt that Aquinas' treatment is something of a seamless robe, for one must at least acknowledge the possibility of conceiving existence (*esse*) as he does, on the analogy of act or activity, to allow that such a characterization could capture what we mean by divinity, however remotely or "formally." I shall indicate ways in which that can be made plausible when I treat of *simpleness* in relation to creation. For now, some tentative concessions need to be made to allow the main lines of the argument to be sketched out.

So simple a One would exist without needing a cause of its existing, so its being simple would not be a merely negative feature, like lacking parts. Indeed this way of characterizing divine simpleness makes it equivalent to *aseity*, yet goes on to spell that out in terms of its *existing* "by its essence" (*per se*). Other things that one would be inclined to call *necessary* may therefore be usefully characterized as "pertaining to every possible world," yet such considerations remain conceptual. Were such things actually to exist as part of *this* world, then they would either pertain to its structure, and so enjoy the simpleness proper to formal structure without a claim to separate existence, or they would be brought into existence, and in that sense be "composed." (Aquinas presumed the heavenly bodies and angels to be such objects, so he used his distinction of essence from existence to distinguish them from divinity while acknowledging their everlasting status.)

It should be becoming clear how much Aquinas' specific articulation of divine simpleness as the identity of God's essence with the divine act of existing seems tailored to a characterization of God as creator: the One who bestows existence. Let us first, however, see how *eternity* emerges from simpleness so conceived, by way of necessary implication and as an articulation of the sense of *simpleness* developing here.

This One whose essence is simply to-be cannot be limited by quantity (since it is not bodily) nor by genus or species, since its essence – to-be – "overflows" both genus and species. So what is simple is also unlimited or, more traditionally, infinite. Nor can such a one be temporal, since it does not come to be, and so is not subject to motion or change, of which time is the measure. So what is simple must be beyond

---

Institute of Medieval Studies, 1968); and my "Essence and Existence; Avicenna and Greek Philosophy," in *MIDEO* 13 (= *Melanges de l'Institut Dominicain des Etudes Orientales*)(1985), as well as *Knowing* (note 10).
[17] ST 1.3.7.

change – not unmoving, as the traditional term "immutable" is often taken to mean, but beyond the categories of *kinesis* or *stasis*. (Such an avowal, however necessary as a consequence, will require a notion of *activity* which is not motion if it is to be plausible – again the seamless-garment aspect of this treatment of divine simpleness.)

We have not quite concluded, however, to God's eternity, but only to the fact that divinity, to be the "beginning and end of all things," must lie beyond change. What does eternity add to this? Boethius' classic definition suggests the answer: "the possession all-at-once (*tota simul*) of unending *life*." Whatever is eternal, in the full-blooded sense in which that is intended when claimed as a formal feature of divinity, must be alive – existing or actual, if you will – and not merely the sort of thing to which temporal becoming is irrelevant, as it is to mathematics.[18] God's eternity, then, specifies the modality proper to an activity which is not a movement, and it is this dimension which the variant "timeless" omits. If God's eternity entails *timelessness*, as derived via the argument that divinity lies beyond becoming, it remains the case that the timelessness entailed is *not* what we associate with mathematical entities or truths. And since "timeless" is inevitably closely connected with such things as these, to which becoming is irrelevant, it seems at least rhetorically misleading to speak of God as timeless, as it is certainly inaccurate to equate eternity with timelessness.

So God's eternity, on this account, also prepares the way for asserting the One to be creator, as it underscores the fact that God's nature is simply to-be, by recalling that whatever simply is must lie beyond the realm of becoming, of cause-and-effect, and so be eternally. Aquinas' pregnant analogy: "as time measures becoming, so eternity measures to-be (*esse*),"[19] opens the treatment to the act of creation, for the "proper effect" of what acts in this eternal fashion will be the to-be (*esse*) of things.[20] So the activity of the eternal One will be conceived, not by analogy with timeless entities impervious to time, but in terms of what makes the world to be. And since "what is" is *now*, the One who makes things to be will be primarily and essentially (*primo et per se*) present. The metaphor of *presence* can be a useful one to flesh out this analogy to present existence.[21]

---

[18]   Hence Kretzmann and Stump distinguish *eternity* from mere *atemporality*: "Eternity" (note 5), p. 432.
[19]   ST 1.10.4.3.
[20]   ST 1.8.1; 45.5.
[21]   See John S. Dunne's evocative treatment in *House of Wisdom* (New York: Harper and Row, 1985).

Finally, I have spoken throughout of "the One." For the conception of divine simpleness which I have been elaborating not only grounds the distinction of God from the world, but also articulates the faith of those religious traditions which have embodied that distinction in a doctrine of creation – that God is one. And not merely in the sense that there happens not to be another answering to the specifications of divinity, as we have but one sun, but in the sense that this notion of divinity entails uniqueness. Although the assertion that God is one seems to go without saying since the Athenian philosophers undermined the Acropolis, it remains doubtful (at least to me) whether treatments of God which avoid securing the nature of their subject can do anything more than *presume* there to be but one God. The exposition of divine simpleness offered here is presented as a challenge to anyone purporting to speak of God when treating, say, of divine knowledge. If divinity, and with it the distinction of God from the world, be not secured in some fashion such as this, how will we know we are treating of God? And if not this way, what are the alternatives?

Difficulties with Eternity

The difficulties which philosophers have found with eternity are two-fold: (1) arriving at a proper conception of an eternal entity, and (2) relating such a being to temporal affairs. The first difficulty shows up immediately in our language, which appears to be irremediably tensed. Attempts to construct a tenseless verb inevitably founder on relating the action depicted to what is happening now, and sacrificing all connection with the token-reflexive "now" leaves one with a thoroughly abstract form of discourse – since whatever happens, happens now. Yet it must also be noted that these difficulties have arisen in relation to a purportedly *timeless* discourse. What would happen were one to discriminate God's eternity from timelessness, in the manner suggested?

   This eternal being could hardly be thought of as one to which temporal occurrences were irrelevant, since they exist by virtue of its eternal to-be. It follows, of course, that there is only one such – God – and that such a One, as the source of the existence proper to each temporal existent, would better be imagined *inside* the becoming which time measures than *outside* it. There is, to be sure, a specific sense in which the eternal One is timeless (or "outside time") as well, namely the fact that the present tense applied to such a one never becomes the past, as it does with everything else. So, while there has to have been a first moment in time marking the beginning of the created universe, we cannot properly say that God *created* the world but that God *creates* the world. (The Creed sidesteps this issue nicely by using the noun instead: "We believe in one God . . . Creator of heaven and earth. . . .") Since the reference point, however, is normally not the divine action but its effect, religious language can properly speak of "the great deeds God has done on behalf of God's own people."

It is no less true, of course, that we cannot speak a language whose present never becomes past, any more than we could function with an idiom pretending to be tenseless. So attempting to construct such a language would produce countless puzzles, as we tried to make it do what our tensed discourse does. Yet there is no need to construct a language for God, but only to draw attention to strategic disanalogies with our tensed discourse. Kretzmann and Stump have been helpful in assembling reminders for discussions of the way God knows what will happen. Often misleadingly referred to as "the future," as though there were a determinate scenario waiting in the wings, the object of God's knowing what will be the case has spawned more than philosophical puzzles, in provoking acerbic theological controversies. The very thought that God knows what I will do can evoke a frisson of terror, as well, in the religious soul.

Much current discussion of God's knowledge concentrates on whether and how God knows "the future" without pausing to reflect on the ambiguities in that term – like the hapless soul who gave up a prestigious post for a future one (which "failed to materialize," as we say). The presumption of a determinate scenario for what the case will be appears to subserve a characteristic form of argument. God must know everything that is the case, for divine omniscience permits no surprises. Cast in terms of knowing which propositions are true, along with the corollary that once something is true, it is timelessly true, God is then said to know what will take place since omniscience requires that God know which side of a disjunction is true, lest God be surprised.

The switch to propositions allows one to let go of one's tenses here, giving the discourse its scrambled air, which becomes further confused as "true propositions" seem to refer only indirectly to what *is* the case. As a result of these maneuvers, one can sidestep Aristotle's quandary over future contingent events – a discussion which shaped Aquinas' treatment of the matter. Aristotle, for whom a true statement asserts what is the case, acknowledges sufficient determinacy regarding what might happen to offer a general description with its negation, insisting that one or the other would indeed be the case (the law of bivalence). But no one can know whether the sea battle will occur tomorrow or not (which of the disjuncts "is" the true one), until it occurs. We can predict, of course, as a BBC spokesman acknowledged in the midst of a news blackout in the Falklands crisis: "there will have been casualties." But predictions are not statements. So strictly speaking, no one can know what will take place, so long as we keep true assertion linked to fact. Not even God can, concurs Aquinas, since "the future" does not yet exist, and what does not exist is not there to be known.[22]

Holding on to one's tenses, then, seems to be linked closely with keeping true discourse tied to states of affairs: what *is* the case. Those who forego both, as do proponents of "middle knowledge," seem caught in a stranger paradox than the one at least some of them thought they were escaping. The paradox they would avoid is the one the wary reader will have associated with Aquinas: since God cannot know what *will* happen, but must know everything, all that was, is, or will be must be present to God eternally. The logic is impeccable, since only what *is* the case can be known to be the case, but one is at a loss to say just how what has not yet happened can be *present* to God. We are faced with an equivocation on "present" which can be resolved only by articulating the sense proper to an eternal present, plus its relation to the present of tensed discourse – "what is the case" – both of which lie quite beyond one whose discourse is tied to tenses.

How could proponents of "middle knowledge" be caught in a paradox stranger than this one? Because their presumption of a determinate scenario also requires that what will be the case be present to divine knowledge, yet be so without benefit of the strategic disanalogies with tensed discourse which accompany asserting God to be eternal. As a result, God can be said to know beforehand what the case will be, since God knows which of each pair of disjuncts is true. But the last "is" must be a timeless one, so God can be said to know "the future" even though what God knows has not yet taken place. Chary of a resolution involving an eternity which lies beyond our capacity properly to conceive, they need to rely nevertheless on a notion of *timelessness* which allows them to state something quite inconceivable: namely, *what* I will do before I have done it. Eternity, as one of the terms in the earlier paradox, at least lies *beyond* our powers of conception; while a timeless affirmation of the free actions of an actual subject *while* that subject is yet a possibility defies reason: *de posse ad esse non valet illatio.*[23]

---

[22]   ST 1.14.13.

[23]   See the observations of Anthony Kenny in *God of the Philosophers* (Oxford: Clarendon Press, 1979), pp. 70–1.

By avoiding characterizing divinity in those ways which assure its distinction from the world and hence entail divine eternity, or else by denying such a formal feature in favor of an everlasting God in time, the claims of divine omniscience have nonetheless forced these philosophers into admitting into divine knowing a quality of timelessness akin to eternity, and also to create an object of knowledge "midway between" what is actual and what is merely possible. Hence the term "middle knowledge." It should be clear how such a treatment prefers propositions to statements regarding what is the case, so that it can speak of true propositions abstracted from what the case *is*. If proponents of divine eternity equate that condition with timelessness, then the difference between the two positions may be largely tactical: where one puts the emphasis. If, however, eternity belongs to God alone as the One whose essence is simply to-be, and as such is the source of each thing existing, then the resolution in terms of eternity will involve an ontology centered on existence and actuality. It is in these terms that we shall now examine divine simpleness.

The Case for Divine Simpleness

The simpleness proposed offered more than a mere denial of multiplicity in divinity, but was positively articulated by insisting that God's nature is simply to-be (*esse*). Aquinas, in his treatment, offers further reasons why no other mode of composition can be found in divinity – potency/act, matter/form, genus/species, substance/accident – but the positive reason underlying every negation is the identity of God's essence with God's very existing. The greatest obstacle to accepting this account as coherent lies in trying to conceive what is meant by existing, or *esse*. It cannot be an accident of substance, since it is presupposed to the notion of substance as *that which is*, whereas accidents presuppose substance. Nor can it be a merely formal feature like *identity*, since such features hold indifferently of possible and actual things, whereas we mean by *esse* the *act* of existing: that which makes something to be here and now.

Here is where Aquinas' maneuver recommends itself. Existing is to be conceived as a constituent feature of whatever is, as toads are constituted toads by the constituent structure called toadness. In the case of *esse*, however, this constituent feature is not merely formal but actual. So Aristotle's analogical complements of potency and act are recapitulated a step beyond matter/form to allow the essence to be realized in an existing individual. The analogy of *act* cannot be further analyzed, as

Aristotle saw, but can be displayed. What we call actions are paradigmatically actions of existing subjects, so the *ur*-action, if you will, is the existing of the acting subject.[24]

One cannot get *behind* this fact of existing, any more than one can *explicate* why the arrival of a newborn infant is always more than the sum of the processes which brought it into being. What now exists is one capable of acting, and in the case of humans, of taking responsibility for one's actions. That is the surplus which must be recognized ontologically even when one cannot analyze it any further. A strategic way to recognize it is to conceive existence as *act* (not *an* act) perfecting the essence as form does matter, by realizing the nature in an existing individual. As the *ur*-act, then, accounting for the constitutive fact that individuals are agents, existing will not be relegated to the status of a mere *given*, or of a presupposition. It will be the source of all further capacities for development and self-actuation which characterize such an individual. (In other words, certain ranges of action are typical of certain types of things, but only the existing individuals of the species can *do* them.)

This last move is the crucial one. If one accepts it, the account given of divine simpleness can be made quite plausible, whereas without it – with a notion of existence as a mere given or presupposition – simpleness remains a puzzle. If one begins with properties, for example, rather than with an acting individual, one will be puzzled to know how two distinct properties, like knowing and willing, could be identified with the divine essence, as simpleness demands, without thereby losing their distinctness in becoming identified with one another.[25] The assertions of simpleness seem incompatible with an elementary application of logic. Moreover, Aquinas' response to this objection appears, from such a perspective, to be a semantic slight of hand: "the words we use for the perfections we attribute to God, although they signify what is one, are not synonymous, for they signify it from many different points of view."[26]

If we assume the primacy of existing individual agents, however, the difficulties can be met and Aquinas' response found to be insightful. For then what we call properties will be located as distinct powers in a subject capable of acting. Where the subject in question is the uniquely divine one, however, which is act without potency, then the distinct acts

---

[24] A further way to display that activity which characterizes the being of an individual is to attend to the way in which judgment crowns the activity of knowing: see my "Essence and Existence" (note 16) or *Knowing* (note 10).

[25] See Alvin Plantinga (note 4), pp. 37–8.

[26] ST 1.13.4.

(knowing and willing) need not be rooted in separate powers. And one should be able to give an analysis of knowing along the lines of the commendation in Genesis 1: "and God saw that it was good," in which a single knowing act, carried to its term, reaches its fruition in the enjoyment of what is – insofar as it is – then the knowing and willing which are distinct acts for us will be but the articulations of a single act of knowing in God.[27] (The only further premise required here is the unproblematic one that an act of knowing "carried to its term" can well be but one act in a mind sufficiently powerful – by analogy with one who "sees" conclusions quickly.)

What seems more perplexing, in fact, is the multiplication of acts of knowing and of willing by the objects known and loved. It was this hurdle which forced Avicenna and Gersonides (though Muslim and Jew, respectively) to limit God's knowing to the "definitions and order of things," whereas al-Ghazali and Maimonides knew they had to defer to Qur'an and Torah to affirm God's care of each individual "without being able to say how."[28] What can we say? That in knowing God's own to-be, God knows and takes pleasure in bringing forth individuals "according to their kinds."[29] If this activity is conceived as a selection among scenarios, it will require a distinct act of will, and the articulation would have to be: in knowing God's own to-be, God knows and takes pleasure in what God *chooses* to bring forth. Yet if the activity is rather understood as a practical knowing, by analogy with doing or making (as *creation* strongly suggests), then no distinct act of choosing will be needed, since the object made is the term of artistic knowing, as the action performed forms the conclusion of a practical syllogism.[30] Choices are entailed, certainly, in

---

[27] Such is the thesis of Bernard Lonergan, whose *Verbum: Word and Idea in Aquinas* (Notre Dame IN: University of Notre Dame Press, 1967) articulates Aquinas' epistemology in such a way as to allow it to develop Augustine's mental analogy for the Trinitarian processions in God.

[28] The formula "without [being able to say] how" (*bi-la kaifa*) is a classic recourse of al-Ghazali in such matters: see Simon van den Bergh, *Averroes' Tahâfût al-Tahafut* (London: Luzac, 1969), pp. 151–2, which incorporates al-Ghazali's original *Tâhafût al-Falâsifâ*, ed. Suliman Dunya (Cairo: Dar al-Ma'arifa, 1980), pp. 153–4. Or the new translation by Micheal Marmura: *The Incoherence of the Philosophers* (Provo UT: Brigham Young University Press, 1997), pp. 77–8. For the others, see Chapter 4 of the present volume "Maimonides, Aquinas and Gersonides on Providence and Evil."

[29] Edward Booth, O.P., *Aristotelian Aporetic Ontology in Islamic and Christian Writers* (Cambridge: Cambridge University Press, 1983) shows how Aquinas' ability to formulate God's creative activity in so neat a fashion relies on his appropriation of pseudo-Dionysius.

[30] James Ross makes this fruitful suggestion, among others, in "Creation II" in *The Existence and Nature of God*, ed. Alfred Freddoso (note 9).

human execution, but they subserve the intention coming to realization in the object.

That God's self-knowledge of God's own essence as the to-be in which things can participate in being, after their own fashion, becomes a practical action of creation is of course a free act on God's part, but again, freedom need not (and I contend, ought not) primarily be considered as freedom of choice.[31] What turns a contemplative *delectatio* into a making defies our articulation, but it need not demand a distinct "decision" on God's part. In other words, the sense in which creation is at once gratuitous yet utterly fitting, according to the axiom that "good diffuses itself," reminds us that divine freedom may be better understood on the model of Zen "resonance" than on that of a western penchant for *decisions*.[32] Or to put it another way, the most significant decisions of our lives seem less *made* than they are "taken," as most western languages put it. If the good moves us by drawing us rather than by constraining us, so that following the bent of one's nature can be at once natural and free, why cannot creation be similarly understood?

These considerations are meant to persuade us of the plausibility of a simple divine nature whose unitary act of loving knowing of itself issues in a making (creating) of the universe. Many questions remain, of course, and proper arguments need to be supplied as needed, but enough has been said to suggest that the effort to supply them is worthwhile. The articulation of simpleness as an essence identical with its to-be (or "act of existing") is clearly the critical piece in the pattern. For without the premise that the to-be of a thing is the source of all its activity (and hence of whatever perfects it), we would not be supplied with a unitary perspective or with the heightened sense of *act* needed to speak of creation as the free culmination of divine loving knowledge of itself. We shall see in a moment that this same premise offers fruitful links both with mystical aspirations and with subsequent Trinitarian developments in Christian theology. For the moment, however, it is worth warning that such a simpleness also entails a divinity that is radically unknowable. The very attempt to conceive the *esse* which comprises divinity will have alerted many; the fact that a normal subject/predicate sentence will *ipso facto* be

---

[31]   Kretzmann and Stump concur, with a careful presentation of Aquinas' strong alternative views on freedom, in "Absolute Simplicity" (note 5).

[32]   Such a strategy would suggest ways of responding to Norman Kretzmann's quandary regarding Aquinas and the gratuity of creation, in "Goodness, Knowledge and Indeterminacy in the Philosophy of Thomas Aquinas", in *Journal of Philosophy* 80 (1983), pp. 631–42. For similarly fruitful suggestions, see Etienne Gilson, *Le Thomisme*, 5th edn (Paris: J. Vrin, 1938), pp. 183–5.

ill-formed of God clinches the matter. At this point, the analogous reaches of our discourse have to be pressed into service, yet the fact remains that they are there to be so.[33]

Without some such attempt to articulate what distinguishes God from the world of which God is the principle and free bestower of its being, we seem to be left with mere assertions that God is without cause, or *a se*.[34] It does not help to insist that God commands all, for one can still wonder whether the being capable of commanding all is in fact creator of all. And if the sense in which God "necessarily exists" is left to compete with that of necessary truths – if one fails to distinguish existential from logical truth – then God can be made to look much like Plato's demiurge, fashioning the world according to the forms. Whereas on the pattern of a God whose essence is to-be, necessary truths assume a properly formal role as the manners in which created things can participate in such *esse*.[35] The critical fact remains, however, that a treatment of divinity which looks only to divine attributes (or properties) without attempting to articulate the uniqueness of the divine nature – announced in the faith-claims of Jew, Christian, and Muslim that God is one – should leave one wondering whether one is discussing divinity or not. And if the tenor of the discussion, besides, leads readers to suspect one to be referring to "the biggest thing around," then the suspicion may well indicate a fatal flaw in the enterprise.

Simpleness, Eternity, and Religious Life

"Process theologians" regard a divinity beyond change (and hence eternal) who is "pure act" to be inherently unresponsive and antithetical to the God presented to Jews and Christians in the Bible. Some would even hold this "classical doctrine of God" responsible for secularism in the west, since no sensitive individual could respond to such a God.[36] Perhaps enough has been said here to suggest that the "classical doctrine" they

---

[33] This is the burden of Ross' *Portraying* (note 7). For a theological application, see Roger White, "Notes on analogical predication and speaking about God," in *Philosophical Frontiers of Christian Theology*, eds Brian Hebblethwaite and Stewart Sutherland (Cambridge: Cambridge University Press, 1982), pp. 197–226.

[34] Here is the weakness of al-Ghazali's critique of Ibn Sina, in his *Tahâfût* (note 28), pp. 191–2.

[35] See *Knowing* (note 10), chapter 4.

[36] This is a subsidiary thesis of Schubert Ogden in *The Reality of God, and Other Essays* (New York: Harper and Row, 1966).

revile bears little relation to a thinker as classical as Aquinas. In fact, once one takes *esse* to be the source of all perfections, one finds divine activity to be thoroughly "intentional" in character, relating to itself and its creation with an understanding love which is the quintessence of responsiveness. Moreover, in the measure that the animating spark of one's own being can be said to be a participation in the very to-be of the One from whom all existence flows, there can be said to be in each of us what John of the Cross calls the "centre of the soul."[37]

One way to God, then, could be by way of disciplines of mind and heart directed to that "centre" or source of one's life. More over, the understanding proffered of eternity as itself at the heart of temporal existence rather than removed from it, suggesting the metaphors of *presence* and *present* life, underscores how God's simpleness – conceived as pure *esse* – can open the way to an invitation to live present to God in the present of one's life, in a way mindful of spiritual disciplines in diverse traditions. And for Christians, the fact that the divine to-be expresses itself in a knowing which becomes a *delectatio* opens the way to exploiting the analogies for triunity offered by Augustine and developed by Aquinas, wherein Father, Son, and Spirit are likened to the articulation of our knowledge in a word which brings intrinsic enjoyment as it expresses what is good, true, and beautiful.[38]

All this by way of suggestion, since the process theologians' criticism is taken even if it misidentifies its target. Philosophical considerations regarding divinity will fail in their ultimate aim of clarification if they end up presenting a God to which one cannot respond with one's whole person. For if divinity means anything, it must mean "the beginning and the end of all things, and especially of rational creatures," and nothing less than "the love which moves the sun and moon and all the stars" (Dante) can present itself as the ultimate end of rational creatures. Such at least is the claim of every religious tradition, and something which many rational creatures come to appreciate in their lifetime. In the Islamic tradition, al-Ghazali's criticism of the writings of "the philosophers" came pointedly to this: that they (and especially Ibn Sina) offered a scheme culminating in a God whom one could not worship, for the One presented could not properly be called Creator or Lord.[39] Similarly, my concern in

---

[37] John of the Cross, *The Living Flame of Love*, Stanza 1, pars 9, 14; Stanza 4, par. 3; cf. *Collected Works*, trans. K. Kavanaugh and O. Rodriguez (Washington DC: Institute of Carmelite Studies, 1979), pp. 582, 584, 643.

[38] See Bernard Lonergan, *Verbum* (note 27).

[39] al-Ghazali, *Tahâfût*, pp. 148–9; van den Bergh, pp. 124 ff, Marmura, pp. 65 ff (note 28).

this article has been to offer a sketch of a way in which philosophers treating of divinity might so distinguish God from the world as to assure that the One from whom all things come would also be the One to whom rational creatures could wholeheartedly respond.

Chapter 2

THE UNKNOWABILITY OF GOD IN AL-GHAZALI

The main lines of this exploration are quite simply drawn. That the God whom Jews, Christians, and Muslims worship outstrips our capacities for characterization, and hence must be unknowable, will be presumed as uncontested. The reason that God is unknowable stems from our shared confession that "the Holy One, blessed be He," and "the Father almighty, creator of heaven and earth," and certainly "Allah, the merciful One" is *one*; and just why God's oneness entails God's being unknowable deserves discussion, though that will occur as we move along.[1] The issue facing us is the one which preoccupied al-Ghazali: how does a seeker respond to that unknowability? The root meaning of the Arabic word for "student" (*tawlib*) means "seeker," and that attitude of "seeking the face of God," along with the indescribability of the face, will be presumed throughout our discussion. That's why we are stuck with the clumsy term "unknowable" rather than its more euphonious Greek form "agnostic." For Western agnostics are such largely because they cannot find God sufficiently compelling, while they "would not have the impudence to claim to be atheists" – as one contemporary seeker puts it.[2] So theologians feel it necessary to enclose the term in quotation marks when discussing, say, Aquinas' "agnosticism" regarding divinity. Yet a genuine *unknowing* does lie at the heart of the inquiry of the Jew, Christian, or Muslim seeking after God; indeed, it is the unknowing which distinguishes a search for God from lusting after idols. So let us follow al-Ghazali in an effort to discover the lineaments of both search and seeker after an unknowable God.

[1] For the general point, see my *Knowing the Unknowable God: Ibn Sina, Maimonides, Aquinas* (Notre Dame IN: University of Notre Dame Press, 1986); for specifics regarding al-Ghazali, see Fadlou Shehadi, *Ghazali's Unique Unknowable God* (Leiden: Brill, 1964).
[2] Jan-Pierre Jossua, *The Condition of the Witness* (London: SCM, 1985), p. 14.

Finding the Proper Mode

One characteristic way of responding to such a divinity is to postulate or produce a scheme which will render it accessible. This was supplied to the philosophically minded Muslim world in the Neoplatonic scheme whereby all of reality is conceived as emanating from the One. It was al-Farabi who elaborated the manner of origination from "the First," as he preferred to call the source of all, and did so with such care that Ibn Sina could take it over whole cloth, with a few minor adjustments. Celebrated by Ibrahim Madkour, a contemporary Egyptian philosopher, as the distinctive contribution of Arabic philosophy, such an elaborate scheme cannot but strike us a gratuitous setting for science fiction.[3] That is in part, of course, because its ptolemaic astronomical base has been supplanted, so that heavenly speculation must give way to verification. Yet speculation remains governed by cogency, and it does seem odd on the face of it that philosophers could think to bridge the hiatus from one to many merely by adding nine (or ten) intermediaries. The heavenly bodies might have suggested such stepping stones, but could hardly warrant postulating them in the role reserved for spheres in the cosmic scheme.

So there must have been a yet deeper motivation, since it was the Greeks who taught us to value consistency. Let me suggest that motivation to have been the intellectual ordering of the universe, much as Leibniz' and Newton's dreams of a universal *mathesis* inspired the seventeenth century. Inconsistencies pale in the presence of a potentially fruitful vision, and rightly so, for the hope is that the subsequent "research program" will iron them out. What the Neoplatonic emanation scheme promised was a cosmic ordering which mimicked the powerful Aristotelian syllogistic, so that suitably powerful intellects would be enabled to traverse the path in reverse, and arrive at the One from whom all comes. So fitted to one another are the structures of psyche and cosmos that thinkers may ascend an intellectual ladder from earth to heaven, by retracing the path which brought the universe into being.

It is just that pretension which Ghazali set out to expose and destroy in his *Tahafut al-Falasifa*.[4] His most trenchant arguments show the logical

---

[3] Ibrahim Madkour, *La place d'al Farabi dans l'Ecolephilosophique musulmane* (Paris: Librairie d'Amerique et d'Ouest, 1934), p. 14. For al-Farabi's development, see *Al-Farabi on the Perfect State*, ed. Richard Waizer (Oxford: Clarendon Press, 1985); for Ibn Sina, see *Avicenne: La metaphysique de Shifa*, trans. G. C. Anawati (Paris: J. Vrin, 1978, 1985), *al-Shifa: al-Ilahiyat*, ed. I. Madkour and G. Anawati (Cairo: Government Printing Office, 1960).

[4] A fine translation of Ghazali can be found in Simon van den Bergh, ed. and trans., *Averroes' Tahafut al Tahafut* (Oxford: Oxford University Press, 1954); *Tahafut al-Falasifa*, ed.

impossibility of ten or any number of mediators to resolve the disparity between the one and the many. To attenuate differences is not to bridge logical divides. In fact, as Ghazali saw, the effect of the scheme is precisely to render divinity part of the cosmos, as the ambiguity in al-Farabi's "First" indicates, and thereby undermine the distinction of the One from many so firmly underscored by his confession of faith. This perception is displayed in his ostensibly less cogent arguments that emanation evacuates genuine agency. Ibn-Rushd finds these jejune, as well he might, since "agent" is a thoroughly analogous term, and Ghazali does fail to specify his primary analogate. It is not difficult to supply, of course, as the Lord of heaven and earth to whom creating the universe is a free act. Moreover, since the Muslim *falasifah* aspired to offer an elaboration of creation, Ghazali's arguments prove to be more telling than they first looked. And it was of course that pretension on the part of Muslim thinkers which he wanted to expose. He was not addressing Greeks to whom the distinction of the One from all the rest remained in umbrage; he was addressing his fellow believers in their activity as philosophers. And while he scored some telling points against them as philosophers, his arguments are the more trenchant against their adaptations of philosophy to explicate a shared belief in God.

Here we encounter an historical-cultural fact about Ghazali himself, and as Louis Gardet would lead us to believe, about Islam as well.[5] Early Muslim philosophers, notably al-Kindi and al-Farabi, tended to adopt as "philosophy" a synthesis of Aristotle with Plato (through the spurious "Theology of Aristotle") woven into a relatively seamless explanatory scheme. Developed as it was, there was little chance to put it to work in explicating assertions of the Qur'an, whose imagery also lent itself more to elaboration in terms supplied by Arabic poetry or by Iranian thought. Islamic philosophers could not draw on anything like the efforts of early church writers in the Christian east and west to formulate in a philosophical idiom the implications of Jesus' life and teachings. In this sense, philosophy was a part of Christian self-understanding from the beginning, as different individuals sought to put it at the service of a faith-assent and so enrich from within our understanding of divine revelation (Augustine); whereas it presented itself to Islam as an independent explanatory system.

S. Dunya (Cairo: al-Maaref, 1980) and a new translation by Michael Marmura in *The Incoherence of the Philosophers* (Provo UT: Brigham Young University Press, 1997).
[5] Louis Gardet, "Rencontre de la philosophie musulmane et de la pensée Patristique," in *Révue Thomiste* LV (1947), pp. 45–112, esp. pp. 87–94. And so emerged the situation exploited by Averroes: cf. Leon Gauthier, *La théorie d'Ibn-Rochd sur les rapports de la religion et de la philosophie* (Paris: Leroux, 1909).

There were certainly parallels in the Christian world, as Peter Brown notes in explicating Augustine's description of his encounter with "Platonism" as an alternative to following Jesus in the church.[6] Yet the very fact that we register Augustine's reaction as strange reminds us that it was a local phenomenon; Clement of Alexandria, Gregory of Nyssa, and others had already demonstrated how to read Plato as breaking ground for God's revelation in Jesus, precisely by displaying how his writings could usefully be employed in showing that revelation to be the highest wisdom – or "true philosophy."

Islamic philosophers tended, however, to work in relative independence of the Qur'an, sometimes pausing to try to persuade us that, say, Qur'anic assertions regarding God's role in creation could be understood in an emanationist sense.[7] Ghazali will have nothing of that. Moreover, since this collective endeavor of "the philosophers" had come to epitomize the activity of intellect in the Muslim world, Ghazali could only conclude that we cannot entrust ourselves to intellect ('aql) in the sense of relying on its discursive powers to orient us to what is real and true (haqq). Nor can we dispense, however, with its discriminatory power, which Ghazali himself uses quite deftly to destroy what he regarded as a pretense on the part of philosophers to construct an alternative to revelation. Yet the stage is set for what we might call al-Ghazali's "turn to the subject." His Ashar'ite convictions already predisposed him to forbear looking for traces of the creator in the order and structure of the world, since one could not conclude anything from the regularities of nature. Moreover, the emanationist model for necessity reinforced those same convictions, since such a universe inevitably stood over against the creating power of Allah, and so appeared to limit that power. Once an intelligibility intrinsic to natural species had been articulated in an emanationist model, other ways of explicating creation so as to accentuate its inherent intelligibility had difficulty emerging. So Ghazali eschewed using reason to elaborate a philosophical account of creation, focusing instead on developing an anthropology explicit enough to serve as a vehicle for our search for God, and organizing Qur'anic materials to assemble a cosmos rich enough to provide the setting ground for such a journey. That is already a great deal, to be sure, and it is striking that he never senses the need to offer any justification for *these* constructs. It is as though the enterprise of the philosophers, while discredited as an explanatory-scheme-cum-way-to-God alternative to the Qur'an, nonetheless licensed (and perhaps even

---

[6]   Peter Brown, *Augustine of Hippo* (Berkeley: University of California Press, 1967).
[7]   See the relevant expositions in al-Farabi and Ibn Sina (note 3); for an appraisal, Louis Gardet, *La pensée religieuse d'Avicenne* (Paris: Vrin, 1956), pp. 41–51, 202–3.

demanded) a similarly luxuriant world constructed out of cosmic and human powers, to offer seekers after God something of a map for their journey.

The Heart at the Center

Ghazali's response to the unknowability of God, then, and partly in reaction to the philosophers' scheme to render divinity accessible, was to teach us how to place discursive reason at the service of the heart, as minister to its king.[8] For the "heart is predisposed for the disclosure in it of the Supreme Reality (Truth) present in all things."[9] Nowhere does he offer a systematic psychic anatomy of the seeker, but in that place in the *Ihya'* where he proposes to explicate four terms often used to refer to that in us which responds to the lure of the unknowable One – heart (*qalb*), spirit (*ruh*), self/soul (*nafs*), and reason or intellect (*'aql*) – each of the last three is said to be given its inner orientation by the *heart*, which (in another place) is said itself to be a divine thing (*amr rabbani*).[10]

So as discursive reason functions properly when at the service of the heart, it is the individual's response to the divine invitation to become God's servant which directs and absorbs al-Ghazali's philosophic efforts. And since everything becomes subordinated to that primary task, speculative reason subserves practical reason: learning how to undertake the journey of a seeker, with whatever knowledge may be needed for that. Moreover, the "wayfarer knows only his own station which he has reached in his journey: he knows it and knows what station is behind him. But he does not have an encompassing knowledge of the reality of what is before him."[11] It is enough for him, Ghazali implies, as wayfarer, that he "believe in it with a faith in the unseen." Furthermore, "hearts preoccupied by anything else than God cannot be entered by the knowledge of God Most High's glory" (*ibid.*). And while Ghazali does not expressly

---

[8] I shall be focusing on his mature development in the *Ihya' 'ulum al-din* (Cairo, 1967), an outline summary of which is available in G. H. Bousquet, *Ghazali: vivification des sciences de la foi* (Paris: Max Besson, 1955), and relevant portions of which are supplied in Richard McCarthy, *Freedom and Fulfillment* (Boston: Twayne, 1980), Appendix v; reissued by Fons Vitae, Louisville KY in 2000 as *Deliverance from Error and Five Key Texts*. References to the *Ihya'* will be by book, *bayan* (or explication) and page number, followed by Bousquet (B) or McCarthy (M): for this reference, see bk III, *bayan* 3, p. 9, McCarthy 371 (= III, b. 3, p. 9, M 371).

[9] *Ibid.*, III, b. 8, p. 24, M 378.

[10] *Ibid.*, III, b. 1, pp. 4–6; M 365–8; III, b. 6, p. 19, B 208.

[11] *Ibid.*, III, b. 4, p. 11, M 374.

identify speculation as a distracting preoccupation, it can be seen not to have led to the truth about God and God's universe in the philosophers, and he does insist elsewhere that only exceptional persons – prophets, in fact, gifted with God's special power – can engage both in worldly sciences and in those of the heart.[12] Finally, there would be no real incentive to engage in cosmic speculation if the order and structure of things offered no regularities in which we might hope to discover traces of divinity. As we shall see, however, when the initiative lies with the heart, countless things can be read as icons of the divine maker.

The way of putting reason at the service of faith, then, has been set. It will be a way of practice and of interiorization. Not the task of transforming speculative reason so that philosophy itself might serve as a vehicle of insight into matters divine, but rather to harness the discerning powers of reason to the inner task of becoming the sort of person I am called to become. The operative power in that activity will be the heart, for it is natural to the heart to respond to God's command (*'amr*). The goal of understanding God and God's world is clearly subordinated to the practical aim of aligning one's entire self to the response of an untrammeled heart. Yet the subordination is a tactical one, for with that alignment will come an understanding far surpassing the necessary truths it is native to intellect to know. What is revealed to the pure of heart, whose intellectual efforts are bent on detecting and detaching the veils of concern from their hearts, are the mysteries of the *malakut*: the spiritual world, quite invisible to intellect (*'aql*) alone.[13]

Such a strategy for arriving at a right understanding of God and God's world contrasts clearly with the more speculative program of an Aquinas, who was concerned to take philosophical understanding itself – in the Aristotelian and Neoplatonic forms in which it came to him – and make it over into a servant of religious understanding, and so develop the hybrid knowledge of theology.[14] In Aquinas' cultural world, the aspiration to elaborate a *logos* (or *scientia*) of God – a *theo-logy* – was at once laudable and possible. That is, the task represented a noble cultural goal, and conditions were favorable to accomplishing it. Without detracting a bit from

---

[12]   *Ibid.*, III, b. 7, pp. 22–3, B 210.

[13]   *Ibid.*, III, b. 7, p. 22, B 209. On *malakut*, see A. J. Wensinck, "On the Relation between Ghazali's Cosmology and his Mysticism," in *Mededeelingen der Akademie von Wetensehappen* LXXV (1933), pp. 183–209, summarized and extended in ch. 3 of his *La pensée de Ghazali* (Paris: Adrien-Maisonneuve, 1940).

[14]   On the status of theology as a "subalternate science" (or "form of knowledge") see Aquinas, *Summa Theologiae*, part 1, question 1 (vol. 1 in T. Gilby, ed., London: Eyre and Spottiswoode, 1963), also M.-D. Chenu, *La théologie comme science au XIIIe siècle* (Paris: J. Vrin, 1957).

his singular achievement, one must also say that Aquinas was the right person in the right place at the right time – and extraordinarily responsive to his heart's desire.

Ghazali, however, is better compared with Augustine, and later with Bonaventure, Pascal, and Kierkegaard. With Augustine primarily, and not simply because his *Munqidh* invites comparison with the *Confessions*, but because the need on the part of both to compose such a work shows the primacy each gives to the inner task of responding to a divine invitation to become what one is called to become. Ghazali's preoccupation with *yaqin* (or certitude) in his autobiographical piece may suggest Descartes' *Discourse* to us, but unless one is disposed to understand Descartes' travails as far less cerebral than he presents them himself, their respective concerns are as divergent as their subsequent odysseys and resolutions.[15] Which is not to deny that each sought a *point d'appui*, but where Descartes construed that to be an indubitable starting point, Ghazali sought a sure harbor. Augustine's opening summation of the universal sense of his own quest: "our hearts are restless until they rest in thee", fits Ghazali neatly, as does the faith assertion explaining that inquietude: "thou hast made us for thyself, O Lord." So the task is given – inbuilt, as it were – in God's forming creatures whose self (or soul-*nafs*) comprises intellect (*'aql*), spirit (*ruh*), and heart (*qalb*). And since that self images the creator precisely in those "parts" whose natural disposition is to respond when that creator speaks, there can be no higher task than the one entrusted to each person: to order and to use those powers to facilitate the kind of response which will make oneself into as perfect a divine image as possible.

Responding to an Unknowable God

How does the unfolding of that task both respect and reflect God's unknowability? The easy answer to that question is to note how, for Ghazali, the task consists in developing in oneself the qualities displayed in the 99 names of God. Such is the ostensible goal of his treatise "explicating the meaning of the beautiful names of God" – the *Maqsad*.[16] But does not that response jeopardize God's unknowability in presuming that

---

[15] Farid Jabre, *La notion de certitude selon Ghazali* (Paris: Vrin, 1958) shows just how superficial are the similarities with Descartes, as Ghazali adopts a "performative resolution" to his problem (p. 126), "practicing the art of certitude" (p. 130). Moreover, Ghazali characterizes his situation of radical doubt as an *illness*, rather than enjoin such doubt upon us all as a *method*.

[16] Fadlou Shehadi, ed., *al Maqsad al-asna fi Sharh ma'ani asma' Allah al-Husna* (Beirut: Librairie Orientale, 1971), relevant portions in McCarthy (note 8), appendix iv; English

we can know God to be merciful, compassionate, just, and the true/real One, etc.? It need not, of course, since it is precisely its manner of being merciful, just, or compassionate which gives divinity its proper unknowability. So perhaps that is why the objection does not arise for Ghazali. However, there must be some *traces*, some pattern or shape so that the mercy we recognize in our local holy man can be related to that of Allah.[17] Without that presumption, and especially in the face of its denial, his project has no reasonable hope of realization. Which suggests that such enterprises of practical reason presuppose, at least for us, a modicum of speculative understanding. We have seen a left-handed recognition of this demand in his anthropology-cum-cosmology postulated to enable the essential task to proceed. But what is it that prevented or inhibited Ghazali from assuming the speculative task as well as the practical one, and thereby putting philosophy itself, as well as the discerning powers of reason, at the service of a quest for religious understanding?

I have already suggested that the model of philosophical understanding available to him was less one of inquiry than of logical and cosmological schemes promising necessary truths about the universe and its origin. This could not but strike him as "cheap grace," and in that his religious instincts served him well. For once Allah had been assimilated to "the First" from which all else necessarily flows, exit the formal fact of divine unknowability, together with the ecstasy demanded of those who would align themselves with that unknowable One. One might suppose that the "intellectual mysticism" of an Ibn Sina simply left him cold.[18] Moreover, Ghazali did not seem to be philosophically minded enough to see how, once having demolished the emanationist ladder, some other speculative points of linkage might be discovered. He is content, for example, to characterize divinity as what alone has no cause, but misses the point of the philosophers' insistence that such a One cannot then be thought of (in quidditative terms) as "having an essence."[19] In other words, whatever has no cause, and thus needs no cause, can be shown from that fact alone to enjoy a unique ontological status. Ghazali shows no desire to exploit this formal fact about divinity to underscore philosophically the distinction of such a One from all that originates from it, and so elaborate an alternative metaphysics to that offered by the Islamic philosophers.

---

translation by David Burrell and Nazih Daher: *Al-Ghazali on the Ninety-Nine Beautiful Names of God* (Cambridge: Islamic Texts Society, 1995).

[17] Cf. Shehadi (note 1), pp. 101–14.

[18] Gardet (note 5), pp. 153–96, esp. pp. 185–96.

[19] *Tahafut al-Falasifa* (note 2), discussion 8, pp. 180–92; van den Bergh, pp. 222 ff; Marmura, 113; also Shehadi (note 1, p. 1), pp. 41–2.

What seems to us to be so natural a step for a thinker clearly did not present itself to Ghazali as an imperative. Perhaps it was a matter of constituencies, and of the expectations students have of their teachers. The university, at whose origins Aquinas attended, offered a soil quite different from the cathedral schools and monastic oratories out of which it had emerged. The *disputatio* may have had its roots in Islamic *shar'ia*, but its exercise in the West encouraged master and pupil alike to bold forays of questioning.[20] What was the process of teaching/learning like in which Ghazali participated? The fact remains that he had available another cosmological/psychological scheme which allowed him to affirm the affinity of human understanding for things divine, yet locate the homing instinct not in the intellect but in the heart. And in a heart which, purified of its own urges – notably desire and anger – would respond to the divine as imaged in the particulars of this world. A purified heart will readily read things in the world as icons of that real world in which it is at home. Not unlike Augustine noting, in the tenth book of the *Confessions* (after the crucial turning of book eight), how things now said to him: "we did not make ourselves."[21]

If that be the program, two questions spontaneously arise. How can we go about purifying the heart? That is al-Ghazali's question and his answer is the main part of the program of the *Ihya'*. The second question is ours: how does he know all that he pretends to know about the heart and the intellect and the true world in which our hearts would be at home? He would be likely to say: from the Qur'an. That is, it would have to have been revealed, since what we know by natural inclination is too simple and basic.[22] Yet it would be more accurate to say: from those who have conformed their lives to the Qur'an. For such ones, there is a process of authentication, like a way of coming to know-by-faith, which confirms the existence of such a world by its direct presence to us. This is the famous *dhawq* or taste of things divine, which is self-authenticating because it implies the presence of the real world of the *malakut*.[23] How do assertions about *dhawq* function for Ghazali, however, without claiming more than they can sustain? They can only purport to be vehicles for self-becoming and not directly statements about reality. They certainly do not

---

[20]   George Makdisi, *The Rise of Colleges: Institutions of Learning in Islam and the West* (Edinburgh: Edinburgh University Press, 1981), pp. 128 ff.

[21]   *Confessions*, Bk 10, ch. 6; on singular things and events as icons for Ghazali, cf. Wensinck, *La pensée* . . . (note 13), pp. 90–7.

[22]   *Ibid.*, III, b. 7, p. 21, B 209.

[23]   W. Montgomery Watt, *Muslim Intellectual; a study of Al-Ghazali* (Edinburgh: Edinburgh University Press, 1963), esp. his critical remarks at pp. 168–9.

compete with emanationist statements in attempting to delineate the structure of the world and of its coming to be. They are couched more in the language of invitation: take these steps and discover the outcome for yourself. Nowhere does he describe the world of the *malakut* except to link it with the angels, and present it as the goal and native home of the searching heart. It is up to the wayfarers to discover its geography.[24]

So if God be unknowable, the way to God is unchartable, except as a set of invitations to set out on a journey of self-becoming, which defines our central task in life. As useful as other forms of knowledge may be, this practical one regards our own destiny, and we are the highest beings inhabiting the material world. Insofar as any of those other forms of knowledge, however, would purport to carry us to the same goal as this divine knowing-cum-practice – to a knowledge of God – then we would be misled. So philosophical speculation, in the measure that it would attempt such a thing, would be misguided. But what about its exploring the cogency of the claims on which the heart's journey rests? His answer here is a practical one, respecting the capacities of human inquirers. It is one thing to respond to the instincts of our hearts, and quite another to scrutinize the psychological and cosmological claims made in describing the heart's trajectory. Most of us are unable to do both at once. So best leave such analysis to the prophets, who are able to combine speculative inquiry with wholehearted personal response since they are fortified by the "holy spirit."[25] For the rest of us, such inquiry can only deflect us from the essential task of following the way revealed to the Prophet. So while the primacy of that task does not in principle supplant efforts to elaborate a speculative philosophical synthesis, it tends to discourage them in practice.

Critical and Comparative Perspectives

So the upshot of God's unknowability, for Ghazali, is to render speculative inquiry into God and the things of God effectively incompatible with the essential human task of responding wholeheartedly to the lure of the One – from whom all things derive. For such inquiry is bound to fall short of its goal, and to the extent that it pretends to carry us to that

---

[24] For the inherent relation between knowing and acting in these domains, see: *Al-Ghazali on Faith in Divine Unity and Trust in Divine Providence*, trans. David Burrell [= Kitab al-Tawid wa'l-Tawkkul from *Ihya' 'ulum al-din*] (Louisville KY: Fons Vitae, 2001), and Timothy Gianotti, *Al-Ghazali's Unspeakable Doctrine of the Soul* (Leiden: Brill, 2001).

[25] *Ibid.*, III, b. 7, p. 24, B 210.

goal, we will be misled and diverted from setting out on the path which can take us there. Yet a wholehearted response cannot be a mindless one, so the discerning power of intellect needs always to be at hand. So no one dare accuse al-Ghazali – or Pascal or Kierkegaard, for that matter – of being anti-intellectual. But others of us can, and some among us must try to explore the assertions they do make by the light of reason. Were we to undertake that inquiry without neglecting our hearts' desire would we not be placing our intellects that much more at the service of the heart? In Ghazali's case, did a picture of doing philosophy which deals only with necessities and so underestimates other forms of understanding, lead him to conflate a proper subordination of goals with a subordination in epistemic authority?

One may legitimately argue that the quest of the whole person to relate oneself rightly to the cosmos outstrips the deliverances of reason in specified ways, without calling its proper authority into question.[26] Furthermore, Ghazali himself deftly employed argument where it served his purposes. Yet if his own understanding of the task of philosophical inquiry had been shaped by the view of speculative reason displayed in the cosmic emanation scheme, that enterprise would certainly appear inimical to the personal task of rightly relating oneself to one's creator. For conceiving creation as emanation from the First by way of necessary consequence could only compromise the transcendence of the One from whom all things come. So the mode of rational inquiry after which emanation was modeled could not be a reliable guide in one's quest for a right understanding in order to respond rightly to divine demands.

Were philosophical inquiry capable of a more supple and analogous manner of proceeding – say, in acknowledging its own limitations and in turning that acknowledgment into a way of understanding a transcendent reality – then such a reason could be directed by the heart to an inquiry into existence itself as well as assist in the existential task of becoming a faithful servant of the One. In his forays into theodicy as well as his effort to prove God's existence, Ghazali did venture on that route.[27] In that respect, he may be compared with Thomas Aquinas. But in his overall attitude to reason, he is more fruitfully considered with Augustine,

---

[26] Cf. Diogenes Allen, *Three Outsiders: Pascal, Kierkegaard, Simone Weil* (Cambridge MA: Cowley, 1981).

[27] For a critical assessment of Ghazali's venture into proving God's existence, see S. de Beaurecueil and G. C. Anawati, "Une preuve de l'existence de Dieu chez Ghazzali et S. Thomas," *MIDEO* (= *Melanges de l'Institut Dominicain des Etudes Orientales*), 3 (1956), 207–58; for Ghazali's theodicy, see Eric L. Ormsby, *Theodicy in Islamic Thought* (Princeton NJ: Princeton University Press, 1984), p. 11.

Bonaventure, and Pascal, whose characteristic strategies employed reason to show up its limitations. Aquinas had his own struggles with a philosophy heavily beholden to Avicenna, much of it masquerading as a developing of Augustine's thought.[28] But Ghazali was too close to that current of thought, which also assumed for him the form of an opposing camp. As a result, he did his best to master it, offered an exquisite summation of its findings in the *Maqasid*, and chose the route of practical reason to bring together intellect and heart, reason and faith. One unforeseen result of that choice can supply a controversial upshot of this exploratory inquiry.

I have already noted how powerful a picture the emanation scheme presented. So much so, indeed, that the very one who effectively demolished its pretenses would turn around to offer a substitute for it in his more natively Islamic picture of the *malakut*. (Something similar may be said of Aquinas, who consistently argued against any created participation in the act of creation, yet who nonetheless can be found relying on the speculative framework supplied by Avicenna to account for God's action in the world.[29]) My suggestion now is a more radical one and less textually supportable. It relies rather on one's assessment of the *tone* of Ghazali's treatment of reason serving the heart's desire, and it regards what I take to be a stringent intellectualizing of that desire. It is as though the heart must become more and more like the intellect, as intellect (in its highest meaning and function) is subsumed into heart. Then Ghazali's decision to eschew exploiting the speculative role of intellect meant that those functions would, *en revanche*, so shape the heart's response as to crowd out the affections to ape a more intellectual synthesis. That is an evocative observation, based on my assessment of the cerebral character of his quite effusive writing on the heart's response. One index of that cerebral turn is his characteristic way of dealing with desire (*shahwa*) and with anger (*ghadab*) – Aristotle's concupiscible and irascible appetites.[30] It is as though the personal task must take on the character of an intellectual synthesis as well. God's unknowability will then be protected, since divinity is only accessible as the goal of a personal becoming (and transformation), but that process itself will be described so as to attribute to it a greater degree of *knowing* than one normally associates with the heart, as affections are suffused with light! For some, indeed, this intellectualizing of *heart* leads

<hr/>

[28]   Cf. E. Gilson, "Pourquoi S. Thomas a critiqué S. Augustin," in *Archives d'histoire littéraire et doctrinale du moyen âge* 1 (1926–7), pp. 5–127.
[29]   See B. J. Lonergan, *Grace and Freedom* (London: Darton, Longman and Todd, 1971), p. 98.
[30]   *Ibid.*, III, b. 3, pp. 8–9, M 72.

them to mistrust Ghazali's directions towards a religious-mystical way, as lacking the intrinsic authority of an authentic seeker on that way.

In any case, the main lines of al-Ghazali's account of the essential unknowability of God, together with an appropriate response to that situation, are clear enough. Given the fact that "God is a being necessarily existing of Himself (al-mawjud al-wajib al-wujud bi-dhatihi),"[31] it should be clear that this "peculiar divine property belongs only to God and only God knows it." Moreover "it is inconceivable that anyone know it save Him or one who is His like, since He has no like, no other knows it." On such an account, "only God knows God" (ibid.). So the resources of philosophy confirm God's uniqueness or tawhid: the utter distinction of the One from all else: "everything the exercise of which is possible," which does in fact exist from that One "according to the best ways of order and perfection".[32] Since nothing but God's creative power can account for the fact that "what is possible in itself" in fact exists, however, no rational scheme can hope to penetrate that divinely bestowed order and perfection.

Having destroyed the emanation scheme with its pretended conceptual bridge from necessary to contingent existence, Ghazali must eschew any pretense to know the nature of divinity, and rely on the access provided by the "names of God." This allows him two routes: the manifestly inadequate one of comparing divine with human attributes, and the clearly impossible one of identification with divinity by assimilating those attributes to oneself. Ghazali carefully examines the way of identification, alluding to al-Hallaj ("I am the Truth" – an attribute reserved for God, who alone is true/real) and citing Abu Yazid (al-Bistami): "I sloughed off myself as the snake sloughs off its skin: then I looked, and behold, I am He!"[33] Strictly speaking, such assertions can only be false, for "a speaker's assertion that the creature becomes the Lord is a statement which is self-contradictory,"[34] but out of respect for the speakers Ghazali allows them a poetic license and excuses them as uttered under the "influence of ecstatic rapture."[35] But that simply underscores the fact that the way of immediacy "is something impossible for a creature and closed to all save God,"[36] leaving us with the names which can do no more than suggest what God

---

[31] Maqsad 47 [ET 35], M 342–3.
[32] Maqsad 47 [ET 35], M 342. See Ormsby (note 27) for a thorough and illuminating presentation of the dispute over al-Ghazali's "best of all possible worlds."
[33] Maqsad 166 [ET 153], M 357.
[34] Maqsad 164 [ET 151], M 356.
[35] Maqsad 168 [ET 155], M 358.
[36] Maqsad 53 [ET 40], M 344.

is like, since they name attributes of this inaccessible One whose knowers'
(al-'arafin, a Sufi allusion) know "that they do not know Him."[37]

He insists that the names of God, licensed by the Qur'an or at least
not forbidden therein, signify a reality in God, but the relevant philosophical theorems, together with the experience of "the knowers," warn
us that we cannot comprehend how (la bi'l-kaifa) those features qualify
divinity. So our use of these names cannot tell us anything about God.[38]
But they can function as lures for us, inviting us to become ever more
merciful, compassionate, and just, thus calling us to a perfection which
admits of countless degrees and unending progress. If the road of identification is closed, the journey of ever-increasing assimilation is not only
open but demanded of whomever desires to come to know God. For
the closer one comes, the more one experiences the difference (as "the
knowers" testify), and we can invoke God's names the more surely, the
more acutely we realize that our conception of the attribute in question
cannot be a sure guide to its reality in God.[39] This epistemological rule
enjoins upon would-be knowers of God the journey of the Ihya', so
Ghazali's celebrated accomplishment of aligning the Sufi mystical path
with the way of conventional Muslim practice is clearly displayed. If his
resolution of the speculative (or theological) issues is closer to that of
Moses Maimonides than to that of Aquinas, I have tried to suggest why.
Yet such differences should not obscure the conviction these three religious thinkers shared: that the resources of human reason should be
employed in whatever ways one can, always respecting their integrity, to
display the incommensurable "distinction" between the One and all else
that exists. The unknowability of God is a necessary corollary of a shared
belief in the universe as God's gracious gift.[40]

---

[37] Maqsad 54 [ET 42], M 344.
[38] Maqsad 192–6 [ET 177–81].
[39] Maqsad 192–6.
[40] For Maimonides' and Aquinas' deeper unity on this issue where they manifestly divide,
see my "Aquinas and Maimonides: A Conversation about Proper Speech," in Immanuel XVI
(1983), pp. 70–85. On "the distinction," see Robert Sokolowski, God of Faith and Reason
(Notre Dame IN: University of Notre Dame Press, 1982/Washington DC: Catholic University of America Press, 1995). I am especially grateful to Fadlou Shehadi for alerting me
to the ambiguities present in Ghazali's many uses of 'aql, and have tried to incorporate our
discussion into my text. James Kritzeck also helped me avoid some historical and cultural
howlers. On the underlying issue of God's unknowability, see my Knowing the Unknowable
God: Ibn-Sina, Maimonides, Aquinas (Notre Dame IN: University of Notre Dame Press,
1986).

Chapter 3

WHY NOT PURSUE THE METAPHOR OF ARTISAN AND VIEW GOD'S KNOWLEDGE AS PRACTICAL?

While this question is put primarily to Moses Maimonides in the light of his praise for the artisan image as a way for us to render what lies quite beyond our comprehension – God's mode of knowing[1] – it must also be put to Aquinas, who boldly adopts the image as his master metaphor to render God's knowledge of the universe, yet fails himself to pursue it in any great detail. My focus, however, will be on Moses ben Maimon (Maimonides), with some help from his friendly commentator and critic after more than two centuries, Levi ben Gershom (Gersonides). And I shall put the question to his writings in both senses of its rhetorical impact: (1) why might he *not* have pursued the metaphor? i.e., what stood in the way? and (2) what might he have gained had he done so?

Maimonides' Model for Knowing

The answer to the first way of formulating our question seems relatively straightforward when we recall that the Rambam[2] identifies the divine image (*zelem*) in us with "intellectual apprehension"[3] or the power by

---

[1] *The Guide of the Perplexed*, III. 21. Unless otherwise noted *The Guide for the Perplexed* will be cited from the M. Friedlander trans. (New York: Dover, 1956), primarily because his terminology is more standardly philosophical than Pines'.
[2] Rambam is a reference to *Rabbi Moses ben Maimon*.
[3] *Guide*, I.1.

which "man distinguishes between the true and the false."[4] In commenting on Genesis 3, he not only identifies the image of God with our capacity to possess a science "of necessary truths," but contrasts this with "the science of apparent truths (morals)" in which "right and wrong are the terms employed . . . : it is the function of the intellect to discriminate between the true and the false."[5] We have only to reflect that Aristotle makes his distinction between two "ways of arriving at truth" in the *Nicomachaean Ethics* (VI.3) – speculative and practical – as a preliminary step towards legitimizing ethical inquiry precisely by warding off objections that it cannot yield the certitude associated with science (i.e., the demonstration of essential properties as flowing necessarily from natures), to remind ourselves once again how beholden Maimonides is to Ibn Sina.[6] In this sense, in fact, Maimonides' philosophy rightly belongs with "Islamic philosophy," since his cultural ambience is clearly the "Islamicate."[7]

Maimonides argues that "*the* function of the intellect is to discriminate between the true and the false," not good and evil. Thus, "Adam possessed [understanding] perfectly and completely" but "was not at all able to follow or to understand the principles of apparent truths," until he had transgressed a command "with which he had been charged on the score of his reason." Only then did he obtain a knowledge of apparent truths. Maimonides bases this remarkable statement on the verse "and the eyes of both were opened, and they knew they were naked" (Genesis 3:7). The line is carefully parsed to reveal that Adam "received a new faculty whereby he found things wrong which previously he had not regarded as wrong."[8] Maimonides' sharp dichotomy between knowledge and opinion as applied to matters of fact and matters of morals is, of course, quite at variance with Aristotle, who speaks of one intellectual faculty whose distinct functions – knowing (speculative) and doing or making (practical) – are determined by the end in view (*Nicomachaean Ethics* VI.2).

So far as I know, Maimonides does not ever identify this "new faculty," although the natural place for him do so would be in the third part of the *Guide*, where he explains the place of the Torah in the life of men (sic), insisting that "there is a reason for each one of the precepts . . .

---

[4]   *Ibid.*, I.2.
[5]   *Ibid.*, I.2.
[6]   Maimonides' references to Aristotle (e.g., II.19) are often in fact allusions to Ibn Sina.
[7]   Marshall Hodgson introduces the term in *The Venture of Islam* (Chicago: University of Chicago Press, 1974), pp. 39–45.
[8]   *Ibid.*, I.2.

although there are commandments the reason of which is unknown to us, and in which the ways of God's wisdom are incomprehensible."[9] He contends that his belief in the law as manifesting God's wisdom – and not merely God's will – is shared by "the common people as well as the scholars," and he moves only to block speculation purporting to show the utility of the particular, detailed means of each of the 613 commandments of the law. Clearly, he argues, "the general object of the law is twofold: the well-being of the soul and the well-being of the body."[10] Thus the goal of the Torah is a practical one, and its function for the people of God would be analogous to one of the roles Aristotle gives to practical reason: to discern right from wrong. So one might naturally have expected the relationship of God to God's people, as displayed in the bestowal of the Torah, to have offered Maimonides a model for the initial gift of existence and all that follows from it in creation. That he does not do so – so far as I know – offers another striking example of how much he was beholden to Ibn Sina's single-minded devotion to speculative reason as the paradigm for knowing and, correspondingly, for the relation between the universe and its source.[11]

But why then the encomium for "the knowledge which the producer of a thing possesses concerning it"? For such a model is suggested by the Rambam for the kind of knowledge God possesses of creation: "Note this well, for I think that this is an excellent idea, and leads to correct views; no error will be found in it; no dialectical argument; it does not lead to any absurd conclusion, nor to ascribing any defect to God."[12] It is difficult to imagine higher praise for a conception whose merits Maimonides has just noted: "our knowledge is acquired and increased in proportion to the things known by us. This is not the case with God. [Like the artisan,] His knowledge of things is not derived from the things themselves . . . on the contrary, the things are in accordance with His eternal knowledge." Yet this contrast, derived from Avicenna, is the only one to recommend the artisan image. When carefully examined, Maimonides' commendation proves to allow that the artisan image is conducive "to correct views" not in that it affords an adequate model for "this kind of knowledge [which] cannot be comprehended by us," but rather in the

---

[9] *Guide*, III.26.
[10] *Ibid.*, II.27.
[11] On Ibn Sina and the paradigm of speculative reason, see my *Knowing the Unknowable God* (Notre Dame IN: University of Notre Dame Press, 1986). The point is even stronger if Warren Zev Harvey's interpretation is correct: "A Third Approach to Maimonides' Cosmogony-Prophetology Puzzle," in *Harvard Theological Review* 74 (1981), pp. 287–301.
[12] *Guide*, II.21.

negative sense underscored by the modifiers following: that it will not mislead us.

So once again, the Rambam uses his dialectical skills to protect the God of Abraham, Isaac, and Jacob from a philosophic reason which can be relentlessly reductive when it tries to make human sense of God's ways. Yet here again I would ask whether the image cannot be pursued in a more fruitful, genuinely *leading* way. Was Maimonides perhaps forestalled from doing just that simply by his Avicennian intellectualism? For on such an account, the artist's knowing cannot be construed as real knowing; only the emanation of conclusions from premises – in the pattern of demonstrative reason – promises knowledge. If God's knowledge will not conform to the speculative pattern, we must simply acknowledge that "the knowledge attributed to this essence has nothing in common with our knowledge . . . so we have no correct notion of His knowledge."[13] We cannot look elsewhere in human knowing for a more acceptable model. For there is nowhere else to look, since the "knowledge of the producer"[14] cannot claim to be knowledge at all.

Gersonides located the nerve of the Rambam's thesis of "sheer equivocity" regarding all divine attributes in his inability to reconcile God's knowledge of future contingents – notably free actions – with the free response demanded by the Torah.[15] His own response, equally beholden to Ibn Sina, was to limit God's knowing to all that is "ordered and defined,"[16] trying to persuade us that there is no more to know. It is to Maimonides' credit that he could not take this tack, which he identified with Aristotle.[17] But let us explore the ways which could have opened to him had he allowed himself to pursue the image of the artisan.

The Artisan's Knowledge

I have suggested that the Rambam was unduly influenced by Ibn Sina in accepting a deductive paradigm for knowing, Aristotle's pattern for science, which had inspired Ibn Sina's cosmological picture. The universe emanates from the One in the way that conclusions in a syllogism follow

---

[13] *Ibid.*, III.20.
[14] *Ibid.*, III.21.
[15] Norbert Samuelson, *Gersonides on God's Knowledge* [= *Wars of the Lord* III] (Toronto: Pontifical Institute of Medieval Studies, 1977), pp. 204–9.
[16] *Ibid.*, p. 232.
[17] *Guide*, III.17.

logically from first principles.[18] Evidence for Maimonides' intellectualism abounds, notably in his treatment of prophecy[19] and of providence over individuals.[20] Yet it would seem that his treatment of the Torah[21] could have opened the way to making practical knowing more respectable, since observance of the law would account for human well-being.[22] In this respect, at least, the attunement to divine wisdom which aligns individuals with God's providential care could apparently be achieved by observance as well as by the "intellectual mysticism" one associates with Ibn Sina.[23] Yet a concluding chapter of the *Guide* insists that "true worship of God is only possible when correct notions of Him have previously been conceived," since it is "the intellect which emanates from God unto us [that] is the link that joins us to God." The passive construction, to be sure, would allow that these notions could be passed on in various non-conceptual ways: through ritual or ethical practices. Yet it is this principle which encourages him to reassert "that Providence watches over every rational being according to the amount of intellect which that being possesses."[24]

There is a clear priority in favor of that "knowledge of God, i.e., true wisdom [which] demonstrates by proof those truths which Scripture teaches by way of tradition." This is "the only perfection which we should seek," since "having acquired this knowledge [we] will then be determined always to seek loving-kindness, Judgment, and righteousness, and thus to imitate the ways of God." So the *Guide* ends where it began, identifying knowing with speculative knowledge, and clearly subordinating the formation of character to that "real wisdom [which] proves the truth of the law."[25] Accordingly, the manner in which the Torah shapes human life "to imitate the ways of God" will not emerge as a fruitful model for understanding divine "providence extending over His creatures as manifested in the act of bringing them into being and in their governance as it is."[26] Such understanding will only derive from that knowledge of God which Maimonides called "true wisdom" and which could *prove* the truths of

---

[18]   This is how I try to make the emanation scheme plausible in *Knowing* (note 4).
[19]   *Ibid.*, II.26.
[20]   *Ibid.*, III.17.
[21]   *Ibid.*, III.26–50.
[22]   *Ibid.*, III.27.
[23]   The phrase is Louis Gardet's in *La pensée religieuse d'Avicenne* (Paris: Vrin, 1956).
[24]   *Guide*, III.51.
[25]   *Ibid.*, III.54.
[26]   *Ibid.*, II.54, Pines.

scripture. Yet it was precisely that pattern of demonstrative reason which forced him to conclude that we can have no understanding of God's knowledge – that "only the words are the same."[27]

Let us examine the features by which he sets divine knowledge apart, to determine whether a more favorable ranking of practical knowing might have offered greater hope for modeling God's knowledge. The stakes are high since the speculative paradigm to which Maimonides is committed threatens his program with a double inconsistency. Authentic human perfection lies in "the knowledge of God [and] of His Providence,"[28] yet such knowledge is denied us by his insisting that we cannot know God but only "qualities of actions emanating from Him."[29] And since the most perspicuously divine activity we can know would be God's bestowing of the Torah, practical knowing would seem to offer a model at the very point where speculative knowledge must fail. The ways in which God's "knowledge is distinguished from ours according to all the teaching of every revealed religion" are five: (1) it is one yet embraces many objects, (2) it applies to things not yet in existence, (3) it is infinite in comprehension, (4) it remains unchanged although comprehending changing things, and (5) "according to the teaching of our Law, God's knowledge of one of two eventualities does not determine it, however certain that knowledge may be concerning the future occurrence of the one eventuality."[30]

By Gersonides' reading, it was the last of these which forced Maimonides to an agnostic position regarding all attributions of perfections to divinity. Yet in the chapter we are citing, he focuses on the fact "that God's knowledge is not different from His essence" and concludes that "as we cannot accurately comprehend His essence so we have no correct notion of His knowledge."[31] The same applies to God's "management . . . and intention" (or perhaps better: *governance* and *purpose*). Such notions "are not the same when ascribed to us and when ascribed to God." Without recounting in detail Maimonides' arguments on equivocity,[32] it should be clear that this generic observation will not suffice to render the discrepancy between divine and human knowledge so great as to prevent utterly our discoursing about divine knowledge. So Gersonides' reading

[27] *Guide*, III.20.
[28] *Ibid.*, III.54.
[29] *Ibid.*, I.60.
[30] *Ibid.*, II.20.
[31] *Ibid.*, III.20.
[32] *Ibid.*, I.51–61.

must be sound. Maimonides must be shying away from comparisons of divine and human knowledge so as to avoid the conundrum of necessitation of contingent events by God's eternal omniscience. Now we ask, how could shifting to a practical paradigm for knowing help to overcome the apparently necessitating consequences of God's knowing "the future occurrence of the one eventuality"?

The main lines of a response are available in Aquinas, and in terms quite consonant with Maimonides' treatment, whose lineaments Aquinas generally followed, however critically.[33] For Aquinas, nothing which has not yet occurred can be an object of knowledge for anyone, including God, for there simply is nothing to know. Not even God can know what is not yet present. At this point Aquinas invokes two devices: one which Maimonides neither invokes nor rejects, eternity; and the other which he praises, the practical knowing of an artisan. These must function together. For the mere mention of eternity, while presuming a speculative model for knowing, produces a mental cramp, or antinomy, when we try to ascertain how what has not yet occurred might nonetheless be *present* to God "in eternity."[34] But what has not yet taken place can certainly be present in the divine intention.

For God knows what God intends to do, as artisans know what they intend to do – without there being anything to know as the object of speculative knowing. Fourteenth-century Christian thinkers, following after Aquinas, began to fear this strategy, finding it too closely patterned on the pot-potter image, and so threatening to human freedom. Yet Aquinas remains serenely untroubled by any potential conflict with his forthright assertions about human freedom, since he finds no reason to understand freedom on the model of autonomy.[35] For like everything else in the created universe, human actions are dependent upon the Creator, whose proper effect is existence and the activity which follows upon existing.[36] Yet that apparently innocent formulation of the article of faith in

---

[33] Cf. my "Aquinas and Maimonides: A Conversation about Proper Speech," in *Immanuel* 16 (1983), pp. 70–85; Chapter 4 of the present volume "Maimonides, Aquinas and Gersonides on Providence and Evil."

[34] See Aquinas, *De Veritate* 2.12, *Summa Theologiae* 1.14.13; cf. my "God's Eternity," in *Faith and Philosophy* 1 (1984), pp. 389–406.

[35] Cf. Joseph Incandela, "Aquinas' Lost Legacy: God's Practical Knowledge and Situated Human Freedom," Ph.D. dissertation, Princeton University, 1986.

[36] Cf. my *Aquinas: God and Action* (Notre Dame IN: University of Notre Dame Press, 1979); for an approximation to this by Maimonides, see Lenn E. Goodman, "Determinism and Freedom in Spinoza, Maimonides, and Aristotle," in F. Schoeman, ed., *Responsibility, Character, and the Emotions* (Cambridge: Cambridge University Press, 1987), pp. 144–8.

God as creator embodies Aquinas' own invocation of the Rambam's insistence that a divine activity is utterly unlike its human counterpart. In this case, it is that " 'to be made' or 'to make' are said equivocally in this universal production of things, and in other productions."[37] Yet the fact that the term can be used formally, if not descriptively, rests on his identifying existence (esse) as neither a feature of things nor a substance, but the principle of anything's actually existing. This represents, of course, Aquinas' move beyond Aristotle, for whom existence is a concomitant of form, and forms are eternal. For Aquinas, however, God's creative activity has an effect proper to it, and the artisan image offers a model for divine knowing without pretending to tell us how God does it.

Sophisticated Rambam readers will remind us, of course, that Maimonides could not countenance such an analogous use of terms,[38] but I have argued elsewhere that he should have no substantive difficulties with an understanding of analogous terms which is as "negative" regarding descriptive features as Aquinas' is.[39] More conventional philosophers will profess to find both analogy and the via negativa incomprehensible, but at some point in our discourse about God incomprehensibility becomes a desideratum rather than a complaint. Then the question becomes a strategic one: why here, where Aquinas locates it, rather than there where Mainionides did? The answer is equally strategic. Aquinas' approach would allow us to exploit the expressly biblical images of the artisan, which the Rambam praised. Moreover, adopting the model of knowing congruent with these images could have given him a way of formulating God's knowledge of what is to come, which would not appear so downright contradictory to our understanding of what it is to know. In fact, one might reconstruct Maimonides as advocating an account of divine knowledge whereby God knows the particulars through their ideas, i.e., through His intentions. This would not be incompatible with the proposal of practical reason nor contradictory to our ordinary ideas of knowledge. But developing that would involve integrating the practical model he proposes into his treatment in ways in which he does not actually do. Were he to have done so, the possibility of an analogous rather than an utterly equivocal account could have arisen – and that would certainly have fulfilled the goal of his project better than he was able to do with the paradigms available to him.

---

[37] In Phys. 8.2 (1974).
[38] cf. Guide, I.56.
[39] See: "Maimonides and Aquinas: A Dialogue about Proper Speech," in Immanuel 16 (1983), pp. 70–85.

Indeed, Menachem Kellner offers us a way of so reading Maimonides,[40] and that is to regard the *Guide* itself as a journey. One may then read the final chapters, with their clear *halakhic* allusions, as the terminus of a gradual transition from Neoplatonic priorities regarding reason to a more distinctively Jewish understanding of *imitatio Dei*: becoming like God by acting as God would have us act. As we can know divine attributes of action, so we have been given to know how God would have us act to become God-like. The Rambam's insistence, even in these final chapters, on the priority of reason would then be understood as our need to employ philosophy as a guide in undertaking this journey. We must put speculative reason in its proper place: indispensable, yet finally in the service of right action. That such a reading would be in tension with the opening chapters of the *Guide* itself would only highlight the point and purpose of the journey it outlines for us to take. Needless to say, I find this reflective reading attractive, chiefly because it places particular statements in the context of the whole work, read as the *Guide* it purports to be. My own proposal would then become the task of reading back onto Maimonides' accounts of providence and creation his concluding exaltation of practical reason, and so fleshing out the model he proposes[41] but does not actually develop.

---

[40] In his *Maimonides on Human Perfection* (Atlanta: Scholars Press, 1990).
[41] *Guide*, III.21.

Chapter 4

MAIMONIDES, AQUINAS, AND GERSONIDES ON PROVIDENCE AND EVIL (WITH A BOW TO DOROTHY SAYERS)

Since the issue of God's knowledge of individuals only arises in the Abrahamic faiths, we may surmise that it becomes an issue only in the face of a Pantokrator. If one seldom finds it raised in more recent times, that can only represent collective prudent counsel, for the history of each tradition records, one after another, the shipwrecks of those who essayed it, as well as bitter aftermaths in their respective religious communities. The more bitter, I believe, as certain stages of this inquiry lead one to dilemmas so harsh that atheism alone could offer plausible rest to the spirit. Against such a history of testimony, then, and in such a climate, why should one even be tempted to pursue the issue? Because there is hope that an approach which resolutely keeps to the path of grammar, and from that vantage-point explores alternative images, might offer a way to go on. For one could go on at least to recover those classical figures who were astute enough to say no more than could be said, and so discover a ground from which one's espousing (or not) one's Jewish, Christian, or Islamic faith would be a human response rather than an exasperated reaction. So the issue occupies that middle ground which reason shares with faith: acutely posed only in the presence of a creator, it also offers a stumbling block for anyone wondering how to acknowledge oneself a creature in the face of *such* a creator.

The book of Job remains the classic religious document to criticize inadequate accounts believers might offer for their God's conduct. There is, unfortunately, no comparable document in Islam, for the simple reason (I suspect) that Job presses to its limits a practice which the Bible countenanced as early as Abraham yet which is nowhere licensed in the Qur'an: argument with the Holy One. Both Moses ben Maimon (Maimonides) and Levi ben Gershon (Gersonides) treat Job as a proto-philosophical treatise, finding each interlocutor espousing positions known to them historically, which also rather neatly represent available logical alternatives. In their resolutions, Maimonides sides with the Torah: "that the various events are known to God before they take place" but that such "knowledge of one of two eventualities does not determine it;"[1] while Gersonides stands with "philosophic thought," leaving God ignorant of what will happen except as "ordered and defined."[2] Yet both reflect the inability of their Muslim conversation partners to conceive human freedom except as a check on divine omnipotence.

Aquinas is positioned historically between his Jewish colleagues, and conceptually in a tradition more practiced in grammatical reflections. These allow him to reconcile a respect for scripture and divine transcendence with the demands of logic, and direct him to identify the difficulties we have in articulating God's knowledge of particulars with the fact that "we cannot speak of divine knowing except in our mode of understanding, using tensed discourse," while "divine knowing is measured by eternity."[3] So "God knows contingent things as each one of them is itself in act."[4] Such is the grammar of the matter, which demands closer analysis, for it apparently asserts that what (in time) will happen is the same as what (in eternity) is happening. Such analysis will show, among other things, how Aquinas' direct assertions accord with Peter Geach's flat denial that God sees the future,[5] a conception fostered by Aquinas' misleading example of a strategically placed lookout. His primary image is in fact quite other – of artisan to artifact;[6] and assisted by Dorothy Sayers' Mind of the Maker I shall suggest how one might make that into a working image.

In presenting these three characters I shall respond more to systematic concerns than to chronology. For while Maimonides stands in the twelfth century, Aquinas in the thirteenth and Gersonides in the fourteenth, the communication networks so functioned as to put Gersonides into closer contact with Maimonides than with Aquinas. There were of course cul-

---

[1]   Moses Maimonides, The Guide for the Perplexed (New York: Dover, 1956), 3.2.
[2]   Norbert Max Samuelson, ed., Gersonides on God's Knowledge (Wars of the Lord III) (Toronto: Pontifical Institute of Medieval Studies, 1977), p. 4.
[3]   de Ver. 2.12.
[4]   ST 1.14.13.
[5]   Peter Geach, Providence and Evil (Cambridge, 1977), p. 57.
[6]   ST 1.14.8.

tural and linguistic reasons for this proximity. It is arguable, for example, whether Gersonides read Latin, even though he lived in Provence. Moreover, given the links of Jewish learning with Muslim Spain, he appears to be more beholden to Averroes than to Western scholastics. It is perhaps the influence of Averroes – that highly systematic thinker whom the West called simply "the Commentator," to acknowledge his fidelity to Aristotle – that gives to Gersonides' writing that directness and clarity one associates with the early scholastics. In this respect he can certainly be said to have assimilated the thought patterns of his time. Yet for all that, as we shall see, his philosophic mode remains beholden to that thought world which he shares with Maimonides; one from which Aquinas learned but to which he remained an outsider: Islamic philosophy. In another respect, however, Maimonides and Aquinas are closer to one another in spirit than Gersonides is to either: in their respect for the life of the faith community as a factor in theological reflection. In this respect Gersonides offers a more purely philosophical interpretation of the issues than they do, and in so doing gives inadvertent testimony to the Islamic position on these vexing questions.

What is fascinating is that each specifically comments on the book of Job.[7] And if the two relatively short chapters which Maimonides contributes in the *Moreh Nebukim* (*Guide for the Perplexed*) cannot rightly be called a commentary, it remains true that they inspired Gersonides to compose his quite extensive work, for he found them the only sensible thing he had been able to turn up on that "strange and wonderful book."[8] Moreover, Maimonides' manner of reading the book shaped Levi ben Gershon's, for each assigns distinguishable philosophical positions to Job's friends and each assimilates the argument of Elihu, the last interlocutor, to his own. Aquinas is more sensitive to the literary genre of the work, often pausing to remark on its poetic features. He is drawn in this direction because he expressly proposes a literal treatment of the work, thereby breaking from the pattern of allegorical interpretation of Job fashioned by Gregory. Maimonides too remarks that it is a "great poem,"[9] but in offering his "explanation" of it imagines it to be a philosophical treatise.

---

[7] Moses Maimonides, *The Guide for the Perplexed* (note 1); Thomas Aquinas, *Expositio super Job ad Litteram* (Romae: Ad Sanctae Sabinae, 1965); Levi ben Gerson (Gersonides), *Commentary on the Book of Job*, trans. A. L. Lasson (New York: Bloack, 1946). I shall employ the Friedlander translation of Maimonides, unless the more recent and literal rendering of Schlomo Pines (Chicago IL: University of Chicago, 1963) be indicated.

[8] Here Gersonides acknowledges his lineage despite his critical stance towards the earlier philosopher. See Gersonides (note 7), 3.22–3.

[9] *Guide*, 3.22.

The positions which Maimonides and Gersonides associate with each of Job's friends are more important for what they reveal of these thinkers' respective preoccupations than for what they assert. Maimonides divides the house among Torah-believers holding human beings to a strict justice since they are invariably the cause of all evil befalling them (Eliphaz), the Ash'arites who hold that divine will causes everything (Zophar), and the Mu'tazilites who must contrive a recompense for every action, good or evil – Bildad.[10] Gersonides finds these latter two positions unworthy of philosophic consideration, and finds a logical way of assigning the three roles. If one queries, in sympathy with Job, why the just should suffer and the evil prosper, there are three plausible ways of dealing with the complaint. One can admit it and locate responsibility with men (Eliphaz), or contest the complaint: on the part of the subject – they are not really just/evil (Zophar), or of the predicate – they are not really suffering/prospering (Bildad). And, he tries to argue in all fairness, each response can be presented quite plausibly. Yet not quite, of course, as the narrative shows.

What proves disappointing, however, is that Gersonides makes no effort to show why he can call Elihu's position his own. By this time he seems to have lost interest in the dialogue, nor does his position, as we shall see, bear any relation to it. And Maimonides' explanation for Elihu's superiority turns on an obscure interpretation of a passing reference to the intercession of an angel. What is far more interesting, in fact, is the different attitudes which Maimonides and Aquinas assume towards Job himself (who plays no defined role in Gersonides' presentation). Maimonides turns his fierce complaints into an ideology, identifying him with Aristotle, for whom there in effect is no special providence for individuals. The denouement of the drama then becomes "the Revelation that reached Job and explained to him the error of his whole belief."[11] God's commendation (Job 42:7) then envisages the Job who was converted. And this was accomplished only when "he had acquired a true knowledge of God." In fact, "so long as Job's knowledge of God was based on tradition and communication, and not on research [= by the way of speculation (Pines)], he believed that such imaginary good as is possessed in health, riches and children was the utmost that men can attain."[12]

For Aquinas, the situation is exactly the opposite. Job is the just man *par excellence* and it is his friends who constantly confuse temporal goods

[10]   *Ibid.*, 3.23.
[11]   *Ibid.*, 3.23.
[12]   *Ibid.*, 3.23.

with beatitude, thinking at once that Job *must* have done evil since *everything* has been taken away from him. (We might characterize their positions as a mechanical application of Deuternomy!) Aquinas pictures Job as exercised, indeed, that his lot has so radically changed, yet possessed of an unerring sense for what one may and may not *say* about God's ways with us, for his heart is focused on the true good, God, and his mind clear about his eternal destiny. Vociferous as is his complaint, he never wavers in essentials, and so is deserving of God's commendation – indeed of God's response. Job's own retraction (Job 42:6), says Aquinas, repents rather of the *way* he has spoken in that it could have given scandal, or may reflect such a keen appreciation of God's justice that he recognizes how far he is from the mark – much as saints can genuinely call themselves sinners.[13]

In the end I am afraid that the fact of these commentaries is more significant than their impact on the thinking of any of our protagonists, all of whom more or less evacuate the dramatic impact of the poem by assimilating it to a treatise. Maimonides' attempt to identify the remonstrations of Job's friends with diverse philosophical positions defies the most discerning reading of the text. In this respect Aquinas is the more faithful reader, since he never finds them making more than minor variations on the same tired ideology. In the measure that Gersonides' followed the lead of his predecessor, he too mislocates the dramatic center. Aquinas will identify it accurately – in the contrast between the "hymn to wisdom" (Job 28) and the Lord's actual address (Job 28–34): "since human wishes will prove insufficient to comprehend the truth of divine providence, it was necessary that this dispute be determined by divine authority."[14] It is the actual speaking – God's responding to Job – which offers the dramatic point of the poem: the determination by divine authority. Yet Aquinas does not exploit this "performative" dimension, assured as he is (from the earlier "hymn to wisdom") that "wisdom can attune us to the *ratio* of divine providence: that spiritual goods are given to the just as the better [reward] while temporal goods may go to the unjust, but these are of course quite worthless (*caduca*)"![15]

And in this wisdom-teaching they all, as we might expect, concur. Moreover, some such orientation will certainly be present in any theological treatment of this classic complaint, yet one would have hoped for a clearer recognition that the "spiritual goods" in question really amount to a personal relationship between the one so vigorously complaining and

---

[13]   Aquinas *Expositio* (note 7), 212, 218.
[14]   *Ibid.*, 199.
[15]   *Ibid.*, 155.

the Lord of the universe – a relationship effected by that One's actual response to the plaintiff. That is how one could exploit the *performative* character of the poem. Maimonides and Gersonides are kept from doing this by their deliberate recasting of it as a treatise, Aquinas by his insistence on Job's holiness throughout and by locating that primarily (if not principally) in his right *belief* about immorality. For since that teaching is available to wisdom (philosophy), the confirmation which God's response brings is prevented from adding anything substantive to the argument.

Maimonides will read the sense of the Lord's response, which "describes the elements, meteorological phenomena, and peculiarities of various kinds of living beings," as serving "to impress on our minds that we are unable to comprehend how these transient creatures come into existence . . . and that these are not like the things which we are able to produce. Much less can we compare the manner in which God rules and manages his creatures with the manner in which we rule and manage certain things."[16] To be sure, this "lesson [which he takes to be] the principal object of the whole book of Job," concurs with Maimonides' way of resolving the dilemmas which arise when we simultaneously affirm God's foreknowledge and responsible human freedom, yet it also comes close *as a reading* to incorporating the drama of the poem: what is most significant is not *what* God says but the impact on us of God's saying it. Namely, that "we should not fall into the error of imagining His knowledge to be similar to ours, or His intention, providence, and rule similar to ours."[17]

Yet Rabbi Moses (as Aquinas always called him) had already arrived at that place, and this time it is Gersonides who will show how unstable a position it is. All three of them will affirm with Isaias, certainly: "as the heavens are higher than the earth, so my ways are higher than your ways,"[18] yet neither Aquinas nor Gersonides will want to conclude therefrom that "our knowledge . . . has only the name in common with God's knowledge."[19] In fact Gersonides judges that his predecessor's notorious agnosticism regarding divine attributes actually stems from this specific impasse.[20] For Maimonides accepts "that God's knowledge extends to things not in existence . . . but the existence of which God foresees and

---

16   *Guide*, 3.23.
17   *Ibid.*, 3.23.
18   *Isaias*, 55.9.
19   *Guide*, 3.20.
20   Norbert Max Samuelson, ed., *Gersonides on God's Knowledge*, (note 2), pp. 130–9; also Samuelson, "The problem of future contingents in medieval Jewish philosophy," in *Studies in Medieval Culture* VI and VII (Kalamazoo, MI: Western Michigan University, 1976), pp. 71–82, esp. pp. 79–80. References to the *Wars of the Lord* by book and chapter: 3.2 = Book 3, chapter 2.

is able to effect." Yet he also insists: "according to the teaching of our law, God's knowledge of one of two eventualities does not determine it, however certain that knowledge may be concerning the future occurrence of the one eventuality."[21] For if it did, human choice would be rendered otiose, and the entire structure of the covenant "set[ting] before you life and prosperity, death and disaster" (Deut. 30:15) would collapse. So Maimonides must conclude that "as we cannot accurately comprehend His essence, and yet we know that His existence is most perfect, . . . so we have no correct notion of His knowledge, because it is nothing but His essence, and yet we are convinced that . . . He obtains no new knowledge . . . and [that] nothing of all existing things escapes His knowledge, but their nature is not changed thereby; that which is possible remains possible."[22]

As we shall see, all the assertions are in place for a resolution uncannily similar to that which Aquinas will propose, with the one crucial difference that Maimonides fails to factor in the decisive relation of time to eternity. By letting our locution go by uncriticized – "that the various events are known to Him *before* they take place"[23] – Maimonides misses an opportunity radically to qualify the comparison of God's knowledge to ours, and must move to the yet more radical denial of any comparison whatsoever. Yet, as Gersonides will show clearly, that is more than a radical move, it is a self-defeating act of desperation. For if one were to carry it out, one would be prevented from using any reference to God's knowing in an argument. And since Maimonides' treatment of providence (in the preceding chapter) did appeal to such knowledge to argue that nothing actuated by the Creator should be concealed from him, Gersonides' critique finds its mark.[24]

Before leaving Maimonides to consider Gersonides' constructive alternative, we should attend to an earlier chapter where he criticizes inquiries into "the purpose of Creation." Taking his lead from Ibn Sina (Avicenna), he reminds us that "a final cause must exist for everything that owes its existence to an intelligent being: but for that which is without a beginning, a final cause need not be sought . . ."[25] Whether one argues from creation or from the eternity of the universe, "there is no occasion to seek the final cause of the whole Universe" since its originator does not act

[21]   *Guide*, 3.20.
[22]   *Ibid.*, 3.20.
[23]   *Ibid.*, 3.20.
[24]   Samuelson (note 2), pp. 155–9.
[25]   *Guide*, 3.13. The background for this axiom can be found in Etienne Gilson's classical article: "Pourquoi St. Thomas a critiqué St. Augustin," in *Archives d'histoire litteraire et doctrinale du moyen âge* 1 (Paris: Vrin, 1926–7).

according to a purpose. The most we can say is that "each [species-] being exists for its own sake" and that "each part [of the universe] is . . . the product of God's will"; in short, that "God saw that it was good" (Gen. 1:4). There is then no sense in trying to ascertain God's *intentions* in creating and guiding the universe as a whole, i.e., in the order among its parts, since that order is not susceptible of functional language, which would be our way of explaining it.

We should continue to affirm and to admire the existence of a divine order – indeed we must presume *order* in any inquiry – and pondering it allows us to "obtain a correct estimation of ourselves."[26] Such, we recall, was his way of taking the Lord's response to Job. Yet we are not thereby licensed to construct a functional theodicy – say of a "higher good" resulting from this disaster or that – in fact, we are effectively blocked from doing just that. What I find so fascinating about this chapter is not only its astute conclusion, but the fact that we can watch Maimonides engage in a discerning discrimination between God's knowing and ours, and doing so with philosophical acumen and religious sensitivity. Moreover, this chapter contains the germs of a criticism of Gersonides' position quite as trenchant as the way his successor logically dismantles Maimonides. Even more trenchant, in fact, for these observations call into question the properly *explanatory* value of any emanation scheme purporting to relate God to the universe.

Yet that is exactly what Levi ben Gershon will propose, and try to align with the Torah as well. He will do so by arranging the alternatives as his philosophical context allows him to do, and opposing himself not only to Maimonides' self-defeating conclusion, but to his stated features of divine knowing as well – what we might call the *givens* of the Jewish tradition. Asking the generic question whether God knows contingent particulars, he divides the house between "the Philosopher and his followers" and "the great sages of the Torah."[27] The sages, including Maimonides, insist that God knows "contingent particulars as particulars"[28] while those followers of Aristotle whom he chooses to treat admit that "he only knows himself" yet argue that "in His knowledge of Himself He knows everything which exists insofar as it possesses a universal nature. The reason for this is that He is the *nomos*, the order and the arrangement [*nimus, seder, yoser*] of existing beings."[29] This second position, indistinguishable from

[26]   *Guide*, 3.14.
[27]   Samuelson (note 2), p. 98.
[28]   *Ibid.*, p. 101.
[29]   *Ibid.*, p. 100.

Ibn Sina, will become that of Gersonides as well. Yet he must first show how the position of the sages, best displayed in Maimonides, is incoherent; while his own scheme answers to the very concerns of the tradition which their assertions intended to convey. This will be difficult, for Gersonides – never one to conceal an implication, however, unwelcome – warns us that on this position God "does not know particulars."[30]

The ploy is not a difficult one for philosophers, of course, who only need to show that such knowledge does not constitute a perfection, so that God's lacking it will not amount to a deprivation in divinity. Yet such an argument will sound very odd, especially in a tradition which produced the book of Job. Gersonides has a general principle for dealing with that oddness, however, and its formulations appear to come directly from Ibn Rushd (Averroes): "whenever the Torah, according to what appears from the external meaning of its words, disagrees with some things which are clear from the point of view of Philosophic Thought, it is proper that we should interpret them in a manner which is in agreement with Philosophic Thought."[31] He claims, moreover, that this principle adequately formulates Maimonides' stated intent and normal practice in the *Guide*, so that deviations have to be seen as contradicting his own principles.[32] Yet it is doubtful whether the text from the introductory letter to Joseph Ibn Aknin will stand so unilateral a reading, and the most fruitful principles of interpretation allow actual practice to determine the sense of a criterion offered.[33] Yet Gersonides must call his predecessor's practice into question to justify his own.

The rest is quite routine, following directly from God as defined to be "the *nomos*, the order and the arrangement of existing things."[34] So we can say that God knows particulars, though not *as* particulars; God knows them in "the respect in which they are ordered and defined."[35] The rest of his treatment amounts to saying this in different ways, which testify to its source yet which offer little clarification: "in knowing things as emanating from His essence, God knows their intelligible orderings," for God knows the "orderings from which these acts [of creating] emanate, and which are performed instrumentally by Active Intellect and the heavenly

---

[30] *Ibid.*, p. 100.
[31] Cf. Samuelson (note 2), pp. 300–1. *Gersonides*, 301 n. 620, citing from Ibn Rushd's *Kitab fasl al-Maqal*.
[32] Samuelson (note 2), p. 302.
[33] *Ibid.*, pp. 303–6 n. 621.
[34] *Ibid.*, p. 101.
[35] *Ibid.*, p. 232 n. 346; also Samuelson, "Gersonides' account of God's knowledge of particulars," *Journal of the History of Philosophy* X (1972), pp. 399–416.

bodies."[36] In the fourth book of the *Wars of the Lord* he will go into greater detail concerning the role the spheres play in guiding those attuned to them towards the good and away from misfortune.[37] Yet what becomes essential there is not God's care but our aligning ourselves with that order so as to receive its benefits. The theory of prophecy familiar from al-Farabi and Ibn Sina becomes his way of tapping into divine providence. And as for the order which particulars do have, it "is just ultimately and a good ordering."[38] The end of the argument – and of all argument!

Before moving to Aquinas, we should consider a dimension of Gersonides' responses to Maimonides in which he appears to utilize that special form of equivocation which Aquinas developed as *analogy*. In fact, he asserts that there is a particular fashion in which God's knowledge is equivocal with ours: "by priority and posteriority."[39] This is the famous *per prius et posterius* of Aquinas, and his manner of elaborating it reminds one of Aquinas' adopting the Neoplatonic scheme: *per essentiam/per participationem*: " 'knowledge,' 'existent,' 'one,' 'entity,' . . . are said of God priorly and of other beings posteriorly . . . because His existence, His oneness, and His entity belong to Him essentially, and from Him emanate the existence, the oneness and the entity of every existing thing."[40] Yet when he puts the scheme to work, the real differences among things, which analogy was crafted to handle, disappear: "there is no difference between the knowledge of God . . . and our knowledge except that the knowledge of God . . . is more perfect than our knowledge."[41] Just what Maimonides feared: the distance between creator and creature becomes one of degree. And feared wisely, for Gersonides' conversation partners were the same as his, and the clarity which they sought from philosophy would be purchased by an unalterable faith in a single stratum of meaning underlying the various uses of a term: "the distance in meaning between these predicates and those like them, when they are said of Him . . . is like the distance between His level of existence . . . and their level of existence in terms of the perfection and excellence of being. I mean to say that they are said in a more perfect way of God . . . than the way in which they are said of what is other than Him."[42] He has said enough, certainly,

[36] Samuelson (note 2), pp. 239–40.
[37] Levi ben Gerson, *Les Guerres du Seigneur, Livres III et IV*, trans. Charles Touati (Le Haye: Mouton, 1968), pp. 133–5, 149–50.
[38] Samuelson (note 2), p. 257.
[39] *Ibid.*, p. 186.
[40] *Ibid.*, pp. 186–7.
[41] *Ibid.*, p. 188.
[42] *Ibid.*, pp. 223–4.

to realize that he thinks there to be something common to all things, something called "being," which is realized essentially in God and in which creatures participate. There is good evidence that this does represent Ibn Sina's position, and even better evidence that it was never Aquinas.[43]

So the very feature of Gersonides' thought which brings him closest to the scholastic tradition in the west shows him rather beholden to the scheme of intelligible emanation which Ibrahim Madkour celebrates as the specific contribution of Arab philosophy.[44] What I find to criticize in such a pattern is not its source – the medievals can teach us all a lesson in accepting truth wherever it is to be found. What this preoccupation with order and definition in characterizing God's knowledge leads us to overlook, however, is precisely the master image associated with a creation story: that of the craftsman. Gersonides cites this expression but only uses it to show how "the heavenly bodies are His instruments,"[45] and he soon transmutes it into that of "an architect of a house [who] should know the form of the bricks and the beams."[46] So in the end his description is of speculative knowing, even if the image the tradition offers insists on an active, working knowledge.

Maimomides explicitly invokes the image of an artisan to show what "a great difference [there is] between the knowledge which the producer of a thing possesses concerning it, and the knowledge which other persons possess concerning the same thing."[47] He even goes on to note how every object is dually related: "to our knowledge and God's knowledge of it. His knowledge of things is not derived from the things themselves . . . on the contrary, the things are in accordance with His eternal knowledge . . . Now "this kind of knowledge cannot be comprehended by us, certainly, as he insists, yet one would also agree with him "that this is an excellent idea, and leads to correct views . . ."[48] But what more is an analogy supposed to do than what Maimonides has done with this one?

[43]   For Ibn Sina see Louis Gardet, "Les notes d'Avicenne sur 'La théologie d'Aristote,'" in *Révue Thomiste* (1951), pp. 346–406; for Aquinas see *inter alia* my *Analogy and Philosophical Language* (New Haven CT: Yale, 1963), ch. 6. On this topic see my *Aquinas: God and Action* (London: Routledge, 1979) and Jean-Luc Marion's "Saint Thomas d'Aquin et l'onto-theologie," in *Révue Thomiste* 95 (1995).

[44]   Ibrahim Madkour, *La Place d'al-Farabi dans l'école philosophique musulmane* (Paris: Librairie d'Amérique et d'Ouest, 1934), p. 14.

[45]   Samuelson (note 2), p. 227.

[46]   *Ibid.*, p. 230.

[47]   *Guide*, 3.21.

[48]   *Ibid.*, 3.21.

I shall follow his lead, in expounding and developing Aquinas' use of this same image, incorporating as well the factor which Maimonides over-looked: the model, proper to divinity, of eternity.

For Aquinas too accepts as his controlling axiom that God's knowledge relates to things not as derived from them but as causing them.[49] More-over, such knowledge extends not only to forms but to matter. For without being able to say *how* this is so, we know that if God knows things other than himself in his essence, then his essence must compre-hend whatever comes into existence through him — and not merely in their universal natures but in their individuality. In this central argument Aquinas warns us not to limit God's knowing by specious comparisons with our own. For the original contrast between our knowing and God's already suggests a powerful image: "natural things are [suspended] between God's knowledge and ours, for we receive ours from those very things which God causes through his knowledge."[50]

This contrast, moreover, offers a way of handling the prickly problem of future contingent events — one touchstone for Maimonides' stark agnos-ticism. For if God knows everything, including future happenings, then their "not-yetness" has effectively been undermined. If nothing is more sure than God's knowing, how can it fail to determine what will happen? Here Aquinas makes some decisive grammatical and linguistic prescrip-tions, which I will first offer in his terms and then present in my own. First a preliminary observation: take care to translate every phrase con-taining "future" as an adjective into a tensed verb phrase — so "my future job" becomes "the job I will take" — and *never* ever let the adjective trans-form itself into a free-standing noun: "the future." (Whoever has lived even a short time among Arabs will recognize that the verbal expression calls immediately for *en sh'allah* "God willing!" — and that's precisely the point of making the translation.) For a "future job" is a quite different animal from a "well-paying job" or a "boring job." Aquinas underscores the difference by noting that not even God can know "the future in itself" — i.e. "what will be the case." For, as he puts it, "what-will-be — as what-will-be — does not yet have being (*esse*) in itself, and *truth* is convertible with *esse*. So, since all knowledge is of something true, it is impossible that any knowing which considers what-will-be in its respect of not-yet-being, can know it in itself..."[51]

---

[49]   ST 1.14.8.

[50]   ST 1.14.8.3. Josef Pieper, "The philosophical act," in *Leisure: the Basis of Culture* (New York: Pantheon, 1952), p. 89.

[51]   *de Malo* 16.7. I have turned his statement about to make the point more dramatically — cf. *de Ver.* 2.12.

Yet he has also affirmed that God does know what-will-happen, so how can he slither out of this one? By insisting, of course, that God knows such things not as what-will-happen, but as happening. For "everything taking place in time is present to God in eternity, and not only to the extent that the essences (*rationes*) of things are present to God, but because his insight comprises all things from eternity, according as each thing *is* in its presentness."[52] Here we have ~~Aquinas' decisive step beyond a theory of emanation to God's knowledge of particulars, accomplished by a direct reference to a mode of being (and of knowing) quite opaque to us: eternity.~~ It is the transformation (in the sense of relativity theory: the Lorentz transformations) effected by this shift of perspectives which will allow him coherently to affirm the five features of divine knowing which Maimonides listed as *givens* (and which Gersonides tried to dissolve).[53] The resulting linguistic recommendation is telling: "if we want to convey the sense of God's way of knowing, it would be better to say that God knows this to be rather than [to say] that God knows what-will-be (*quod Deus scit hoc esse quam quod sciat futurum esse*), because things are never future to him but always present . . . As it is more proper to speak of *providentia* than of *praevidentia* . . . Our difficulty with all this, however, stems from the fact that we are unable to signify divine knowledge except through that mode proper to our own which [inevitably] consignifies differences in time."[54]

We shall examine this "difficulty" more closely, for it would seem to relegate us to that complete agnosticism to which this issue brought Maimonides as well, if there be no way at all for us to signify the mode of knowledge proper to God. And the differences dividing the mode of eternity from time are crucial to Aquinas' assertions, for what-will-happen, "insofar as it is contingent and while it is not-yet, does not exist; yet insofar as it is present, it both exists and is true, and so does it stand before the divine vision."[55] But how can we speak of *something* in so far as it exists, and of the same *something* in so far as it does not? Aspects of existing things we deal with all the time, but what of this "now you see it; now you don't"? Can it improve matters to say: "now God sees it; now *you* don't"? And how can he use the language of "God seeing," anyway,

---

[52] ST 1.14.13.

[53] The five features are "first, that his knowledge is one, and yet embraces many different kinds of objects. Secondly, it is applied to things not in existence. Thirdly, it comprehends the infinite. Fourthly, it remains unchanged, though it comprises knowledge of changeable things . . . ; Fifthly, according to the teaching of our Law, God's knowledge of one of two eventualities does not determine it, however certain that knowledge may be of the occurrence of the one eventuality" (3.20).

[54] *de Ver.* 2.12.

[55] *de Ver.* 2.12.8.

since it is our knowledge which is derived from *seeing* things, whereas God's was said to cause them, like the potter a pot?

Allow me to recast his discussion in my own terms, profiting by some remarks of Peter Geach in his *Providence and Evil*.[56] This will show us how alive this medieval question is today, and prepare the way for a less technical reflection on the controlling metaphor of artisan:

- **For us**: what has happened or what is happening ≠ what-will-happen. Thus we cannot say "what-will-happen is happening." What has happened can be named and hence "does exist in the sense of 'exist' expressed in formal logic by the existential quantifier," whereas what-will happen does not (Geach, 54–5). Thus we can speak of *what* has happened, or of *what* is happening, but not of *what* will happen. Here we must keep the context opaque: what-will-happen; or imaginary: what-(I believe)-will-have-happened.

- **For God**: what-will-happen = what-is-happening (*sub specie aeternitatis*) = what-is (eternally)-happening = what-eternally-happens; since it is present to God after God's mode of being. But there is no *what* (for us) here, any more than there is a *what* (for us) in what-will-happen. Thus two *unknowns* are said to be identical. We respect the fact that they are unknowns by reminding ourselves that it is not proper to say: *what* (in time) will happen is the *same* as what (in eternity) is happening. For as there is no *what* removable from the ". . . -will-happen" context, so there is no *what* removable from the ". . . -eternally-happens" context.

All that Aquinas has done, then, in asserting these two "items" to be identical, is to offer a formal response to the question. Such a response dissolves one difficulty, without however answering the question in terms amounting to an answer for us. For it is precisely those terms which make it impossible for us to articulate (*significare*) the mode proper to divine knowing, since we cannot avoid tensed discourse – except to speak atemporally. So I replaced "is happening" with "happens" lest the "is" connote our present tense, yet of course "happens" does so as well. It remains felicitous to this extent, however, that numbers do not happen. For atemporal discourse is even less appropriate to alluding to eternity than present-tensed discourse, for atemporal discourse renders an abstract realm unrelated to time, whereas eternity must be said to "embrace time."[57] Yet

[56] Geach (note 5).
[57] ST 1.14.13; cf. 1.10.2.4.

one might propose both types of expression as complementing one another, as Aquinas does in giving rules for attributing perfections to God.[58]

If we could conceive a *now* – an "is . . . ing" – which would not as soon as it is said be followed by a "*was . . .*" or always be anticipated by a "*will . . . ,*" we would be on the track, as Augustine suggests.[59] Aquinas uses the abstract expression "presentness" to try to convey this inexpressible feature, as one might speak of "the now." Moreover, he invokes the notion of the present to handle another difficulty as well – two at once, in fact, both of which especially vexed the Islamic philosophers: the necessity attributed to God's knowing of anything, plus that individual's proper contingency (and in human affairs, freedom). By rendering divine knowledge of events on the model of unmediated vision, Aquinas is able to ascribe to them (as known by God) that necessity which attends our knowing that Socrates is seated when we see him seated. Two texts, roughly ten years apart, will suffice to indicate how Aquinas is employing the model of vision:

A. The order [of past to future] is not to be found between divine knowledge and any contingent thing, but divine knowledge is always ordered to a thing *as* one present is ordered to something present (*de Ver.* 2.12).

B. A contingent thing known in itself, as present, becomes infallibly an object of certain knowledge, as with (*utpote*) the sense of sight, e.g. when I see Socrates seated.[60]

From the model, to be sure, he will go on to speak of the "vision of divine knowing (*visio divinae scientiae*) measured by eternity . . . which sees whatever takes place in time not as future but as present,"[61] "because God's insight comprises (*intuitus fertur*) all things from eternity, according as each thing *is* in its presentness."[62] The language is as direct as it need be, certainly, "to say that God sees future events as they are in themselves, in their presentness, and not *as* future."[63] Yet it is precisely such a statement

[58] cf. ST 1.13.1.2, 1.3.4.1.

[59] *Confessions* 11. 11.

[60] ST 1.14.13.

[61] *de Ver.* 2.12.

[62] ST 1.14.13. My translation of *eius intuitus fertur super omnia ab aeterne, prout sunt in sua presentialitate.* Thomas Gornall, S.J. emphasizes the visual metaphor: "because he eternally surveys all things as they are in their presence to him," *Summa Theologiae*, vol. 4: *Knowledge in God* (New York: McGraw-Hill, 1964), p. 49.

[63] Geach (note 5), p. 57.

which Peter Geach convicts either of misperception or of patent self-contradiction. And one could only agree, were Aquinas in fact ascribing to God the role of "ideal spectator." Yet the contextual evidence would argue otherwise, despite his infelicitous example in both places of the strategically placed observer.[64]

All one needs to do is ask whether Aquinas is actually contending that God looks out to inspect objects, and the question answers itself. We are clearly in the presence of a model designed to make a very specific point, and not a controlling picture of divine knowing, for God's knowledge is not derived but causal,[65] comprehending things in the divine essence by granting to each its to-be.[66] The point of the visual model is clearly stated in a work contemporary with the *Summa* yet later than the question cited here: in *Questio Disputata de Malo*. Asking whether demons can know the future, Aquinas is drawn to resume his treatment of God's knowing individuals in response to an objector. He notes that "providence does not remove contingency, however certain the knowledge may be or efficacious the will, for divine knowing (*scientia*) is related to future contingents as our eyes are related to contingents in the present: as we see Socrates sit when he is sitting, yet his sitting is not simply necessary."[67] It is, however, conditionally necessary, since given the fact of his sitting – a fact observed – it is necessary that he be sitting. This form of necessity may sound odd to us, yet it should not, for in most elegant form it secures Descartes' *cogito*, and Aquinas is always careful to note his sources in Aristotle.[68]

This simple yet central point must be the sole purpose of the visual simile, for Aquinas is willing to overlook the immense and often decisive gap separating knowledge derived from things from that which causes them, in order to make it. Moreover, his explicit commentary on the model recalls just that difference, for "the divine will, as universal cause of all being, of course transcends the order of necessity and of contingency."[69] So Aquinas does not use the simile with sense knowledge to suggest that God sees the future, but only as a way of showing us how the mode of necessity ascribed to things known by God is quite com-

---

[64] Cf. ST 1.14.13; *de Ver.* 2.12. This image is introduced in *de Malo* "*potest accepi conveniens similitude ex ordine locali*" (16.7).
[65] ST 1.14.8.
[66] ST 1.14.12.
[67] *de Malo* 16.7.15.
[68] Jaake Hintikka, "*Cogito ergo sum*: inference or performance," in *Philosophical Review* LXXI (1962), pp. 3–32; Aristotle, *On Interpretation*, 9 (19a23).
[69] *Ibid.*

patible with their contingency. And when he goes on to extend the simile to include a well-placed observer, he fails as expositor and as teacher by allowing himself to be caught in an unwarranted implication of a quite limited model, and so misleading his auditors.

In fact, such a critique arises from Aquinas' own treatment when he explicitly likens God's knowing to that of artisans with regard to their artifacts: "just so is the knowing (*scientia*) of God related to all created things."[70] And as if to underscore how different this simile is meant to make divine knowing from human science, he offers a suggestive image of "natural things as [suspended] midway between two knowings (*scientia*), God's and ours."[71] Our science is derived from those very things which God's knowing causes. Yet if we recall that each of these knowings is a relational activity, it will not be the case that the things known will be identical. For we will be able to apprehend what the current state of scientific development (in the broadest sense) makes accessible to us, and when relevant, such knowledge will always be subject to the temporal modifications of past, present, and future. So it is that Aquinas understood things to be constituted as objects of human knowing.[72]

How, then, is the thing which we know constituted from the other side, as it were, as an object of divine science? Surely that we do not and cannot know – as Maimonides insisted and Aquinas confirmed.[73] Yet we can say some things about this inexpressible relation, things already noted: (1) that it is more like art than what we call science, practical rather than speculative, as artisan to artifact; and (2) that it "is *measured* [not by time but] by eternity, which is itself all-at-once, and yet includes all of time without missing any part of it."[74] Both of which observations, of course, only underscore just how unknown to us is the object-as-known to God, for the relation of artist to artifact is only slightly less mysterious than the strictly incomprehensible manner in which eternity is said to include all of time.

The *inclusion* image stems from Augustine, whose great breakthrough in understanding such matters came when he realized that "spiritual things contain that in which they are, as the soul contains the body."[75] When Aquinas tries to articulate this particular containment of time by eternity,

---

[70]   ST 1.14.8.
[71]   ST 1.14.8.3.
[72]   Bernard J. F. Lonergan, *Insight* (London: Longmans, 1957), ch. 8, "Things."
[73]   *Guide* 3.20; *de Ver.* 2.12.
[74]   *de Ver.* 2.12.
[75]   The words are Aquinas' in ST 1.8.1.2, but the source is Augustine, in *Confessions*, Bk 7, chs 15, 20.

however, he misleads us by using a temporal expression: "eternity is the measure of permanent being (*esse*) while time is the measure of motion."[76] Inevitable as it is that "permanent" will slip in, as he already stated in *de Veritate* 2.12, it is misleading here nonetheless. The most satisfying expressions seem to be metaphors: the *tota simul* of Boethius, and the *nunc temporis* of Augustine, although Aquinas is less happy with the latter, since he recognizes that it is inherently related to the token-reflexive status of a temporal subject, itself susceptible of descriptions in past, present, and future.[77]

Where, then, do we stand? Firmly within time, and quite unable to prescind from that modality in anything that we know or say. Yet for all that, we are able to affirm without misperception or contradiction that what-will-be is known-by-God as what-eternally-happens. For such a statement does not suppose God "to perceive what really is future not *as* future but as present,"[78] since there is not a unitary *what* to bridge the gap between eternal and temporal knowings.[79] Similarly, it does not assert that "what God sees is *both* future *and* simultaneously (since in itself it is just as God sees it) also present,"[80] since we have no way of removing a *what* from the two diverse contexts of knowing. Yet such grammatical reminders clarify, if they do, by dividing rather than uniting. Can anything afford us a glimpse of the mode proper to divine knowing, even if its eternal character be opaque to us? Here I believe the image can serve us – of artisan to artifact – notably as Dorothy Sayers has begun to develop it in her minor classic, *The Mind of the Maker*.[81]

Originally published in 1941, the work has been successively reprinted ever since. For in it, a creative writer seeks to reflect upon her own activity to elaborate the metaphor which all three of our thinkers acknowledged to be the controlling one. Yet she proposes to *make* something of

---

[76]   ST 1.10.4.

[77]   ST 1.10.4.2.

[78]   Geach (note 5), p. 57.

[79]   As Thomas Gornall in his book *Knowledge in God* (note 62), p. 347 n.1, notes: "It is always ultimately in terms of eternity that St Thomas explains God's knowledge of the creature's free acts. What is known in eternity is known not as past or future but in God's presence, with the hypothetical necessity which belongs to what is actual and present. Nor does St Thomas treat the question of God's knowledge of the free acts of possible but not actual creatures." On the latter question, I would agree with Anthony Kenny's critique in *The God of the Philosophers* (Oxford: Clarendon, 1979), p. 71; though I am presenting here a position at variance with his regarding the coherence of speaking of God's knowing something "in eternity."

[80]   Gornall (note 64), p. 347.

[81]   Dorothy Sayers, *The Mind of the Maker* (Grand Rapids MI: Eerdmanns, 1963).

it, asking how one's own experience of creativity might inform the philosophical reflections of those standing in a tradition which affirms creation. We cannot underestimate the difficulty of the task, even for the creator of Lord Peter whose imagination was also up to the task of translating Dante's *Divine Comedy*. For anyone who has questioned artists about their work knows they prefer to keep a prudent if not a holy silence. And as for those who write about others' creations – literary critics and art historians – it is fair to say that such writing can claim no discernible mode. Where it is insightful, it comes close to wisdom, for it manages to convey to us something of the creative spark itself. Where it is not, it stumbles awkwardly between pretention and pedantry.

It is when she focuses on the relation between a novelist and her characters that I find Sayers most illuminating.[82] She reminds us that there is no contradiction between an author's creating a character, and the character's developing a life of its own. In fact, such is a common experience reflected more recently in the alternate endings which John Fowles included in his novel *The French Lieutenant's Woman*. There is a malleability yet there are limits, and the network of relations which develops begins to spin its own world, even when this is not expressly highlighted, as Charles Dickens was wont to do. Human freedom in the hands of God? Why not?, the reflective author asks.

As a thoroughly intentional activity, her primary analogate for human creativity introduces more harmonics than Jeremias' pot and potter (Jer. 18). She goes on to put the analogy to work. Not only could we think of ourselves as characters being composed by the divine author – note the emphasis on the present as the closest tense we have to the eternal. But the book of the world – the universe, really – includes us all. There are no readers outside this book of nature.[83] Moreover, while individuals die, there is as yet no conclusion to the story; a felicitous way of explaining why Wolfhart Pannenberg must always remind us of the "proleptic" character of events in this world.[84] So we are asked to conceive existence –

---

[82]   This image is also employed by James Ross in *Philosophical Theology* (Indianapolis IN: Bobbs-Merrill, 1969), pp. 250–72, though he insists he is not drawing an analogy but illustrating a metaphysical principle (p. 268). Yet since his use of this "principle" invariably turns on counter-examples which rely uniquely on the author-character *analogy*, one must wonder what other access he has to the principle – perhaps one of "intellectual emanation"!

[83]   Sayers (note 81), p. 103.

[84]   One may now understand why Wolfhart Pannenberg, who cannot escape invoking the limit-notion of "universal history," must always use the complementary "proleptic" to characterize things as we know them.

most plausibly human existence – as being part of a story always being composed by its divine author, which we read, when we can, *as* characters within it, and whose end is beyond our grasp. So she begins to elaborate the image which our philosophical theologians could assert but failed to develop.

Moreover, in the process she may have offered us some clues to "imperfectly understanding" what Aquinas said was quite beyond us: the relation of time to eternity. He said we could never step outside of the temporal mode of our assertions – much as Kant insisted about our perceptions. Yet is there a way we might reach – or even gesture – beyond that mode, analogous to reaching beyond the determinate realization of a perfection? The most obvious is also obviously unsatisfactory: the "larger view." We saw that Aquinas' image of the far-seeing observer for providential guidance skewed the entire discussion by leading us to think of God not as artisan but as spectator – like us. Grandparents can help a young person, but the conflicting temporal modes will also limit their efficacy. Science fiction – or its analogue in Doris Lessing's trilogy – often juxtaposes timeframes to useful effect, but again the mode remains. Another candidate would be the *now* of ecstasy, or less formidably, the privileged unraveling of liturgical time or of traumatic episodes. An arresting experience always, which can usefully relativize our tyranny to the day-to-day quotidian, yet of these we must say that there is precisely no way to relate them to time. That is why, in fact, they stand out, and often why we treasure them.

What Dorothy Sayers' procedure suggests is that we relate eternity with time on the model of the intentional simultaneity of artist with object-being-made. There is an intensity in this process, which most of us have one time felt, which defies the ordinary course of time. And yet *what* is being produced is a thoroughly temporal object. The artist, *as artist*, is related to the world of created things through her creations; although as individual she is herself part of that world as well. Can we, through that experience, touch something of the *mode* proper to the creator of all? Sayers suggests that we might; she carries us a certain way herself. I have offered just enough for you to pursue it on your own.

The most startling conclusion we might draw from this exercise, however, has to do with its mode. For we have been asked, not to construct tenfold enamation schemes, but to reflect on an experience of creativity open to each of us, even if better exemplified in a few. And we were asked to do so in an explicit attempt to probe what speculative thinkers have recognized to be the controlling image for God's knowing: artistry. Perhaps speculative thought shows its own limits here: by identifying an image and leaving its development to us. And the image itself –

indeed the doctrine of creation – suggests that the creative mode is itself the more perfect mode of knowing, and that all one may ever succeed in doing through philosophical reflection or scientific investigation amounts to approaching things from our side: deriving what knowledge we can from them. It is the creative artist, the artisan, and perhaps – as Aristotle was wont to extend it – the architects of community as well, who actually imitate that intentional activity whereby the creator of all "knows each particular thing, not only as they are in their causes, but even as each one of them is itself in act."[85] Such is Aquinas' most succinct formula for God's knowledge of singulars, yet the way to our appreciating that knowledge lies not through amassing more such formulae, but through reflecting on the modes of knowing proper to us which fulfill this one. Or one's own inner life, in which we each share an inbuilt task – that of becoming oneself, and whose secret lies in discriminating the next step.[86]

The best we have, then, beyond the bare grammatical assertions, are analogies such as these. Yet to begin to explore them is to mine the crucial distinction between God's knowing and ours, recognized by both Maimonides and Aquinas though left quite underdeveloped by each. Yet this beginning alone could offer some useful therapy to counteract our endemic tendency to overlook the warning embodied in the distinction between a knowing that is productive and knowing that is derived, as we invariably treat God's knowing as though it were a knowing *about* something. In that way at least, one might display what one cannot express: the mode of knowing proper to divinity and its otherness from our own.

[85] ST 1.14.13.
[86] Cf. my *Exercises in Religious Understanding* (Notre Dame IN: University of Notre Dame, 1974), chs 4 (Kierkegaard) and 5 (Jung).

Chapter 5

AQUINAS' DEBT TO MAIMONIDES

I want to focus on three areas in which Aquinas' articulate manner of utilizing philosophy to develop doctrinal positions made significant and lasting advances in philosophical theology. In each of them, however, his contribution has not proven to offer the kind of plateau from which subsequent thinkers can henceforth be presumed to begin their own inquiries. Many of us would be pleased were that the case, but the resolutions which he proposes appear to be more "dialectical" than that. Anyone continually trying to "show the independence of dependent things," as Chesterton epitomized Aquinas' task, will doubtless have to stretch ordinary categories beyond their accustomed use. This helps to explain why each generation of thinkers must reappropriate Aquinas, and why the officially sponsored attempt to make a timeless synthesis of his thought in the early decades of this century (Thomism) was seen before too long to have betrayed the spirit of his inquiry. The three areas are: the analogical character of language and especially of religious discourse and expression, the centrality of creation and of divine practical knowing, and the inner compatibility of divine providence with human freedom. The last issue exemplifies most directly Chesterton's observation, while the first issue has remained the least understood (if betimes the most celebrated) of his achievements; yet it is his keen grasp of the philosophical issues surrounding creation which forms the centerpiece of his synthesis. So much so, in fact, that so astute a commentator and philosopher as Josef Pieper has identified creation as "the hidden element in the philosophy of St. Thomas."[1] Beginning our exposition with analogy, however, will provide a way to illustrate the role which creation plays for Aquinas, as well as highlight his distinctive way of characterizing that divine activity.

[1] Josef Pieper, *Silence of St. Thomas* (New York: Pantheon, 1957), p. 47. There is a new edition of Pieper's book issued in 1999 by St Augustine's Press in South Bend, IN.

Analogous Uses of Language

Maimonides was clearly working without a developed notion of analogical discourse. In those chapters of the *Guide* where he canvasses the vexed discussion of divine attributes,[2] the Rambam briefly mentions a position between equivocal and univocal uses of a term, only to reject it:

> The terms "knowledge," "power," "will," and "life," as applied to Him, may He be exalted, and to all those possessing knowledge, power, will, and life, are purely equivocal, so that their meaning when they are predicated of Him is in no way like their meaning in other applications. Do not deem that they are used amphibolously [either]. For when terms are used amphibolously they are predicated of two things between which there is a likeness in respect to some notion, which notion is an accident attached to both of them. . . . Now the things attributed to Him, may He be exalted, are not accidents.[3]

This is an expression of Maimonides' celebrated agnosticism regarding our knowledge of God, together with his reasons why some intermediate way cannot be found.

The background here is Aristotle's classification of the ways in which terms can be used to signify (in Categories 1), while the foreground is a tangled controversy among Muslim thinkers regarding how one might responsibly apply ninety-nine names to the one God. The intramural Islamic controversy over "divine attributes," moreover, was further complicated by debates with Christian theologians wherein trinitarian "modes" and "persons" in God were often assimilated to *attributes*. So Maimonides had a difficult task of clarification facing him if he was to help his student Joseph find his way through the philosophical issues as they had been raised in that discussion, to relate himself properly to the confession that "the Lord, our God, is one." Moreover, given the understanding of amphibolous terms available to him as a way through the difficulties involved, he would have to reject the offer. For it entailed a third "likeness" somehow *between* the divine and the human, and extrinsic to both. The thought of something between God and creation repelled him

---

[2] *The Guide of the Perplexed*, trans. Shlomo Pines (University of Chicago Press, 1963), 1.50–61.
[3] *Ibid.*, 1.56. For "amphibolous terms," see H. A. Wolfson, "Amphibolous Terms in Aristotle, Arabic Philosophy and Maimonides," in *Studies in History and Philosophy of Religion 1* (Cambridge MA: Harvard University Press, 1973), pp. 455–77.

as much as later it would Karl Barth, nor could anything be said *accidentally* of the One without compromising the primary confession of the community's faith.

Maimonides' position on this matter is relevant both because Aquinas develops his own position in explicit opposition to Maimonides[4] and because the reasons which he offers for rejecting an intermediate use of language between equivocal and univocal meanings indicate how distant was the thought-world he inhabited from that which Aquinas could presume.[5] For in the West a century or more of preoccupation with the diverse uses of language in the scriptures had prepared the ground for the fruitful ways in which Aquinas would develop Aristotle's rather cryptic remarks on "analogy," whereas the Islamic philosophers with whom Maimonides (and his friend Joseph) were conversant had been engaged on a more architectonic enterprise, and the rabbis in Moses' own tradition had been content to remind themselves how frequently "the Torah speaks in the language of men." A systematic grappling with religious language would certainly demand greater sophistication than that regarding the structures inherent in our use of terms attributing perfections to God.

Aquinas was able to call upon and to expand some key distinctions already articulated in the "speculative grammar" developed during the century preceding him.[6] And the merit of recent studies on analogy in Aquinas has been precisely to call our attention to the way he roots his treatment in our linguistic capacities.[7] So, by way of offering a constructive alternative to Maimonides' radical agnosticism, while also eliminating those features that had made an intermediate solution unacceptable to his predecessor, Aquinas insists:

> Words are used of God and creatures in an analogical way, that is in accordance with a certain order between them. . . . In this way some words are

---

[4] For citations of Aquinas, *Summa Theologiae* (= ST), always cited from the Blackfriars edition (London: Eyre & Spottiswoode, 1964), where questions 12–13 of the First Part are translated by Herbert McCabe. ST 1.13.2.

[5] For an imaginative presentation of their differences, see my "Aquinas and Maimonides: A Conversation about Proper Speech," in *Immanuel* 16 (1983), pp. 70–85.

[6] See M.-D. Chenu, *Théologie au douzième siècle* (Paris: Vrin, 1957), much of which has been translated by Jerome Taylor in *Nature, Man and Society in the Twelfth Century* (Chicago: University of Chicago Press, 1968).

[7] The initial work in this vein was that of Ralph McInerny, *The Logic of Analogy* (The Hague: Mouton, 1961), followed, in a representative selection, by my *Analogy and Philosophical Language* (New Haven CT: Yale University Press, 1973), two illuminating articles by Patrick Sherry, "Analogy Reviewed," in *Philosophy* 51 (1976), pp. 337–45 and "Analogy Today," *ibid.*, pp. 431–46; as well as James Ross' masterful *Portraying Analogy* (Cambridge: Cambridge University Press, 1981).

used neither univocally nor purely equivocally of God and creatures, but analogically, for we cannot speak of God at all except in the language we use of creatures, and so whatever is said both of God and creatures is said in virtue of the order that creatures have to God as their source and cause in which all perfections of things pre-exist transcendently.[8]

Aquinas' understanding of "this way of using words [which] lies somewhere between pure equivocation and simple univocity"[9] will require neither an intermediary between God and the world nor a predication of God that is accidental. Instead, he focuses on the ordering that relates creature with Creator, and suggests that certain words may be especially useful to articulate that order – namely, those that express the perfections that accrue to creatures from their source, and orient rational creatures to that same source as their goal.

It is all here, compressed in Aquinas' lapidary prose: the elasticity which ordinary usage demands of certain terms, and the capacity those same terms have for invoking the intentional orientation of spiritual creatures toward the creator as their final end. So the "fact" of creation is presumed as a premise in the argument, and we are invited to recognize how the fact that normative terms require us to distinguish the "mode of signifying" from the "thing signified" points to a transcendent dimension in our ordinary usage. For we could never aspire to a more just society, if "just" merely described arrangements to which we could point. That certain terms possess, in their *ordinary* usage, this transcendent dimension is, then, a constitutive feature of those intentional creatures who require such a language to "go on," and so a feature of creation itself.

Aquinas will then be able to insist that such terms can "signify what God is although they do it imperfectly," and also show how their distinct meanings do not imply a plurality of features in God. What enables him to untangle the issue which had so vexed Islamic thinkers is his attention to language, coupled with an explicit reliance on the *order* following upon creation: "Since we know God from creatures, we understand him through concepts appropriate to the perfections creatures receive from him."[10] The language of perfections must outstrip itself, as we have seen, so we are entitled to project it responsibly to its transcendent source without having to claim a thorough understanding of that use: "such terms signify what God is . . . imperfectly." One reason we cannot attain an adequate grasp of the transcendent application of these terms is that such

---

[8] ST 1.13.5.
[9] *Ibid.*
[10] ST 1.13.4.

perfections must "pre-exist in God in a simple and unified way," since asserting that God is just is not so much to discover that God is characterized by justice as to remind ourselves of its source.

Moreover, the other side of that reminder is to return to where we began to note how "what pre-exists in God in a simple and unified way is divided among creatures as many and varied perfections."[11] So it is not the mere "fact" of creation that is presupposed in this argument, but the dynamic orientation of intentional creatures to their source. Normally associated with pseudo-Dionysius, a fifth-century philosophical theologian who provided Aquinas with a way of incorporating the power of Neoplatonism without adopting its luxuriant hierarchical schemes, this ordering from and to a creator not only accounts for the very structure of the *Summa Theologiae*, but also provides the key for Aquinas' remarkable articulation of dependent beings as independent agents.

Creation and Practical Knowledge

Medieval discussions regarding the eternity of the world versus its beginning in time reflect a religious concern that divided Jewish, Christian, and Muslim thinkers sharply from their pagan predecessors. Aristotle and the Greeks had maintained the eternity of the world because they had no way of conceiving it as a whole, but could only *presume* it as a given – as the context for whatever else might be said or thought. This was a very sensible position indeed, for who could pretend to be able to think the world as a whole – as Kant would later contend, albeit for different reasons? And if it sounds pretentious to try to conceive the world as a whole, how preposterous to try to think what "it" would be like *before* it! So the only assertion coherent with the original presumption was that the world itself had always been.

Indeed, the contrary assertion – that it had been created in the moment when time thus began – would require access to a perspective beyond the world. Affirming creation required faith in a revelation, and revelation presupposed one revealing. As Maimonides put it: "as for us, the matter is clear . . . : that all things exist in virtue of a purpose and not of necessity, and that He who purposed them may change them."[12] Necessary emanation from the One does not count as creation, for on that picture the First is not clearly distinct from the ensuing series, so the Oneness of God

11   *Ibid.*
12   *Guide,* 2.19.

is jeopardized. Aquinas will concur with Maimonides in contending that one may be unable to demonstrate from such a purposeful dependence clearly "in favor of the world's having been produced in time,"[13] yet the fact remains that the presumption in favor of an eternal world has also been swept away.

The philosophical problems, however, have only begun. Ibn Sina had tried to reconcile Qur'anic assertions about creation with a pre-existent (and eternal) matter because he could see no other place to locate the *possibility* that what came to be *would* come to be. (Aquinas distinguished *real* possibility from nonrepugnance, and so required no *location* for the latter beyond the mind of the maker.) Even a clear conception of *creatio ex nihilo*, however, would similarly founder on identifying the proper effect of the creator, since analogies with human making inevitably demanded some thing be presupposed. Maimonides did not even attempt this one, beyond the assertions of the Torah, though his endorsement of practical knowing as a useful way of intimating to ourselves the divine knowing which utterly escapes us[14] offers Aquinas his leading analogy of artisan to artifact. Similarly, Ibn Sina's distinguishing existence from the essence of created things will allow Aquinas to identify "*esse* as the proper effect of the first cause."[15] Not, however, before he had painstakingly refined Ibn Sina's distinction, as well as carefully distinguished practical from speculative knowing.

As Maimonides notes, "a great disparity exists between the knowledge an artificer has of the thing he has made and the knowledge someone else has of the artifact in question."[16] The latter form of knowledge corresponds to our way of knowing "the things from which we acquire the knowledge [we have] of them," whereas "the things in question follow upon [God's] knowledge," as the artifact an artisan. The analogy is hardly a novel one; creating is usually proposed as a making or modeling. Besides Genesis 2, we are also reminded of Jeremiah: "as clay is in the potter's hand, so you are in mine, House of Israel" (18:6). What makes it a bold comparison, however, is to think of God so related to all there is as artisan to artifact. For the knowledge involved is too inarticulate to satisfy the philosopher in us, while the relationship of clay to potter is too passive and mute to meet the demands for independent agency which we associate with freedom.

---

[13] *Guide*, 2.21.
[14] *Ibid.*, 3.21.
[15] ST 1.45.5.
[16] *Guide*, 3.21.

Aquinas, therefore, will need to specify *what* it is which can properly be said to come forth from God, as the shape of the pot does from the potter's hands. Maimonides' context evoked a parallel concern: "to explain to you . . . that what exists indicates to us of necessity that it does exist in virtue of the purpose of One who purposed it; and to do this without having to take upon myself what the Mutakallimun have undertaken – to abolish the nature of that which exists and to adopt atomism."[17] How can one safeguard the integrity of created natures while acknowledging the creator's sovereignty? Aquinas refines the distinction introduced by Ibn Sina at the heart of all created being to identify the effect proper to God's creative action: the very existence of things.[18] The distinction of essence from existence was not unknown to Maimonides; he in fact invokes it to characterize God as the One whose "existence is identical with His essence and His true reality" – unlike everything else where "existence is an accident attaching to what exists" (1.57).[19] But as his literal adherence to the language of Ibn Sina suggests, Maimonides had not yet seen how one might characterize this "accident" as a constitutive principle of created being.

That was to be Aquinas' signal achievement, elaborated in a work that is probably his earliest, *De ente et essentia*, and used notably to characterize the uniqueness of God,[20] and in his treatment of creation. Rather than characterize existence as an accident of things, Aquinas extends Aristotle's constituting principles of potency and act to "propose that existence itself be compared to the essence which is distinct from it as act to potency" so that "existence (*esse*) is the actuality of every form or nature."[21] Although our speculative inquiries direct themselves invariably to determining *what* something is, our lives are usually more affected by the fact that it exists. In any case, existing bestows an actuality which no amount

---

[17]   *Ibid.*, 2.19.

[18]   A telling summary phrase can be found in ST 5.4.3: "And this is how things receiving existence from God resemble him; for precisely as things possessing existence (*inquantum sunt entia*) they resemble the primary and universal source of all existence." For Ibn Sina, see Fazlur Rahman, "Essence and Existence in Avicenna," in Richard Hunt et al., eds, *Medieval and Renaissance Studies* 4 (London: Warburg Institute, 1958), pp. 1–16; Charles Kahn, "Why Existence Does not Emerge as a Distinct Concept in Greek Philosophy," in Parviz Morewedge, ed., *Philosophies of Existence* (New York: Fordham University Press, 1982), pp. 7–17; and my "Essence and Existence: Avicenna and Greek Philosophy," in *MIDEO* (= *Melanges de l'Institut Dominicain des Etudes Orientales* [Cairo]), 17 (1986), pp. 53–66.

[19]   See Alexander Altmann, "Essence and Existence in Maimonides," in *Studies in Religious Philosophy and Mysticism* (London: Routledge and Kegan Paul, 1969), pp. 108–27.

[20]   In a passage reminiscent of Maimonides: ST 1.3.4.

[21]   ST 1.3.4.

of reflection can achieve. It is in this sense that "everything . . . is potential when compared to existence," so much so that we must acknowledge that "existence is more intimately and profoundly interior to things than anything else." For that is precisely how God is present to each created thing: "in a way in keeping with the way in which the thing possesses its existence (*secundum modum quo esse habet*)."[22]

God is present to each existing thing "according to the manner in which it has its existence" because "*esse* (existence) is the proper effect of the first and most universal cause."[23] Since the fact that something exists is not a feature of a thing – not an accident, as Ibn Sina's unfortunate choice of words suggested – we need not fear to identify it as an effect proper to divinity, for there will be no way for us to pick it out, as Robinson Crusoe did Friday's footprint. The situation is paradoxical, not unlike a Zen *koan*: that which is most actual in each thing – what makes it exist – escapes our notice because it cannot be isolated as a feature of the thing. In that sense, then, we cannot talk about it, for what we call features of things are precisely those things we can say about them. On reflection, however, that does not surprise us, since the fact that some thing exists is not customarily listed among its characteristics. It must, then, be a special sort of *fact*, which is exactly Aquinas' point in singling out *esse* as "the actuality of every form or nature" which exists.

By recasting Ibn Sina's distinction as he has, Aquinas is able to offer a coherent characterization of the act of creation without pretending to have described it. That is appropriate, moreover, since the relation of the One who is source of all to all that originates from it will not be susceptible of description since it is not a relation within the world.[24] *Esse* (existence) understood as actuality becomes the vehicle for articulating God's transcendence, as well as what links created things with their creator. It should now be clear how central a role this account of creation plays in the development of Aquinas' thought. We have seen how it offered him a philosophical basis for confidently asserting a transcendent referent for analogous terms: "whatever is said both of God and creatures is said in virtue of the order that creatures have to God as their source and cause."[25]

[22] ST 1.8.1.
[23] ST 1.45.5.
[24] Robert Sokolowski's *God of Faith and Reason* (Notre Dame IN: University of Notre Dame Press, 1982/Washington DC: Catholic University of America Press, 1995) develops this point masterfully in terms of "distinctions." James Ross indicates the quality of metaphysical understanding required, in "Creation II," in Alfred Freddoso, ed., *Existence and Nature of God* (University of Notre Dame Press, 1983), pp. 115–41.
[25] ST 1.13.5.

Although such terms will "signify what God is . . . imperfectly,"[26] that is to be expected since they are being used to signify not an object in the world but the source of all. What is remarkable, then, is not that we cannot speak adequately of divinity, but that we can use our language to speak truthfully of God at all.[27]

Maimonides' concern that the demands of philosophical discourse not undermine the uniqueness and transcendence of God is Aquinas' as well; he has simply discovered a way of enriching that discourse to the point where philosophy can serve our confession of faith in the One while exploiting hidden resources in our ordinary human language. But his philosophical virtuosity will be especially taxed when it comes to showing how human freedom and divine providence are not only reconcilable but enjoy an inner compatibility. For this was the point at which Muslim religious thinkers found it necessary to dissolve created natures into their atomic components (as Maimonides had noted), and at which Maimonides himself found specific corroboration for his agnosticism regarding attributing things like knowing to God.[28] Yet Aquinas will insist that divine providence does not fail even while respecting the realities associated with human freedom.

Divine Providence and Human Freedom

It is this resolution of Aquinas which has proved to be the most contested, as the issue recurred time and again under the rubric of "the problem of evil." If God is all-good and all-powerful, how can we explain the presence of evil in the world? Either God does not care, impugning divine goodness; or God is unable to prevent it, questioning divine omnipotence. The response congenial to Jews and Christians invokes Genesis 3, in which Adam's "passing the buck" to Eve, and Eve to the serpent, offers a paradigmatic account of the way we can abdicate responsibility for our actions so as to allow space for evil. And when self-deception moves to cover-up, evil has a way of prevailing.

Could not God have fortified Adam and Eve, however, to the point of resisting the serpent's enticement? Or as some prefer to put the question, recalling Maimonides' insistence "that He who purposed them may change them,"[29] could not God have foreseen their weakness and supplied

26   ST 1.13.4.
27   ST 1.13.12.
28   Guide, 3.20.
29   Ibid., 2.19.

us with hardier archetypes? Or is human freedom simply a stubborn fact, representing an absolute limit to divine power in creation, which God is pledged to respect? We begin to discern the philosophical issues emerging, and there is certainly more than one way of delineating them and of bringing them together to meet the religious questions involved. I shall sketch Aquinas' delineation and synthesis, alluding to alternative accounts. My own conviction is that he respects the realities in question – created and divine – together with the transcendence attending the relation between them, better than other contenders; but defending that conviction would require more than I can do here. The fact remains, however, that this issue taxes the acumen of philosophers who adhere to the Bible or the Qur'an in a way no other question can, so one's way of dealing with it will exhibit that specific interpenetration of faith with reason, and of reason with faith, which I have suggested as a hallmark of Aquinas' legacy to us.

The theorems, with one exception, are in place. God's knowledge of all that God creates is to be conceived by analogy with the way artisans understand what they are doing, so its mode will be primarily practical. Moreover, the world is not to be thought of as an eternal object over against an eternal God, but a temporal process embraced by God's "eternity [which] comprehends all phases of time."[30] (This affirmation is the most contested, although Aquinas' arguments for eternity as a "formal feature" of divinity are straightforward enough; it is the ineffable relation between time and eternity which makes philosophers question the very notion.)[31] As a result, it is never appropriate to think of God as "foreseeing" anything; all is present to God "in its presentness."[32] If we link these (incomprehensible to us) assertions about God's eternity with the analogy of practical knowing, and recall that what God properly does in creating is to bestow things with their existence, we have asserted an intimate relation between creature and creator – since nothing is more intimate to things than their existence.[33] The result is very like a philosophical articulation of a pot in the hands of a potter, however, an image which seemed to threaten the independent agency we associate with freedom.

Here we need one more theorem to complete Aquinas' synthesis, and establishing it requires a summary analysis of human freedom. There is an irreducibility to human agency which we can characterize as indepen-

---

[30] ST 1.10.2.4.
[31] See Norman Kretzmann and Eleonore Stump, "Eternity," in *Journal of Philosophy*, 78 (1981), pp. 429–58; and my "God's Eternity," in *Faith and Philosophy* 1 (1984), pp. 389–406.
[32] ST 1.14.13.
[33] ST 1.8.1.

dence. It represents our capacity to take responsibility for our actions, to receive both praise and blame: "the buck stops here; *I* did it." Yet we need to resist the temptation to conceive that situation as an indeterminacy which *I* resolve into agency, for then the question simply recurs: How did I decide to do it? Or even: What made me do it? Aquinas had the benefit of Aristotle's analysis of practical reason deliberating over means to ends, which he adapted to accommodate an end beyond the imagination of the Greeks. This analysis confronts our tendency to identify freedom with choice (note how spontaneously we say "freedom of choice"), finding free agents more imbedded in the orientation of their natures to the goods proper to them than a simple indeterminacy model would suggest. In this way, Aquinas will handle the logical fact that one cannot (on Aristotle's analysis) *choose* one's final end – since we deliberate only about means to ends – by observing that we either consent to it, or refuse it.[34] Either action is free, however, even though neither is strictly speaking a *choice*. (We will find this analysis plausible, even if at first it affronts us, by reflecting on the more substantive decisions of our lives: can I be said to have *chosen* my wife, perhaps from a field of candidates? Decisions usually entail choices, but cannot be identified with them.)[35]

If God, then, who is our sovereign good in so intimate a fashion that "in desiring its own perfection everything is desiring God himself,"[36] were to move us to do something, the natural way for God to do so would be as the final cause of our actions. Such was the insight of Augustine, whose reflections on freedom in book 8 of the *Confessions* established that nothing – neither myself nor God – can make me *will* something, unless it draws or entices me. And if I cannot be pushed to will something, but only drawn to do so, not even God can cause me to do something freely, if we are thinking of an efficient cause. Yet God, as my sovereign good, could so draw my will as to bring me freely to consent to the end for which my nature craves.

Such are the main lines of Aquinas' resolution of God's unfailing providential care with human freedom. They imply that any good choice will

---

[34] Frederick E. Crowe, "Complacency and Concern in the Thought of St. Thomas Aquinas," in *Theological Studies* 20 (1959), pp. 1–39, 198–230, 343–95; reprinted in Frederick E. Crowe, *Three Thomist Studies*, ed. Michael Vertin [Supplementary issue of *Lonergan Workshop*, vol. 16, ed. Fred Lawrence] (Boston: Lonergan Institute [Boston College], 2000).

[35] K. M. Sayre, "Choice, Decision, and the Origin of Information," in F. J. Crosson and K. M. Sayre, eds, *Philosophy and Cybernetics* (Notre Dame IN: University of Notre Dame Press, 1967), pp. 71–98.

[36] ST 1.6.1.2.

presuppose an orientation to the end, where the orientation itself is not a choice but a consent to the orientation of one's very being. And where that end is enhanced beyond our imagining, as in the ways revealed by God to Jewish, Christian, or Muslim believers, the consent becomes a response – of faith.

Many questions remain regarding the character of that divine initiative, questions familiar to Christians under the rubrics of "predestination" or the "irresistibility of God's grace." Suffice it to say here that Aquinas' theorem of divine eternity makes the notion of *predestination* as incoherent as "foreknowledge," and that human freedom does retain for him those mysterious reaches where it can renounce its own good. Bare refusal, of course, is seldom available to humans, though the angels' sin can be explained no other way.[37] The limiting case is, however, just that; in the course of human events we find ourselves operating within an orientation originally supplied or freely offered, and our freedom is structured by consenting to the first and responding gratefully to the second.

On the whole, Aquinas has shown himself more philosophically astute than Maimonides, although a cool assessment of his influence on Western thought would suggest that Maimonides' warnings about misunderstandings were more accurate than Aquinas' confidence in human understanding; not simply that his own works were to be condemned for a time so soon after his death, but that his subtle and dialectical ways of resolving faith and reason seem so easily to escape both ecclesiastics and philosophers. What I have tried to suggest, however, is that the attempt to recover that synthesis for oneself is well worth the effort.

[37] ST 1.63.

Chapter 6

CREATION AND "ACTUALISM": THE DIALECTICAL DIMENSION OF PHILOSOPHICAL THEOLOGY

"Philosophical theology" is a descriptor coined in the 1960s by the contributors to a group endeavor, entitled *New Essays in Philosophical Theology*, which meant to bring the tools of analytic philosophy to bear on topics long recognized to be theological in character, yet with considerable philosophical resonance. It was subsequently adopted by those who wished to do just that: bring their philosophical expertise to issues theological, without being thereby constrained to consider the traditional "preambles to faith" that had become the stock in trade of a discipline called "natural theology": the existence of God, the possibility of divine revelation, and the capacity to discourse at all about such transcendent objects.

The model operative here had been one in which reason was invoked to establish the truth of certain claims that were deemed to be presupposed to a reasonable assent of faith. And since reason was supposed to function with evidence available to all, its deliverances were considered "natural," while those of faith were "supernatural," indicating that something more than evidence was at work in the assent of faith. Whatever the preoccupations of the contributors to the *New Essays* symposium, others of us who have adopted that title for our work wanted not only to expand the range of theological topics available for philosophical inquiry, but also to intimate a new model for the relation of reason and faith. Rather than a stepwise pattern that suggested a foundational approach to matters of faith, we preferred to direct our attention to the tradition of Christian theology, as one in which the community had availed itself of reason from the outset in the elaboration of its faith and its own self-understanding. By attending to the explicitly philosophical contributions to that endeavor, those who style themselves "philosophical theologians" have tried to bring some distinctive critical tools to assessing the larger endeavor of Christian theology and especially to adjudicating its claims to truth. Moreover, there are convincing hermeneutic arguments that the medievals never considered the discussions involving the "preambles to faith" to be foundational in character, but rather to be a retrospective inquiry into the presuppositions required for any consideration of the truth of the articles of faith.[1]

It is the assessing and adjudicating role of philosophy, however, that deserves a fresh look today, in the light of recent reflections on the role of tradition in guiding inquiry, and specifically out of respect for the primarily theological focus of the work in this field. For if the mode is expressly philosophical, the issues are theological, and theology operates far more historically than many philosophers are accustomed to proceed. The notions that proved crucial to the early doctrinal formulations of Nicaea and Chalcedon, for example, were themselves forged over three centuries of debate, in which their meaning and intent were shaped to the specific role they were to play in that discussion. Apprising oneself of this conceptual development means entering into the theological tradition itself, at least enough to follow the reasoning presented for modifying the philosophical terms in play, so that the discourse will be assessed in its own terms rather than presuming it to be employing a putatively neutral idiom. Absent such efforts, we cannot presume we are discussing the theological issues we set out to examine, but only a procrustean version of them that we take to be "coherent" within prevailing horizons. But one of the salient contributions of theological questions to philosophy has ever been to challenge the adequacy of current horizons. It is in the interest of good philosophy as well as accurate theology to show how the criteria of assessment are inherently dialectical in a merged discipline like "philosophical theology." What follows intends to illustrate that contention with respect to an avowal shared by Jews, Christians, and Muslims alike: that the universe comes forth from God freely and deliberately.

In the medieval discussion, the operative counterpoint was the scheme of necessary emanation from the One, in which all-that-is flows from that source in much the same way as many premises may be deduced from a single axiom. What the Bible and the Qur'an were presumed to say, however, was that the creator who freely bestowed those revelations also

---

[1] Guy de Broglie, "Le vrai sens de *preambula fidei*," in *Gregorianum* 34 (1953), pp. 345–88.

brought forth the universe as an utterly free gift: neither responding to any need in the creator nor presuming any stuff with which to work. The resulting challenge to philosophy is to find a conceptuality that will articulate how all-that-is is freely originated and exists in dependence on the One. This is indeed an exercise in theology, since those who don't accept this story of origination could hardly be bothered. Yet it is a philosophical exercise as well, since the issues involved are inescapably metaphysical: there could be no witnesses of such an origination. I shall contrast two ways of articulating this situation, arguing that one of them is more compatible with the original assertion of the revelatory sources, and for that reason ought to recommend to us the ontology employed. In other words, rather than simply assess the adequacy of a revelatory statement according to our philosophical horizons, I want to show how the faith horizon can also exercise a normative role in leading believers to prefer one ontology to another.

It is commonly presumed that the alternative to a necessary emanation of the universe from its source is a picture of the creator selecting which universe to create. This picture coheres with our commonly held presumption that choosing is the paradigm for the exercise of freedom. It seems that if there were no choice in the matter, the creator would be constrained, and this universe would be the only universe possible, given the creator it has. I shall argue against the picture, as well as the metaphysics that it suggests: one that privileges possibility over actuality. I will do so from the perspective of affirming the free creation of the universe from the One. Once we are alerted to the fact that this universe is indeed a free gift, rather than the given context of all that we can say or do, we will be even more concerned than Aristotle was to make of individual existing things our paradigm for what-is. The utter freedom of creation not only denies any need on the part of the creator, but also any prior constraints on the part of the world. There is no possibility preceding God's free origination, except by reference to the power of God.[2] So there are no "possible worlds" from which the creator selects *this* one, as though God's action in creating were primarily a matter of will and indeed of choice.

It is true that many who so construe creation do not think of the presence of such "worlds" as a prior constraint on God, since the worlds are rather conceived as products of the divine mind, one of which the divine will "actualizes." Indeed, nothing would seem to enhance the scope of the divine intellect so much as to think of God knowing in detail all pos-

---

[2]   Thomas Aquinas, ST 1.46.1 ad 1.

sible configurations of all possible states of affairs, necessary and contingent, and selecting *this* one! Nothing, that is, except the thought that some
of these states of affairs will involve actions of free individuals, so that
knowing their outcome would presume a determinacy unavailable before
that person existed and performed the action. *Actiones sunt suppositorum*,
as the medieval axiom had it: actions result from existing individuals. To
put it another way: possible configurations may give us a scenario, but not
a history. And we all know that scenarios are parasitic on histories. The
anticipated responses of standard scenarios are distilled from what we know
of behavior in the past. Possibility follows actuality when one speaks of
"worlds," even if in a constituted world, potentiality precedes actuality. Yet
it remains true, doesn't it, that what-is could have been otherwise? Isn't
that what "contingency" comes to? In a universe that is merely given, this
would be the operative sense of "contingency": understanding that some
states of affairs in the world could indeed have happened otherwise, while
others could not. Indeed, distinguishing invariant from variable features of
the world is part of our basic orientation. But when the universe is a free
gift, there is another level of contingency beyond that which presupposes
the actual configurations and then recognizes that many of them are in
fact variable. It is rather the level that acknowledges that all this might
not be at all. Such a recognition represents another level of contingency
because even what happens by "natural necessity" may yet be said to be
contingent in this sense. In fact, "no creature can be said to be absolutely
necessary, for it is necessary only on the supposition that the divine will
has unchangeably decreed its preservation."[3] For "just as before things
existed on their own it was in the creator's power for them to exist, so
now that they do exist on their own it is in the creator's power for them
not to exist."[4]

So it seems that the presence of a free creator adds a dimension to ordinary discourse about possibility and necessity, emphasizing that they are
modalities of existing, which is the free gift of the creator. "Just as bringing things into existence depends on God's will, so also preserving them
in existence. For [God] preserves them in existence only by perpetually
giving existence to them, and were he therefore to withdraw his activity
from them all things . . . would fall back into nothingness."[5] This statement of Aquinas, the sense of which he attributes to Augustine, shows
how crucial it is whether one treats the divine origination as a mere pre-

---

[3] Thomas Aquinas, *Quaestiones disputatae de potentia* 3.17 ad 3.
[4] ST 1.9.2.
[5] ST 1.9.2.

supposition or as a continuing presence. If the originating activity is but presupposed, the universe can be considered, like that of the Greeks, a given. If that activity is indeed pervasive, however, "actuality" takes on a new valence. One may indeed speak about how things might have been, but as possibilities. They remain relative to the power of God to create them, and so say little more than that things could have been otherwise than the way in which they are. How much otherwise is a disputed question, as recent discussion surrounding the "universal constants" attests.

What appears from this perspective to be a fruitless enterprise is to extrapolate randomly from the world that we know into other "possible worlds." The inverse of the complaints of empirical philosophers regarding "God-talk" recurs in this context: such flights of fancy presume that too many of the implications from the actual world to remain as we alter one feature after another of the world we think we know. How little we really know of the intricacies of this world is dramatized by the "universal constants" discussion. In fact, this is the only world we know; we remain quite ignorant of those features which make it into a unified, functioning whole, in short, a world. Aquinas called this pervasive and transcendental feature the "order of the universe as a whole [*bonum ordinis universi*]" and considered it to be the "primary intent" of the creator.[6] Since the various sciences have only begun to explore the synergies proper to ecological interaction, we rightly confess a large degree of unknowing in regard to this order, yet we can perceive enough to marvel at its intricacies. Once again, the positive valence of actuality strikes us forcibly. Even while we know that this world "could be otherwise," we remain unable to identify those features which make it into the world that it is or to tell why they do so. We are reminded of the rhetoric of al-Ghazali and Maimonides in the face of an ostensibly philosophically superior scheme of "necessary emanation": what one really ought to marvel at is the conjuncture of things that we cannot explain yet which make this world what it is, for these patterns – unpredictable by the sciences available to them – display the wisdom of the creator.[7]

Indeed, this accent on the world in which we live as the world that is the free gift of the creator (and so the only *bona fide* "world" that we know) calls into question the utility of modal logic and of "possible world" semantics more generally to articulate the relation of creator to creation.

---

[6]   ST 1.15.2.
[7]   Al-Ghazali, *Al-maqsad al-asna fi sharh ma'ani asma' Allah al-husna, 'al-'adl'*, translated as *Al-Ghazali on the Ninety-nine Beautiful Names of God* (Cambridge: Islamic Text Society, 1992); Moses Maimonides, *Guide of the Perplexed*, 2.19, 2.24, 3.13.

These "worlds" remind one of alternative emanation schemes, replacing "necessary" with "possible," yet retaining the sense that God is "in" each of them. In fact, the "distinction" of creator from creation is what is at stake – what Ibn Sina had identified as the bifurcation in being between necessary and possible.[8] This represented the first attempt of an Islamic philosopher to factor in the difference that an originated universe could make to one's metaphysics. The device that he employed was to distinguish essence from existence in such wise that everything other than the First received its existence from that First, whose uniqueness was assured by the fact that its essence [dhat] was identified with existing.[9] So while Avicenna regarded "possibles" as presupposed to the activity of emanation, what distinguished the necessary being from all that might be (i.e., what is merely possible in itself), as well as from what exists (i.e., what is possible in itself yet necessary from another), is also what makes it unique. While it lacks existence as something "coming to it," it nevertheless enjoys existing as what "belongs to it" – the etymological root of "dhat," the term Alfarabi had already coined for God's unique essence.[10]

Ibn Sina's account of God's necessity and the world's contingency was bedeviled by two interrelated factors. First, there was his way of characterizing existing as "what comes to something" and hence an "accident" (since the Arabic expression for "accident" bears the same relation to the root verb as our term does to the Latin verb "accidere," "to come to"). There was, second, his identification of existing with the "necessity" that obtains among existents by virtue of their emanation from the One. These are connected in that the vague characterization of existing as "what comes to something" makes it into an attribute, which attribute is then identified with a place in a formal scheme. So what we recognize as contingency in existing things, their "precarious" status as existents, is translated into a derivative form of necessity, namely their place in a necessary scheme. What distinguishes all such items from the One that is necessary is simply that each of them is what it is already (as it were) as a merely possible, whereas God alone is such that it could not not be. Now the

[8] See my "Essence and Existence: Avicenna and Greek Philosophy," in MIDEO (= Melanges de l'Institut Dominicain des Etudes Orientales) 17 (1986), p. 366. For the sense of "distinction" here, see Robert Sokolowski, The God of Faith and Reason (Notre Dame IN: University of Notre Dame Press, 1982/Washington DC: Catholic University of America Press, 1995).
[9] Fazlur Rahman, "Essence and Existence in Avicenna," in Mediaeval and Renaissance Studies [London] 4 (1958), pp. 1–16.
[10] See my Knowing the Unknowable God (Notre Dame IN: University of Notre Dame Press, 1986), pp. 16 (Farabi), 39–40 (Ibn Sina).

force of existing as "coming to something" emerges: the item in question is already constituted "before" existing, so that the characterization is relatively apposite, despite the self-referential problems which obviously arise when one so defines existing.

Now we may see the connection between Avicenna's scheme and "possible worlds" treatments of these issues. "Possibles" in both cases are taken to be identifiable prior to their existing (or being actualized) – indeed, to be exhaustively so. (There are subtle differences whether one is referring to "objects" or to "states of affairs," but these are quite compatible with the similarities we shall develop here.) So on both counts, "actualizing" may be thought of as the emerging of something into full-blown reality, or alternatively, as existence (or actualization) "coming to" it, where the *it* is already given. So existence is, in the current jargon, "an on/off property: either you're there or you're not."[11] It should be immediately evident how such a notion jars with the assertion shared by Jews, Christians, and Muslims of a creator who brings all-that-is into being. The picture operative here is more like a demiurge who, instead of fashioning out of pre-existent material, selects among a plethora of "possibles." With the Jewish, Christian, or Muslim God, however, the "possibles" could indeed be the product of the divine intellect, so nothing would be postulated as extraneous to the creator (except perhaps those "necessary truths" that would have to attend all possible configurations). So the mere assertion of a creator who is not a demiurge does not decide the matter. What does come nearer to deciding it is the conception of creation with which one is operating. Since this is usually quite implicit, the alternatives deserve to be developed.

If the creator is the source of all-that-is, and hence of the perfections of things, the creator will be the source not merely of their "existence" (in the "on/off" sense), but of all that emanates from their existing. Operations above all are the sign of something's existing, so it follows that the initial and grounding perfection is existence itself. If that be the case, this utterly "non-qualitative property" of existence will be the "proper effect of the first and most universal cause, which is God."[12] From that divine activity will flow all that comes to be from such creatures. Far from being an initial "floor," an "on/off property," what the act of creation bestows,

---

[11] Christopher Hughes, *On a Complex Theory of a Simple God: An Investigation in Aquinas' Philosophical Theology* (Ithaca NY and London: Cornell University Press, 1989), p. 27.
[12] ST 1.45.5. For the notion of "non-qualitative property," see R. M. Adams, "Theories of Actuality," in *Nous* 8 (1974), pp. 211–31, reprinted in *The Possible and the Actual*, ed. Michael Loux (Ithaca NY: Cornell University Press, 1979), pp. 190–209.

in creating this world, is what makes it to be and to be a world: the existential order that is the only matrix within which action occurs. Since
this bestowal is free (by the shared belief of Jews, Christians, and Muslims),
we are also led to believe that such a One could have created otherwise,
as well as not having created at all. Yet, nothing whatsoever licenses us to
picture the freedom to have created otherwise as a selection among determinate "possibles." In fact, much leads us in another direction: the
inscrutability of the divine wisdom, recently reinforced by astrophysical
reflection on the "universal constants," might make us wonder just how
different this universe could be, in its very structure, and remain a
universe.

However we may decide that (undecidable?) question, the presence of
human freedom would follow as a perfection utterly consonant with the
existential order of a universe conceived as the gift of a free creator. Such
a One would be empowered to create existents whose operations were
natural as well as others whose operations were also intentional. In fact,
the natures of intentional beings would be to be free. Just as the creator
who is the cause of being "imparts to creatures also the dignity of
causing,"[13] so also that same creator makes some such creatures free agents.
That need not inhibit the certitude of providence, for "to be necessary
or contingent are corollaries to being as such."[14] This last assertion is the
crucial challenge to a metaphysics able to articulate the scope of a creator
of all-that-is, and to do so in a way that also articulates "the distinction"
as well. Such a One is not "faced with" necessities any more than subverted by contingencies, for this One need not "negotiate" the world it
creates. What is also needed is a manner of understanding this relationship that avoids the spatial images connected with a "transcendence/
immanence" scheme. It would only be accurate to say that this One is
"beyond" necessity-contingency if we were also prepared to say that it is
so because this is the very One that sustains all-that-is in being, whether
its mode of being is necessary or contingent. So what is required, as James
Ross has been reminding us, is a way to articulate a "cause of being":

> omnipotence is FORMALLY not the power to make states of affairs obtain
> or to actualize the possible. It is the power to *cause being ex nihilo*. . . . Its
> domain is realized with its exercise. What is possible *ad extra* is the result
> of what God does. God's power has no exemplar objects, only a perimeter
> (that is, finite being) plus a limit (that of internal consistency, compatibil-

---

[13]   ST 1.22.3.
[14]   ST 1.22.4 ad 3.

ity with divine being). God creates the kinds, the natures of things, along with the things. And [God] settles for what-might-have-been insofar as it is a consequence of what exists; for example, you might have been wealthier. Thus, there is no *mere* possibility with content (for example, "there might have been only Marticils, silicon-based percipients, native to Mars"); there are only descriptions, actual and potential, that might, for all we know so far, have been satisfied. They do not, however, "pick out" any definite content that, if actual, would satisfy them. All content *ad extra* is caused by God. In sum, God creates the possibility, the impossibility, and counterfactuality that has content (real situations) involving being other than God.[15]

Those who must begin with "possibilities" rather than with the act of creation would locate what Ross calls "definite content" in the "divine ideas," some of which the creator "actualizes" in creating this world. They often appeal to Aquinas' treatment of "divine ideas" to underscore their point.[16] Yet their appeal tends to miss the deft way in which Aquinas altered this Neoplatonic legacy to subserve his accentuating God's creative knowing as practical. It is only in the measure that God is creator that there is need at all for ideas, since the divine intellect as such has no need of "being informed by a plurality of *species*" by which it knows.[17] Indeed, divine simpleness would be violated were that required. Yet once we speak of God freely creating, then ideas become a convenient way for us to articulate the fact that God creates deliberately, and the idea serves as "that which is known, [as] the form of a house in the mind of the architect is something understood by him, to the likeness of which he produces the form of a house in the matter."[18] It should be clear that Aquinas is employing an analogy, and one which underscores the practical dimension of the knowing associated with creating. It is in that context that he then distinguishes two senses of "idea," both of which he acknowledges to be inherited from Plato: "as a principle of the production of things it may be called an *exemplar*, and belongs to practical knowledge; as a principle

---

[15] See James Ross, "God, Creator of Kinds and Possibilities: *Requiescant universalia ante res*," in *Rationality, Religious Belief, and Moral Commitment*, ed. Robert Audi and William Wainwright (Ithaca NY: Cornell University Press, 1986), pp. 315–34, especially p. 318; and Ross, "The Crash of Modal Metaphysics," in *Review of Metaphysics* 43 (1989), pp. 251–79.

[16] ST 1.15; *Quaestiones disputatae de veritate* 3.

[17] See the discussion between William Alston, "Does God have Beliefs," in *Religious Studies* 22 (1986), pp. 287–306, and William Hasker, "Yes, God has Beliefs," 24 (1988), pp. 385–94. Compare John Farthing, "The Problem of Divine Exemplarity in St. Thomas," in *Thomist* 49 (1985), pp. 183–222.

[18] ST 1.15.2.

of knowing, it is properly called a *ratio*, and can belong also to speculative knowledge." This *ratio* "is related to all the things God knows, even
though they never come into existence; and to all the things [God] knows
in the *rationes* proper to each, and as known by [God] in a speculative
way." [19]

This distinction Aquinas had already made in the previous question, in
asking "whether God has knowledge of non-existent things"?[20] He distinguished there between two modes of knowing by their objects: of those
things which were, are, or will be, "all these God is said to know by
knowledge of vision," while of those "which can be produced by God or
by creatures, yet are not, were not, and never will be, . . . God is said to
have . . . knowledge of simple understanding." The use of "vision" to
name God's creating (or practical) knowledge reflects the fact that "in ourselves things seen have a separate existence outside the one who sees."
Such items, then, are present to God as items that God creates; the
"others" need not be so construed: in fact, what knowledge of simple
understanding amounts to is God's knowing "the divine essence . . . as it
can be participated in some degree of likeness by creatures."[21] But in the
case of knowledge of vision, "God, in knowing [the divine] essence as
imitable in this particular way by this particular creature, knows [the
divine] essence as the nature and idea proper to that creature." This
knowing, which is practical, terminates in a particular creature with its
"proper nature," while the first terminates only in a "proper *ratio*," indicating how the divine essence could indeed be participated. That is why
Aquinas calls it "knowledge of simple understanding" and why he notes
that it is speculative in character. It should be clear, then, that Aquinas is
not an "exemplarist," in the sense identified by Ross, according to which
God first knows in a determinate way all the items God could create, and
then chooses among them certain ones to "actualize." Aquinas reserves
the term "exemplar" to the exercise of divine practical knowing and so
to those things which have existed, do or will exist. Beyond terminology,
the critical point is that the creator need not be a platonist to create in a
deliberate fashion. Aquinas' treatment of "divine ideas" cannot be adduced
as evidence for such a contention; indeed it testifies to the contrary. But
how may we formulate that contrary more precisely?

By noting how Aquinas transformed Avicenna's observations about
"existing coming to" things into an ontology that privileges existing over

[19] ST 1.15.3.
[20] ST 1.14.9.
[21] ST 1.15.2.

essence, as *act* of a potency. ~~If existing is not the merest fact about things,~~ ~~but rather the source *of* all their subsequent perfections, then it will follow~~ ~~that existing is the "proper effect of the first and most universal cause,~~ ~~which is God."~~[22] Whatever else there is – natures, powers, inclinations, habits, actions – is dependent upon those individuals' existing which embody them. It should be clear that "existing" here means just that. It is not the denatured "existing in" found in statements like "every object has existence in each world in which it exists."[23] For such statements reduce "existing" to a "property . . . essential to each object, and necessarily so," which property comes down to an object's belonging to a "possible world," so that the very point of Avicenna's original distinction is subverted, and one is constrained to substitute a new word "actuality" for "existence" as we normally use it. The alteration is far more than terminological, as we have seen; it brings with it an ontology that privileges possibility over actuality, and thereby makes it very difficult to understand what "actuality" means, other than to identify the world that happens to be from among all those which could be. ("Contingency" is given a strong sense – this world just "happens to be" – while the very being of the world is given short shrift.)

Alternatively, if what-exists is all we have, and what-is-possible is parasitic upon that, then another dimension is added to "contingency." It is not merely that things might have been otherwise, or that another "world" might have been "actualized," but that those things which exist might not have existed at all. That there might not have been anything at all was unthinkable to the Greeks, and equally so, it seems, to purveyors of "possible worlds," for whom "exists" as we normally use it is a special case of "exists in" (as in "exists in a possible world"). One can always suppose another "possible world." Yet this difference is no doubt illustrative, for as Sokolowski insists, the capacity to think "contingency" in this more radical sense is clearly a function of the affirmation of a free creation. "That the world is now understood as not having had to be, [which amounts to] the denial that God . . . is part of or dependent on the world, . . . is glimpsed on the margin of reason, . . . at the intersection of reason and faith."[24] With that "distinction" comes the corollary that God, as free creator, is the cause of all-that-is, and of the modalities that follow upon being. What we formulate as "necessities" are not thereby made arbitrary;

---

[22] ST 1.45.5.
[23] These citations are from Alvin Plantinga, "Actualism and Possible Worlds," in *The Possible and the Actual*, ed. Loux (note 12), p. 261.
[24] Sokolowski, *God of Faith and Reason* (note 8), pp. 34, 37, 39.

they depend on the divine nature rather than on the divine will, as what God understands must be the case if the divine essence is to be imitated by such a created nature. In that respect, necessities would seem to function more like rules of inference or like the constraints of matter, purpose, and appropriate agency in building something, than like constituent parts of created things. Such formal features differ from other constituents in that things are not made of them.

Moreover, if God's "necessity" is defined by what makes such a creator unique, namely that God's very essence is to-exist, then the primacy of existing will be confirmed in the clearest way possible. The One from which all-that-is comes to be exists in and by itself. What it bestows in creating will be a share in that perfection of existing, so that the very existence of the creature will consist in "a relation to the creator as the origin of its existence."[25] Even if the formulation of necessity as "being true, or obtaining in, all possible worlds" were an adequate account of the modal notion (which Ross challenges),[26] it would hardly succeed in formulating what it is about God's being necessary that further identifies such a One as the creator, indeed, as the free creator of all-that-is. Perhaps that is more than one ought to ask of such an account, but a characterization of God that required a separate premise to assure that such a One is the origin of all-that-is would hardly be adequate to articulate the faith of those who believe in free creation. Some other metaphysical scheme is clearly required. It must be able to characterize a One that need not create and from which all that is emanates. Moreover, since this world is the only world we know, and is deemed to be the one that God freely creates, underscoring the primacy of existing as what individuates by granting a participation in the divine act of existing offers itself as a metaphysical corollary of the original faith.

Furthermore, identifying the existence of the creature as "a relation to the creator," and hence as "what is more intimately and profoundly interior to things than anything else,"[27] including what makes each thing to be what it is (its essence), goes a long way to overcoming the imaginative bifurcation of transcendence-immanence. By reminding us that the "proper effect" of the free creator in things will by definition transcend the causal order of creatures, we are also brought to realize that this same effect will define what is most "intimately and profoundly" interior to created things. The distinction of existence from essence becomes the axial

---

[25]   ST 1.45.3.
[26]   Ross, "The Crash of Modal Metaphysics" (note 15), p. 270.
[27]   ST 1.8.1.

conceptual tool for articulating "the distinction" of God from the world by formulating the relation of creature to creator. Moreover, the conceptual obscurity of the key notion of existing also follows from the scheme itself, for were the "relation to the creator" in which created existing consists to be accessible in terms proper to the created universe itself, that is, if it were identifiable as a feature of the world, then its transcendence would be lost and "the distinction" elided. We see that the essence-existing distinction, as formulated by Aquinas so as to extend Aristotle's axial categories of potency-act, belongs to the same "logical neighborhood" as "the distinction" itself. Avicenna's formulation of existing as some thing "coming to the essence" would be more accessible to reason alone, however incoherent it may be seen to be. Aquinas' distinction seems to be as much "on the margin of reason" and hence "at the intersection of reason and faith," as is "the distinction" of God from the world.[28]

My reliance on Aquinas throughout is strategic rather than doctrinal. If the prime concern of philosophical theology is to elaborate the essentials of a faith-tradition, with special attention to the so-called *preambula fidei*, then it could be argued that the most critical of these is "the distinction" of God from the world. Everything turns on the character of the divinity that one wishes to set forth as existing, as revealing itself, and as guiding the terrestrial course of events. Much of that character is decided in attempting to articulate that One as the free creator of all-that-is. So it was that Aquinas, confronted with an Islamic philosophical tradition that had compromised the Qur'an's clear assertion of a free creation, yet emboldened by the arguments of Moses Maimonides to the effect that no philosopher had been able to demonstrate the "eternity of the universe," managed to find a clear metaphysical way of characterizing such a divinity. Beginning with a description of this One compatible with all three traditions – "the beginning and end of all things and of reasoning creatures especially"[29] – was able to transform Ibn Sina's version of "the distinction" into the more coherent formula of existing as the act to which any essence was in potency. He thereby established "the First" as that One which had no need to create, being its own existence. The One whose very nature is to-exist will, by that fact alone, merit the transcendence

[28] This remark takes a position on a controverted question among students of Aquinas. See the debate between John Wippel and Joseph Owens in Wippel, "Aquinas' Route to the Real Distinction: A note on *De ente et essentia*, ch. 4," in *Thomist* 43 (1979), pp. 279–95, with Owens' response, "Stages and Distinction in *De ente*: A Rejoinder," in *Thomist* 45 (1981), pp. 99–123; followed by Wippel's reply in his *Metaphysical Themes in Thomas Aquinas* (Washington DC: Catholic University of America Press, 1984), pp. 120–32.
[29] ST 1.2 prologus.

that Plotinus could claim for his "One" only by locating it "beyond being," since everything-that-is exists in such a way as to be distinct from its existing. Moreover, by identifying the divine essence with its existing, Aquinas succeeded both in distinguishing God's existing from that of everything-that-is and in relating the creator to all creatures, as participants in that singular act of existing which is God.

One question alone seemed to be left hanging for Aquinas, as he negotiated a path for faith through the philosophical universe of his day. The One of Plotinus (and of Avicenna) was not so much moved by need to emanate the universe, as by an inner necessity of sharing the superabundance of its being: *bonum diffusivum sui est* ("good is diffusive of itself"). If that were so, then the divine freedom in creation would be entirely "natural" to the One. I say that this question seems to have been left hanging for Aquinas. While the identification of divine essence with existing would clearly rule out need, it would not so clearly circumvent this sort of "natural overflow" of goodness.[30] Aquinas says so himself when he indicates why "knowledge of the divine persons [in the Trinity] is 'necessary' for us [to have] the right idea of creation: the fact of saying that God made all things by His Word excludes the error of those who say that God produced things by necessity. [And] when we say that in [God] there is a procession of love, we show that God produced creatures not because He needed them, nor because of any other extrinsic reason, but on account of the love of His own goodness."[31] We can use Aquinas' response to address our immediate question by noting that the ordered processions of Word (Son) and of Love (Holy Spirit) *in divinis* certainly suffices to meet the "spontaneous overflow of goodness" consideration of Plotinus, and it does so in a manner utterly faithful to the pagan philosopher's (as well as Jews' and Muslims') strictures on divine unity. Showing that to be the case would require an excursion into formally Christian theology inappropriate here. It should suffice to note that Aquinas so constructed his treatment of God's triunity as to be compatible with the twin concerns of faith and of metaphysics: the uncompromising unity of divinity as well as the utter impossibility of concluding to the presence of such processions in God. The first concern is one of philosophical theology,

---

[30] Norman Kretzmann's articles to this effect corroborate the fact that this remains an issue for Aquinas. See Kretzmann, "Goodness, Knowledge, and Indeterminacy in the Philosophy of Thomas Aquinas," in *Journal of Philosophy* 80 (1983), pp. 631–49, and "A General Problem of Creation: Why Would God Create Anything at All?," in *Being and Goodness*, ed. Scott MacDonald (Ithaca NY: Cornell University Press, 1984), pp. 208–28.
[31] ST 1.32.1 ad 3.

critical to articulating "the distinction" of God from the world; the second is a matter of faith, identifying the domain proper to God's self-revelation.

Any metaphysical scheme may, and probably will, leave some questions hanging to which the revelatory tradition alone will be able to give adequate response. So also will there continue to be debate regarding which scheme better articulates that tradition. But one thing should be beyond discussion: no tradition of faith can avoid being elaborated from within by metaphysical notions, which alone will be able to capture the transcendent relation of divinity to all-that-is. The criteria of adequacy will always be mutual, as faith seeks understanding, and understanding allows itself to be amplified by revelation. There is no procrustean set of "cutters" that are themselves structured so as to cut either side down to size. Philosophical theology must develop those sorts of skills which foster a dialectical confrontation of criteria from both sides, as each side of the classical faith–reason divide employs intelligence at the service of understanding.

Chapter 7

AQUINAS AND SCOTUS: CONTRARY PATTERNS FOR PHILOSOPHICAL THEOLOGY

It is notorious that theological controversies have philosophical roots, so teachers intent on explicating the controversy will often help students trace the philosophical influences which could lead to opposing theological positions. Yet the "influence" is hardly one-way, since theologians of particular doctrinal persuasions will often be drawn to those philosophical approaches which they find consonant with their beliefs. The relation between convictions and conceptualizations is one of mutual interaction, according to the time-honored phrase of *fides quaerens intellectum*, making the task of philosophical theologian especially demanding. One must be attentive to historical articulations of faith as well as adept at conceptual clarity, since theological inquiry occurs in that space of communal self-understanding where faith seeks an appropriate conceptual articulation while the philosophical notions employed are stretched to accommodate a transcendental reach. Yet anyone who hopes to explicate a theological controversy simply by tracing it to its philosophical roots or by laying bare its conceptual frame has overlooked the dialectical situation which actually obtains.

So philosophical theologians must eschew such one-way pictures, which offer an *ersatz* clarity, while continuing to work toward displaying the conceptual or structural dimensions of theological developments and controversies. Yet where controversy is concerned, their work may not succeed in resolving the conflict so much as in clarifying the opposing philosophical approaches that may well have exacerbated matters. And at that point one may feel oneself faced with a choice between "fundamental intuitions of reality." Indeed, some philosophers even seem content to speak that way, however un-philosophical it sounds to leave root intellectual questions the prey of "choice" and "intuition." As we have insisted, however, a philosophical theologian cannot rest there, but will be constrained to recast the language of choice into the texture of a faith-commitment and try to show how one of the philosophical approaches is more amenable than the other to providing a grammar for the lived language of faith. This exercise is inherently dialectical, working as it does with two sets of criteria, yet it is incumbent on a philosophical theologian to carry it through.

My chapter attempts the task of clarification and will leave the comparative task at the level of suggestion, allowing the reader to complete it. My excuse is space, but the reason is that I am not yet sure how to do it. Perhaps, however, criticism of my analysis will suggest ways of carrying out the comparative stage as well, since the entire process of conceptual clarification in matters theological is dialectical throughout. I have chosen Aquinas and Scotus as representative figures. This is especially appropriate to my appreciation for both the work and person of George Lindbeck – for I have learned equally from both – since he did his doctoral work on Scotus and has focused much of his scholarly life on Aquinas. The valuations are my own, of course, as to some extent my rendering of Aquinas and Scotus will also be, though I shall try to profit from those critics who read earlier drafts of this chapter to help me present my protagonists fairly.[1] In taking two historical figures as embodying two approaches which appear quite irreducible and often incompatible, however, I wish also to make a further point about method in philosophical theology: appropriating the struggles of the giants in our respective traditions offers the most salutary way of developing the set of complex skills required to do philosophical theology.

The theological controversy at issue is the thorny one for Jews, Christians, and Muslims: the relation between divine and human freedom. The One who freely creates the universe holds absolute sway over it, as Job's divine protagonist reminds him in the end. Yet when that same One values only the free responses of those creatures created in God's own image, we can find ourselves hard put to articulate that encounter in a way which adequately respects both free partners. To be sure, the biblical background of covenant (alluded to in the Qur'an as well) offers some pregnant leads, and the narrative portions of the Scriptures provide paradigms for the

---

[1]   I am indebted to Tom Flint for his comments at a joint Philosophy/Theology colloquium at Notre Dame, and to a communication from Douglas Langston (author of *God's Willing Knowledge: The Influence of Scotus' Analysis of Omniscience* [University Park PA: Pennsylvania State University Press, 1986]. For the theological dimensions, I am beholden to Gary Gutting's "The Catholic and the Calvinist: A Dialogue on Faith and Reason," in *Faith and Philosophy* 2 (1985), pp. 236–56.

interaction which may well surpass any attempt at conceptual articulation, yet the challenge continually confronts us.[2] I shall not enter into the particulars of the so-called *de auxiliis* controversy in the Western church, except to say that anyone tempted to identify the Banezian (or "Thomist") position with Aquinas will be severely misled, as Bernard Lonergan has definitively shown.[3] Rather than provide a benchmark, that controversy offers no more than an episode in the continuing inquiry and one especially dogged by conceptual confusions. It will be the burden of my chapter that the critical questions are determined by issues quite a bit prior to freedom, which nonetheless affect how we think about that feature of human (and divine) existence. By choosing Aquinas and Scotus as protagonists, I have in fact identified the critical issue as *existence*, and with existence, quite different views on the ways in which language and world relate; only after which shall I consider the operation of human intentionality concerning action which we characterize as "freedom."[4]

Object Proper to Human Understanding

I said that the approaches would divide on *existence* – concern for it, how to deal with it; relations of language and language user to the world, and the operation of human intentionality – specifically that orientation toward an end which directs our choices and shapes what we mean by freedom (without reducing it to "free choice"). Yet I would like to introduce the contrast epistemologically, to bring the principal actors – Aquinas and Scotus – directly on stage. Consider the responses each gives to the characteristically medieval question: What is the proper object of human knowing? or the object proper to a human knower? Briefly, for Aquinas, it is a "nature existing in corporeal matter";[5] while for Scotus it is the essence taken "absolutely."[6]

[2] For an example of attention to the conceptual fruit of narrative, see Robert Alter, *The Art of Biblical Narrative* (New York: Basic Books, 1981) and A. H. Johns, "Joseph in the Qur'an: Dramatic Dialogue, Human Emotion and Prophetic Wisdom," in *Islamochristiana* (Rome) 7 (1981), pp. 29–55.

[3] Bernard J. F. Lonergan, *Grace and Freedom* (New York: Herder and Herder, 1971), offers comprehensive textual and analytic evidence of the subtlety of Aquinas' position on these matters.

[4] See my *Aquinas: God and Action* (Notre Dame IN: University of Notre Dame Press, 1979), esp. ch. 3.

[5] ST 1.84.7.

[6] ST 1.3.4.2. The *Ordinatio*, ed. Carl Balic (Vatican City, 1954–) will be abbreviated "*Ord*." This observation can be found in Etienne Gilson, *Jean Duns Scot* (Paris: Vrin, 1952),

Some Thomists like to put this in terms of Being (often capitalized): For Aquinas the intellect aspires to know Being. I would rather parse him (and them) by saying: For Aquinas the intellect aspires to know what is the case. Fulfilling that aspiration may well involve a great deal of speculation regarding what might be the case, or what it might have been, but such considerations are at the service of a teleology intrinsic to understanding itself: to know what is.

Beginning in this way, however, hardly seems likely to set up a contrast with Scotus. For Scotus' celebrated concern to know the individual in its *individuality* seems to offer immediate parallels with Aquinas, and to contrast strikingly with my way of characterizing the proper object of human understanding for him: the essence taken "absolutely." The apparent conflict is resolved, however, when we consider how Scotus characterizes individuality – by a property making this a *this*: *haecceity*.[7] So the individual is identified by an individualizing *kind* (or property), thus retaining the focus on essences taken "absolutely." Before exploring this solution, however, let us return to Aquinas' treatment.

In the formula "nature existing in corporeal matter," neither "existing" nor "in corporeal matter" (or "materially") names or expresses a *feature* of things. For "existing" eludes our grasp (as Scotus insists *haecceity* does, yet for different reasons), while "materially" expresses a manner of being rather than something said of a subject. (Strawson, in *Individuals*, locates such things as *presuppositions*.)[8] "In corporeal matter" is something presupposed in those things of which we connaturally speak and with which we customarily interact. What we say of such things is that they exist, are "concrete" entities (as opposed to abstract objects), are spatiotemporally identifiable, and the rest. For Aquinas, since items like these are proper objects for human understanding, they are paradigms for us of what is. These are familiar Aristotelian roots.

What about Scotus? Has he such a paradigm for knowing? Or for substance? The answer, as usual, is less straightforward. Gerard Manley Hopkins celebrates his exaltation of the individual, crediting Scotus with

---

pp. 535 ff. Subtitle numbering of paragraphs herein is attempted to facilitate comparison throughout the text.

[7] Hence "something can be considered a metaphysical individual if it can be identified in a world by virtue of its individual nature" (Simo Knuuttila, "Being qua Being in Thomas Aquinas and John Duns Scotus," in S. Knuuttila and J. Hintikka, eds, *The Logic of Being* (Dordrecht: Reidel, 1986), p. 210; cf. *Ord.* II, d.3 pars 1, q.5–6, n.191). Also *Ord.* II, d.16, q.un., n.5: "*Illud enim individuum, quod nunc est in actu, illud idem fuit in potentia.*"

[8] P. F. Strawson, *Individuals* (London: Methuen, 1959), *passim*.

inspiring his own poetic rendition of "inscape."[9] Gilson, however, links him with Avicenna, where a process of concept formation shaped by Neo-platonist emanation schemes allows the intellect to know the natures of things by its link with the first intelligence from whom essences emanate.[10] Gilson finds this picture imbedded in illumination theories which medieval thinkers associated with Augustine without realizing their Islamic origins. My response is closer to that of Gilson: for Scotus the formula gives the essence of a thing, and formulas are what we connaturally grasp. The evidence for this contention is cumulative: his concern for distinctions and definitions, plus his demand for univocity, together with a confidence that such an approach captures the things we are concerned with. As a result, there is little or no reflection on actual usage; distinctions are more constructed than found.

For Aquinas, however, distinctions are employed to serve a current purpose: to understand what is the case. A distinction made in one context may not serve at all in another.[11] Understanding is contextual and language inherently analogous, so we must scrutinize actual usage to discern how analogous terms are functioning and so be led to understand how things actually are.

How to Attain Clarity About Existing?

One way to highlight the distinctiveness of Aquinas' paradigm (for being and for knowing) – a "nature existing in corporeal matter" – is to compare and contrast it with Aristotle, for whom substance paradigmatically is a material thing of a certain kind.[12] There is no question for Aristotle but that such a thing *exists*, for to be a material thing of a certain kind *is* to exist. Nothing more need be said, or can be said. Why must "existing" be explicitly mentioned for Aquinas, and how can it be expressed?

Aquinas must make existing explicit because something has happened; someone named Moses has intervened: Moses the author of Genesis, and

[9] For the manner in which Scotus' epistemology influenced Hopkins, see W. H. Gardner, ed., *Poems and Prose of Gerard Manley Hopkins* (Baltimore: Penguin, 1953), pp. xxiii –xxv.

[10] Etienne Gilson, "Pourquoi S. Thomas a critiqué S. Augustin," in *Archives d'histoire littéraire et doctrinale du moyen âge* 1(1926–7), pp. 5–127.

[11] Robert Sokolowski, "Making Distinctions," in *Review of Metaphysics* 32 (1979), pp. 652–61.

[12] The *Metaphysics* is not that straightforward, of course (but cf. Bk. Z [104lbll]), yet this does turn out to be the best reading of his discriminating dialectic, and the one accepted by medieval and modern readers alike. For Aquinas, see ST 1.84.7, 1.85.1.

Moses the author of the *Guide for the Perplexed*. The upshot of that intervention was to realize that such things not only might have been otherwise (Aristotle), but that they might not have been at all.[13] It was a Muslim philosopher – Ibn Sina – who gave to both Maimonides and Aquinas the conceptual tools for articulating that new situation, by dividing all that is into *necessary* being and *possible* being according as its existence is underived or derived.[14] As Moses Maimonides employed the distinction, everything derives from underived One; and while he had some difficulties with Ibn Sina's presentation of that originating relationship, the distinction served well enough for him as an articulation of the earlier Moses.[15]

Identifying necessary being with underived existence and possible being with derived existence, however, led Ibn Sina to characterize *existing* as something "coming to a thing," which thing was known, insofar as it was knowable, in its *essence*.[16] The all-important fact of something's actually existing, then, which relates each individual thing to its source in the One, sounds like it is *accidental* to the thing itself. Yet that assertion is incoherent, of course, since accidents must be accidents *of* substance – so what makes something to *be* one of those paradigmatic items cannot be extrinsic to it as accidents are.

So Aquinas (not Maimonides) proposes that we conceive *existing*, not as an ordinary feature (or property) of things, but as a formal or constitutive feature of whatever is – as Aristotle conceived matter/form.[17] One does not notice a thing's matter or form, but rather presupposes that "mode of composition" in constructing the sentences we do construct to speak about it. The constructions themselves *display* the matter/form composition in their subject/predicate structure. Yet the ambiguity Aristotle

---

[13] For a perceptive development of this contrast, see Robert Sokolowski, *The God of Faith and Reason* (Notre Dame IN: University of Notre Dame Press, 1982/Washington DC: Catholic University of America Press, 1995), where he introduces "the distinction" of God from the world as a distinctively Christian achievement.
[14] Ibn Sina, *al-Shifa, al-Ilahiyyat*, ed G. Anawati and S. Zayed (Cairo, 1960), French trans.: G. C. Anawati, *La Metaphysique du Shifa* (Paris: Vrin, 1978, 1986), 1.7. On Ibn Sina, see Fadlou Shehadi, *Metaphysics in Islamic Philosophy* (Delmar, NY: Caravan, 1982), pp. 77–83.
[15] Moses Maimonides, *The Guide of the Perplexed*, trans. Schlomo Pines (Chicago: University of Chicago Press, 1963), 1.57.
[16] Ibn Sina, *al-Shifa* 1.5 (Anawati, 108); on the notorious dictum of Ibn Sina that "existence is an accident," see Fazlur Rahman, "Essence and Existence in Avicenna," in R. Hunt, R. Klibansky, L. Lobowsky, eds, *Mediaeval and Renaissance Studies* 4 (London, 1958), pp. 1–16; also Fadlou Shehadi, *Metaphysics*, pp. 71–118 (note 13).
[17] This is, of course, the thesis of Aquinas' *De Ente et Essentia* (*On Being and Essence*, trans. A. Maurer (Toronto: Pontifical Institute of Medieval Studies, 1982); see my *Knowing the Unknowable God* (Notre Dame IN: University of Notre Dame Press, 1986), ch. 2.

left between *assertion* and *proposition* hides another correlative set of formal (or constitutive) features in which the roles played by matter/form, respectively, are assumed by essence/*esse* (existence). This new proposal of Aquinas allows him to express that each "nature *existing* in corporeal matter" has been made to do so by the creator – the One who brings into being and sustains all that is. This new constitutive feature of things, then, is the sign in things of a relation which links them to their transcendent source and so is best characterized as an *act*.[18]

This final move is at the heart of Aquinas' account of why individual existing things are paradigmatic of what is. It offers justification, if you will, for Aristotle's founding intuition: a justification in that the "proper effect" of the creative activity of the One from whom all else is derived must itself be an act – that is, can only be conceived as an act. This is an analogous use of the term "act," of course, since only existing things can act (*actiones sunt suppositorum*). Yet they can be said to act only because they are (as existing things) already *in act*.

The actuality of existing things, then, derives from the One whose underived (or *necessary*) existence is expressed by identifying essence with existence.[19] And since existing offers the paradigm for actuality, such a One whose nature is to-be will embody all the perfections which flow from existing. Here we have a condensed description of what Gilson and others have called Aquinas' "existentialism." It is no longer Aristotle, yet is certainly consonant with his founding insight: individual existing things are paradigmatic for what is. It is rather an effort to articulate the new mode of contingency introduced by Moses: that the world need not be at all; and the positive effect of this articulation is to treat existing as a perfection – indeed the perfection of perfections, as that from which all others flow.

So Aquinas' manner of both articulating and celebrating existence is hardly "Greek" in inspiration. It is in fact quite unintelligible to those for whom contingency remains bounded by the classical "could have been otherwise."[20] For that view concentrates on formal structures – essences taken "absolutely" – without attempting to articulate what distinguishes the world in which we live. That approach will thus find differentiating fact from fantasy difficult to articulate, presuming that "'histories' of

---

[18] ST 1.45.5. For Aquinas' use of this metaphor (and analogy), see my *Aquinas: God and Action* (note 4), ch. 3.

[19] ST 1.4.1.

[20] For an extended development of this point, see chapter 12 of the present volume, "Creation, Will and Knowledge in Aquinas and Duns Scotus."

possible individuals" could be available, if not to us, at least to God.[21] Indeed something like that must be available to God if God is to know which world God *chooses* to create. So "middle knowledge" scenarios are not only conceptually unproblematic in this approach; they are required if God is to act freely. (So if "middle knowledge" be incoherent on Aquinas' approach, he must have a very different view of freedom, and hence of divine freedom as well. We shall see that he does.)

Scotus will carry us a long way toward constituting this other approach. If Aquinas' thesis about the unity of the virtues is rooted ontologically in his conception of all perfections flowing from existence, Scotus' queries about that unitary thesis suggest that he was beginning to look more at features of things than at things themselves, so that things become conceived as a coalescence of features.[22] Existence functions more as the precondition for things being *what* they are than as the source of a thing's being and becoming. For as we have seen, what makes a thing individual is not its actual existing, but a formal feature corresponding to "this" and called *haecceitas*.[23]

Since language mirrors reality for the medievals, as for the Greeks, it should prove useful to articulate this difference in treating existence linguistically. For Scotus, each item in the sentence "roses are red" names a corresponding element in the world, with the copula standing for existence or being – the precondition for saying anything at all about something.[24] (Correlatively, if crudely, the item which "this" stands for in "this horse is frisky" would be that feature called *haecceitas*.) Aside from its being the first thing known by the intellect and showing up in the copula of every statement, however, nothing more can be said about it.

Aquinas, however, parses "roses are red" differently, as composed of two (not three) items: a subject ("roses") which relates to the predicate ("are red") as matter to its form.[25] So at the structural level primacy is given to the predicate, which is not a name nor should it be thought of as naming a property or feature; it rather predicates that feature *of* the subject. More-

---

[21]   See Knuuttila's way of articulating this position by contrast with that of Aquinas, "Being qua Being . . ." (note 7), p. 210.

[22]   See the dissertation by Bonnie D. Kent: "Aristotle and the Franciscans: Gerald Odonis' Commentary on the *Nichomachean Ethics*" (Columbia University, 1984).

[23]   See William O'Meara, "Actual Existence and the Individual according to Duns Scotus," in *Monist* 49 (1965), pp. 659–69; and Knuuttila (note 7), nn. 6, 19.

[24]   See *In Peri Hermenias* L. 1, *lectio* 5 (ed. 1, 591). For a more extensive commentary on this point, see my *Analogy and Philosophical Language* (New Haven CN: Yale University Press, 1973), p. 108.

[25]   *In Peri Hermenias* L. 1, *lectio* 8 (esp. [9]).

over, the proposition *roses are red* is secondary to the *assertion* "roses are red," for names succeed in referring only as we employ them in asserting a proposition – either explicitly or implicitly (as in one-word answers to questions). On such an account "this" becomes a pure indexical, replaceable by the act of pointing, and hence cannot be a feature of possible worlds (wherein one could speak of "some particular horse" but never of "this horse") but only of the one in which we live.

The primacy of assertion underscores two points made earlier: (1) the primacy of individual existing things, including speakers; (2) the finality of intellect – to come to know what is the case. And it adds a third: the activity of judgment. I assert what I ascertain to be the case, by contrast to what I propose might be the case. While philosophers have a penchant for proposals, Aquinas insists that proposing be at the service of asserting. As a consequence, we are warned off speaking of true/false propositions by analogy with well or ill-formed strings of sentences. A proposition needs to be asserted to be true; even then, of course, it may be denied. Aquinas' observation that what "true" adds to "being" is a relation to intellect[26] does not favor a "correspondence" over a "coherence" view of truth, as these terms are sometimes used currently, for an attestation of the truth of *p* will require a constructive as well as a verifying role for the mind. What it does demand, however, is a distinct intellectual activity – judgment – to assert that *p* expresses the way things are.[27]

Activity then, is the keynote of Aquinas' view of the world and of language use. To understand what something is involves an activity; so it is consonant with his thinking to propose that we understand *existing* on the model of this second activity of the mind (judgment), so that existing is conceived as an activity.[28] Moreover, activity finds expression in structures but is not itself structural. For Scotus, however, structure is primary, as what is articulatable. Some of these essential structures obtain, but that is not what interests him; what is interesting is what could or might obtain.[29]

---

[26] *de Ver.* 1.1.

[27] Bernard J. F. Lonergan has developed the central role of judgment in Aquinas, in *Verbum: Word and Idea in Aquinas* (Notre Dame IN: University of Notre Dame Press, 1968), where he presents a copious and well-ordered collection of texts.

[28] This specific chain of reasoning will not be found in Aquinas; yet it is presented as a summary of Lonergan's careful analysis of Aquinas' "metaphysics of knowing" in *Verbum*, which forms the basis for Lonergan's own constructive metaphysics in *Insight* (London: Longmans, 1957). I have shown how this presents a plausible way of reading the transition from Ibn Sina to Thomas Aquinas, in *Knowing the Unknowable God* (note 17).

[29] Knuuttila identifies the context for this shift in his concern to show how a new theory of modality developed – see "Being qua Being . . ." p. 209 (note 7).

It is doubtful whether "intuitions" can decide between these two approaches, yet if I have characterized them accurately the differences are quite basic. Grasping Aquinas' approach depends on one's appreciating how asserting a proposition differs from entertaining it, as well as the import of that difference. One could mark it but find it of little philosophical relevance. I have tried to identify this impasse by contrasting activity with structure, much as the later Wittgenstein became taken with language use. By identifying judgment as a distinct activity of the mind, which does not, however, alter the shape of a proposition entertained by asserting it, Aquinas found a way of articulating the difference which existence makes without having to locate it as a feature of things. A closer look at this analogy between judging as the premier activity of intellect, and existing as what "is more intimately and profoundly interior to things than anything else" (ST 1.8.1), will help us locate another salient contrast between Aquinas and Scotus.

Existence, Judgment, and Analogy

In the background (for both thinkers) lies Avicenna's distinction in being between the One as necessary and the rest as possible, as well as Aristotle's views on the relation between semantics and ontology – though each of our thinkers will soon divide on their use of Aristotle. Aquinas parses subject and predicate as parts of an assertion, as matter and form are parts of an existing thing. And the manner of being is determined by the form (*esse viventibus est vivere*), as the manner of knowing is determined by the subject matter. So both "being" and "true" will be (and must be) used analogously if they are to be used accurately. Propositions may be the vehicles of truth/falsity, yet the manner of verifying/falsifying them will differ according to the subject matter, so the truth affirmed or denied will be a function of the judgment rendered on the proposition proposed.

Similarly, the assertion that something exists cannot be an ordinary statement about it (since existence is not an accident), but rather expresses the judgment concerning its availability for full-blooded predication: that statements made about it may be verified/falsified in appropriate ways. This precision picks up Aristotle's founding intuition that the paradigmatic sense for "*F* is true of *x*" is of an existing individual, and others are parasitic upon that. Aquinas formulates that intuition in terms of the finality of intellect, and identifies the crowning activity of intellect as a judgment. And since the activity of judging is always at least virtually conscious of its warrants,[30] one can distinguish different uses of "exists" in the assertion that something exists: what Geach calls the "there is" sense – in which elephants exist but mermaids do not, and the "actuality" sense – in which elephants exist but dinosaurs do not.[31] These are not the same, since the *actuality* sense entails the *there is* sense, but not vice-versa; yet they are systematically ambiguous – that is, their relatedness will prove significant as well as their difference.

If the activity of judgment is so central to Aquinas' treatment of knowledge, especially in his attempt to articulate the relation of language to the world, what role does it play in Scotus? The short answer is none. Epistemologically there is no need for a distinct activity of judgment, neither to verify what is the case nor to capture the individual, since (in principle, at least) the individual is knowable this side of its actually existing.[32] (And Scotus acknowledges that what the tradition calls *judgment* has to do with verifying that something is indeed the case.) For, ontologically, Scotus does not conceive existing as the actuality of a thing such that it will differ with each kind of thing (as in Aristotle's *esse viventibus est vivere*), but considers existing rather to be the precondition for concrete discourse, thus distinguishing it from abstract consideration.[33] Again, as we shall see and have seen, the difference lies less in the formulae each uses than in the use to which they put them: the import of their respective articulations. These differences may be captured best by their respective attitudes toward language: is a philosophically precise language univocal or analogous? Here we have two clearly disparate positions. For Scotus, such discourse must be univocal, as the precondition for straight talk and coherent argument. (Besides, what clear sense can we make of "analogical"? And if Henry of Ghent were one's primary interlocutor, that would be a most plausible question.)[34] For Aquinas, however, analogous usage alone reflects the related differences in reality, so he will be preoccupied to show how these

---

[30] This is Lonergan's proposal for understanding the reasonableness of judgment as "virtually unconditioned," in *Insight*, pp. 280–1 (note 27).

[31] For this important distinction, see Barry Miller, "In Defense of the Predicate 'Exists,'" in *Mind* 84 (1975), pp. 338–54.

[32] As William O'Meara puts it (in "Actual Existence and the Individual" [note 23]), "existence does not confer individuality" – cf. my "Creation, Will . . ." (note 20), p. 250 n.18.

[33] For this development, see Gilson's *Jean Duns Scot* (note 6), pp. 454–66. Judgment will of course play a role, but its role has little or no metaphysical import, since it is not language use but language structure which tells us about reality. The formulation of Aristotle is Aquinas', in *Aristotelis Librum de Anima* L. 1, *lectio* 14 [209].

[34] Cf. Gilson's extended discussion of analogy/univocity in Scotus, especially with reference to Henry of Ghent, in *Jean Duns Scot*, pp. 87–116 (note 6).

eminently useful resources of language may be employed in a disciplined philosophical argument. His sense of "analogical" is "systematic ambiguity" guided by astute judgment.[35]

It is clear, then, that Aquinas presumes here the finality of the intellect: to understand the actual world; whereas Scotus focuses on "world" as a conceptual system. That is, Aquinas wants and needs to exploit the analogical resources of language because language is the human instrument of knowing, and the paradigmatic object of human knowing is the individual existing thing. Whatever else may be said to be *known* must be said with respect to that paradigmatic object, and our knowing it will only be completed in the activity of judgment: the activity which relates us to the actual world. (These observations help resolve a dispute among Thomists initiated by Ralph McInerny's insistence that "analogy is a linguistic doctrine" – that is, it regards the resources and uses of language. And indeed it does, but language functions in the ways it does because it allows us to come to grips with the world as it is. However one explains that fact – theologically or evolutionarily, or both – one need not oppose language to the world so much as regard them together.)

Scotus, too, presumably regards language as an instrument of human knowing, and a human instrument of knowing, yet the proper object of human knowledge differs for him. And since essence taken "absolutely" prescinds from existence, there is no need for the language fitted to such an object to function analogously. One need not refer diverse ways of being to a primary sense, since one prescinds from existing in understanding things; one need only multiply distinctions to accommodate the diverse "modes of being."

How, then, ought we conceive the relations between language and the world for Scotus? I am tempted to respond: there is no need to do so, since the formula which accompanies one's grasp of the essence taken "absolutely" will normally be presumed to have captured that essence. Or alternatively, one could be tolerant of diverse formulae, confident one has grasped the nature in question. In either case, closer attention to the use of language, or probing to settle nuances of interpretation, will be considered superfluous.[36] For all that the intellect needs to do is to "univer-

---

[35] That is my thesis in *Analogy and Philosophical Language* (New Haven CT: Yale University Press, 1973), but also see James Ross, *Portraying Analogy* (Cambridge: Cambridge University Press, 1982).

[36] I have been accused of unfairness here, so will leave it to readers to assess this criticism of a prevalent way of doing philosophy today; cf. Alasdair MacIntyre's "Postscript" to *After Virtue*, 2nd edn (Notre Dame IN: University of Notre Dame Press, 1984), pp. 264–78.

salize the common nature, [which] it finds [in the real singular known by the senses] in immediate potency to be universalized."[37]

Since the entire preoccupation is with understanding essences in their relations to one another, there is no discernible difference between possibilities and actualities except that the world in which we live *obtains*. For "the subject must be fully constituted, i.e., be determined to individuality as a *possible* existent," to qualify as an individual, since "Scotus holds that the individual constituent is of the same order as the specific constituent." This will allow Scotus to secure "that existence is of another order, its own, and that, consequently, existence does not confer individuality."[38]

It is but a short way from here to a "middle knowledge" scenario, in which one will speak straightforwardly of God simulating "possible histories," for a virtual inattention to the difference existence makes will lead one to overlook the differences between a *precise* individual and *precisely* one of a kind.[39] Scotus will go on to insist, nevertheless, that "nothing exists but for individuals and there *are* not individuals which do not exist."[40] But the only thing left to secure that insistence is God's will, since the notion of an individual is complete before its actuality, so existing adds nothing intelligible to it.

For Aquinas, on the contrary, it is precisely existence which makes something an individual, so that it can be indicated by an indexical ("this," "that") and given a name.[41] Aristotle's answer to that question – matter – merely distinguished items numerically, and allowed an Aristotelian to speak adequately of individuals as *instances* of a kind.[42] By locating the individuality of living (and hence indivisible) beings in their "act of existing," however, Aquinas not only secured such individuals as paradigms for what exists, but also specified a role proper to existence: that which makes something a real individual.

Moreover, since there are many kinds of things, what it means to exist will differ with each kind (*esse viventibus est vivere*). So the role Aquinas gives to existence demands that it be analogous, varying with the kinds of individuals we encounter or otherwise become acquainted with: plants, snails, water buffalo, human beings, or angels. By contrast, one can see

[37] Gilson, *Jean Duns Scot*, pp. 535–6 (note 6).
[38] O'Meara, "Actual Existence and the Individual," pp. 664–5 (note 23).
[39] Miller, "In Defense . . . ," p. 340 (note 31).
[40] O'Meara, "Actual Existence and the Individual," p. 665 (note 23).
[41] This is the upshot of the argument in *De Ente et Essentia* (note 18).
[42] Where this becomes decisive is in God's knowledge of individuals: see Maimonides' caustic rendition of Aristotle on such matters in the *Guide*, 3.17.

why Scotus appears relatively indifferent to the question of the analogy of being, for the issue is little more than an annoying residue if existence is a mere precondition which adds no intelligibility to the individual.

Typically diverse attitudes toward univocity/analogy in language reflect the differences we have already noted regarding the three issues of (1) the proper object of human understanding, (2) the role which existence does (or does not) play, and (3) recognizing (or not) the distinction between a precise individual and precisely one of a kind. One's philosophical predilections for univocal or analogous discourse also indicate how these three issues are interrelated.

Where the proper object of human understanding is essences taken "absolutely," and existence is quite extrinsic even to individuality, then one is free to insist upon *univocity*. For one need not struggle to convey by one's language a sensitive and accurate rendering of the (actual) world, but is free to inquire among possible connections. "Realism" of this sort, where "true propositions" can be counted upon as the counterpart of each coherent assertion, readily metamorphoses into "coherentism" – a nice puzzle for anyone with a penchant for doing philosophy by "isms."[43]

Where the proper object of human understanding is the nature of existing things, however, and where their existing determines their individuality, one will need to have recourse to a language which contrasts as it compares, in an effort to offer an accurate description of the individual about which one wants to make true statements. The more sensitive and nuanced the description, the better chance one has to verify or falsify it. Therefore philosophical analysis cannot set itself up as a separate discipline, but needs both to employ and bring its skills to bear upon those of the working lawyer or judge, novelist or poet, or the astute historian – each of whom employs analogous expressions in a quite disciplined fashion.

It follows as a corollary that approaches akin to Scotus will see their task as developing "theories of . . . ," while those in the family of Aquinas will exercise their philosophical acumen in sorting out, appreciating, and thereby sharpening our capacities to use the resources latent in ordinary language – resources inherently analogous, as Ross has shown clearly and extensively.[44] These approaches may even utilize the aforementioned "the-

---

[43] Once "true" can be employed as "*true* in a possible world," and coherent assertions are defined by "possible worlds," then it follows that one can speak of "true propositions" without relation to actuality. It is indeed ironic that this variety of "Platonism" is called "realism," but of course that intends, after the usage of philosophers, to call our attention to the fact that statements express propositions, which are presumed to be "real." Yet one has a right to remain baffled.

[44] James Ross, *Portraying Analogy* (note 3).

ories" in their inquiry, but employing them as testimony among others, never dreaming that the "definitions" they contain would offer a more "basic" understanding of an item of reality than any other working language. Put otherwise, analogical discourse needs no univocal *ground*. The demand for such a "ground" simply wants to canonize the requirement imbedded in a responsible use of our inherently analogous language: that we relate such expressions to a paradigmatic sense each time we employ them.

This corollary returns us to the role which Aquinas reserved for judgment. For where understanding is regarded as culminating in a judgment of the veracity of one's proposals, where a statement is deemed to be true in the measure that it offers a faithful rendering of what is the case, then the skills prized and exercised by philosophers will be ones designed to enhance that capacity for judgment. So philosophical training will include dialectical exchange between historically developed positions as a way of sharpening one's capacities for assessment by pitting them against formidable peers. Moreover, the upshot of such a dialectical interchange could offer an appropriately indirect but nonetheless germane introduction to a keenness of philosophical judgment.

Where judgment is not so highly valued, philosophy will consist of carefully developing the logical consequences of quite arbitrary intuitions, as Alasdair MacIntyre depicts much of contemporary philosophizing, and Robert Nozick conveniently exemplifies in his *Philosophical Explanations*.[45] Put otherwise, when we take so little care to discern what others have said, or better, to apprentice ourselves to their way of inquiring to help us develop the skills of philosophical investigation, something must explain that oversight. It would be explicable – that is, it would not amount to an oversight – were philosophy regarded as an exercise in conceptual virtuosity unconnected with sound judgment. Then possible worlds would be as engaging as the actual world, since nothing distinguishes actual from possible except the "mere fact" that it happens to exist.

Two Approaches to Human Freedom

How does this contrast on existence, analogy, and judgment affect our understanding of the operation of human intentionality regarding action, or freedom? It is bound to do so, since one's views on history and human possibility are intimately connected with one's understanding of how we

---

[45] Alasdair MacIntyre, "Afterword" (note 36); Robert Nozick, *Philosophical Explanations* (Cambridge MA: Harvard University Press, 1981).

impinge on what is. Moreover, the current polarities of libertarian and compatibilist overlook a significant middle ground, as will be clear when we see that Aquinas' position will fit in neither camp. (Those who presume the bifurcation to be exhaustive will try to put Aquinas in the "compatibilist" camp, but a recent article by Kretzmann and Stump shows how foreign the presuppositions of this distinction are to Aquinas' analysis.)[46] Finally, it is probably inevitable that a position like Aquinas' be overlooked in a liberal society where *choice* spontaneously dominates discussions of freedom, as ethicists are preoccupied with decisions and economists concerned with trade-offs. What is conspicuously missing from such parlays is a vision of the end or goal of a society, and understandably so, since such questions become procedural in a society where the reigning "theory of justice" finds it both possible and expedient to bracket any discussion of the human good.

Let us first consider Scotus' views on freedom as more in tune with the current discussion. They are firmly "libertarian," presuming freedom to imply a radical "indifference" before a set of options, so that it is always possible to do otherwise in each particular human act which we would call free. For it is *will*, for Scotus, which determines what one does; the role of intellect is to present to the will a list of possible actions from which to choose. As God's will chooses among possible alternative "histories," so our will chooses among alternative scenarios for action.[47]

In the absence of an existential (or prudential) judgment to ascertain the truth of one's understanding of and orientation toward an actual situation, the will must "decide" by a spontaneous act of self-movement. Such an autonomous movement, prepared of course by what understanding delivers to it, yet itself moving us beyond proposals to action, fairly defines *willing* for Scotus.[48] It also marks him as a "modern man," for whom freedom is auto-determination of an "indifferent" power, as in "the church of your choice."

It does not take a great deal of imagination to move a few steps further to see how Luis de Molina, presuming freedom to be autonomy (i.e., the

---

[46] Calvin Normore, "Divine Omniscience, Omnipotence, and Future Contingents: An Overview," in Tamar Rudavsky, ed., *Divine Omniscience and Medieval Philosophy* (Dordrecht: Reidel, 1985), pp. 3–22; Norman Kretzmann and Eleonore Stump, "Absolute Simplicity," in *Faith and Philosophy* 2 (1985), pp. 353–82.

[47] Patrick Lee has given a careful historical development of these issues in "The Relation between Intellect and Will in Free Choice according to Aquinas and Scotus," in *Thomist* 49 (1985), pp. 321–42. But see Douglas Langston's treatment of the issue in *God's Willing Knowledge* (note 1).

[48] Walter Höres, *Der Wille als reine Vollkommenheit nach Duns Scotus* (Munich: Pustet, 1962), pp. 269–74.

ability to do otherwise) and wishing to elaborate a notion of divine omniscience, would have recourse to the fabrication of "middle knowledge."[49] The goal of so elaborate a construction was to sever God's foreknowledge from any casual connection with human actions. The way was eminently prepared by what we have seen of Scotus' ontology of individuals, such that one could coherently conceive of God simulating "possible histories" of "possible individuals." Moreover, the notion of freedom as indifference plus auto-determination left no room for divine subvention except as a form of intervention; no way for God to empower a free act without interfering.

So it is not one's antecedent notion of God so much as one's conception of human freedom (together with an ontology lacking the resources to mark the difference between a precise individual and precisely one of a kind) which finds "middle knowledge" to be an attractive strategy. That dominant picture of human freedom, however, will return to characterize God's free act of creating as a *choice* among possible scenarios.[50] Which only confirms the contention that one's theology is frequently a function of one's anthropology, whether consciously or unconsciously so.

But what alternatives have we? What Joseph Incandela has felicitously called "situated freedom" will allow us to show how Aquinas' views on human freedom are of a piece with his views of creation as (1) primarily an exercise of practical knowledge, (2) whose principal effect is the to-be of things, and (3) itself recovered intellectually in the role which Aquinas assigns to judgment.[51] That is, the picture of a plethora of possible worlds (replete with possible individuals) over against a God whose free act of creating is conceived as choosing one of these scenarios, finds a clear alternative in a conception of God's action in creating as preeminently one of making.[52] The knowledge involved will then be primarily practical knowing, issuing in the *being* of creatures, some of which are so constituted as to act freely.[53] Yet their freedom is conceived not as sovereign indifference, but the principal component of an intentional orientation toward their origin.[54]

[49] On Molina, see the Introduction by Alfred J. Freddoso, trans., Luis de Molina, *On Divine Foreknowledge* (Ithaca NY: Cornell University Press, 1988).

[50] Gilson, *Jean Duns Scot*, p. 323 (note 6).

[51] Joseph Incandela, "Aquinas' Lost Legacy: God's Practical Knowledge and Situated Human Freedom" (Ph.D. diss., Princeton University, 1986).

[52] ST 1.45.3.

[53] Cf. James Ross, "Creation II," in Alfred J. Freddoso, ed., *The Existence and Nature of God* (Notre Dame IN: University of Notre Dame Press, 1983), pp. 115–41.

[54] See Frederick Crowe, S.J., "Complacency and Concern in the Thought of St. Thomas Aquinas," in *Theological Studies* 20 (1959), pp. 1–39, 198–230, 343–95.

And since existence is to be thought of as an act, this specific manner of existing is seen as the source of a specific power or capacity with a correlative *telos* or perfection. And that capacity ought not be thought of as *will* alone, but as an intellectual appetite or orientation toward the end or goal inscribed in a derived existence. Just as judgment is required to bring our considerations up against the actual situation as its final measure, and so ascertain the truth of our proposals, so a practical judgment directs our actions in accordance with the way we have perceived things ought to be.

On this view, no separate step (of *willing*) is required to incline us to what we perceive to be our genuine good, though a distinct "faculty" or capacity must be presumed, since perceiving alone could not generate wanting.[55] Yet that wanting is the result of an orientation of the whole person – intellectual and sensitive as well – toward that One from which its existence comes. Aquinas does not (and need not) conceive *willing*, then, as a separate act, but subsumes it under the practical judgment of a being endowed with intellect and will – that is, with a capacity for understanding and judgment plus a spontaneous tendency toward its proper good.[56] It is the judgment which suffices to elicit and direct the natural inclination.

This analysis allows him to appropriate Aristotle's recursive analysis of means/ends, whereby we find ourselves ever choosing means in relation to ends – in principle, at least, up to that point where we come to an end which cannot itself serve as means to a yet more comprehensive goal. At that point we can no longer properly speak of *choosing*, but of consenting to (or refusing) the end which presents itself as ultimate.[57] Institutionalization, the public face of habit, spares us such a recursive analysis of our everyday actions, but certain junctures in life are called "crises" because they require the kind of judgment we call "decision."

On this analysis, then, freedom cannot be identified with choice, since freedom of choice is rooted in a constituting consent (or refusal) regarding what we judge to be our proper good – that is, in a yet deeper freedom. Nor may we conceive that judgment willfully, but rather as the

---

[55] Here I would disagree with Lee (note 47); see Incandela (note 51) for a close argument against such an "autonomous" view of willing in Aquinas; also Mary T. Clark, "Willing Freely according to Thomas Aquinas," in Ruth Link-Salinger et al., eds, *A Straight Path: Studies in Medieval Philosophy and Culture* (Washington DC: Catholic University of America Press, 1988), pp. 49–56.

[56] See my *Aquinas* (note 5 above), ch. 12.

[57] My source here is Crowe (note 54 above), though I prefer "consent" as a translation of *complacentia*.

practical analogue of Aristotle's remarks about his predecessors "constrained as they were by the things themselves" – since the only goal or good which elicits consent with full spontaneity is the ultimate end.[58] That means, of course, that refusing such a good is tantamount to denying our nature, the complexus of orientations with which we come into being as humans. So it would not be strange were so normative a view of freedom to be alien to a liberal ethos. For if one's ultimate goal be inscribed in one's nature, then freedom is no longer indifference but contains an orientation and a capacity for growth.

Consenting freely to that orientation brings one to a greater measure of freedom, whereas freely refusing it leads one toward enslavement by lesser goods. Enslavement because one is only free to choose goods not ordered to one's final goal *via* a mistaken judgment (i.e., thinking that they are so ordered) or as a consequence of refusing one's own orientation to that good. Such an exercise of freedom will be doubly *situated*, then, in an orientation of our nature and in the light available to us in concrete historical circumstances to judge wisely.

So everything turns, for Aquinas, on practical judgment in analyzing a free act. *Will* is nowhere invoked as a separate action, though it is ever presumed as a distinct faculty or orienting power. If free acts are those by which we constitute ourselves in the character which is ours (as a "second nature"), and are claimed to be free because we assume responsibility for them, then they are at once originating and constituting, like creation itself. So it is not surprising that one's view of human freedom parallels one's view of creation. And so it is here. For Scotus, freedom is accounted "indifference" so that the will decides, while creation is pictured as God's free choice among "worlds." For Aquinas, freedom consists in the response to the orientation of our nature in a concrete practical judgment; and God's practical knowing of what it is God wills to bring forth, in response to the divine nature, is accounted creation.

The general outlines should be clear, then: for Aquinas, the orientation of the intellect to what is true is matched by the will's inclination to what is good. And since the good must be perceived as such, the mediating activity is that of judgment. In speculative knowing we ascertain what is the case; in practical knowing, what is to be made or done. What moves us, in each case, are the "facts of the matter," calling for *assent* in the case of the intellect and *consent* in the case of the will. The power to act freely, and hence to move oneself, for Aquinas, then becomes a function of a person's orientation and inclination to one's proper end.[59]

[58] ST 2–1.15.3.
[59] ST 2–1.15.2.

This will also allow him to conceive of God entering into our actions without interfering. For if God, who is our sovereign good in so intimate a fashion that "in desiring its own perfection every thing is desiring God himself,"[60] were to move us to do something, the natural way for God to do so would be as the final cause of our actions. Such was the insight of Augustine, whose reflections on freedom in the eighth book of the *Confessions* established that nothing – neither God nor myself – can make me will something, unless it draws or entices me.[61] And if I cannot be pushed to will something, but only drawn to do so, not even God can cause me to do something freely, if we are thinking of an efficient cause. Yet God, as my sovereign good, could so draw my will as to bring me freely to consent to the end for which my nature craves.

So freedom is less a question of self-determination of what otherwise remains undetermined than it is one of attuning oneself to one's ultimate end. There are plenty of choices, of course, but these are to be made rationally, by taking counsel regarding the way perceived goods relate to that to which we have already consented. Ends function like principles, guiding the inquiry in which we must engage while taking counsel.[62] So Aquinas' model for free action remains one of inquiry, concluding this time in a performance rather than a proposition: "just as the end functions like a principle, so whatever is done for the sake of the end functions like a conclusion."[63]

Such are the main lines of Aquinas' resolution of God's unfailing providential care with human freedom. They imply that any good choice will presuppose an orientation to the end, where the orientation itself is not a choice but a consent to the orientation of one's very being. And where that end is enhanced beyond our imagining, as in the ways revealed by God to Jewish, Christian, or Muslim believers, the consent becomes a *response* of faith. Many questions remain regarding the character of that divine initiative, questions familiar to Christians under the rubrics of "predestination" or the "irresistibility of God's grace." Suffice it to say here that Aquinas' theorem of divine eternity makes the notion of *predestination* as incoherent as "foreknowledge" and that human freedom does retain for him those mysterious reaches where it can renounce its own good.[64] Bare refusal, of

---

[60] ST 1.6.1.2.
[61] See Augustine, *Confessions*, trans. R. S. Pine-Coffin (Baltimore: Penguin, 1961), 8.8–10.
[62] ST 2–1.14.1.
[63] ST 2–1.14.6.
[64] A close examination of Aquinas' treatment of "predestination" (ST 1.23) will show that he takes it up for completeness' sake. Nothing new is added; the principles have been

course, is seldom available to humans, though the angels' sin can be explained no other way.[65] The limiting case is, however, just that; in the course of human events we find ourselves operating within an orientation originally supplied or freely offered, and our freedom is structured by consenting to the first and responding gratefully to the second.

Concluding Remarks

It should be clear which approach I prefer, as well as my reasons. Yet I hope my inability to keep a poker face did not entail unfairness to the other side. For the aim of this exercise was to delineate as clearly as possible two irreducibly different ways of doing philosophical theology, by showing them to be irreducible. That is, the coherence of each reveals presuppositions incompatible with the other. How might one adjudicate between them? If each proves to be coherent philosophically, then the balance may be tipped, as I have suggested, by a better fit with doctrinal positions. As Thomas Tracy suggests, "systematic consistency may sometimes be less highly prized in theology than the ability to provide a place for enduring (even if conflicting) tendencies in religious self-expression."[66] I would add: notably liturgical expression, where the relation of creature to creator attains cultural expression, and worshippers' presence to God accentuates the actual communication between them.

My preference for Aquinas stems from the way his approach links us with Augustinian restlessness by attending to existence and to its source. And that attention assures us that one is speaking, when speaking of God, of the source of all, and not simply of some "maximal being." It is fair to say that the greatest objection to Aquinas' view turns on the conception of God's eternity. I have tried a look at that question, assisted by Kretzmann and Stump, but there is neither time nor space to deal with it here.[67] One thing must be said, however: God's eternity, for Aquinas,

---

developed elsewhere. So it would be inaccurate to say "there is predestination in Aquinas" just because he devotes a question to it. The general principles are given in his treatment of providence in *De Veritate* 2.12, where he remarks that "God's knowledge of future things is more properly called *providentia* than *praevidentia* [because] it would be impossible for God to have knowledge of future contingents were God to know them as future."

[65] ST 1.63.

[66] Thomas Tracy, *God, Action, and Embodiment* (Grand Rapids MI: Eerdmans, 1984), xi.

[67] Cf. my "God's Eternity," in *Faith and Philosophy* 1 (1984), pp. 389–406, which relies on and extends an earlier article by Norman Kretzmann and Eleonore Stump, "Eternity," in *Journal of Philosophy* 78 (1981), pp. 429–58.

hardly reflects a Hellenic prejudice, but is rather rooted in divine simpleness as "subsistent existence itself." The model is not the atemporal mode of being proper to mathematicals, but the eternal source of the present actuality of existing individuals.

It is equally fair to remark that the "divine foreknowledge" and "middle knowledge" scenarios overlook a crucial distinction between a precise individual and precisely one of a kind. So that leaves us – in fairness – with two ontological and epistemological chestnuts! But what else could one expect in trying to conceive the relation between the One and all that derives from that One? The chestnuts, though, are of different order: God's eternity can be regarded as part of the mystery of divinity, indeed the place where that peculiar unknowableness linked to simpleness makes itself felt, whereas the structures demanded by "middle knowledge" ask us to revise what we mean by *individual*. The doctrinal issue most directly involved is that of creation and how to understand it. For creation remains, for Jews and Christians, the fundamental mystery revealing God to us and us to ourselves.

Chapter 8

FROM ANALOGY OF "BEING" TO THE ANALOGY OF BEING

Ralph McInerny's philosophical reflection has been framed by careful and subtle probings into the analogous uses of language, where the inquiry has been motivated by an irenic yet persistent corrective to the tradition which has called itself "Thomist," taking issue first with the sixteenth-century commentator *par excellence* of Thomas Aquinas, Thomas de Vio Cajetan.[1] From *The Logic of Analogy* (1961) and *Studies in Analogy* (1968) to *Aquinas and Analogy* (1996), his goal has been consistent and unyielding: to show how Aquinas managed to articulate the logical and semantic structure of language in such a way as to display its analogical reaches. Hence his untiring emphasis: analogy is a logical doctrine in Aquinas. That is not to say, however, that attention to analogical uses of language has no metaphysical payoff; it is simply to note that conflating the two risks harming both. More precisely, a precipitate move to metaphysical assertion without careful preliminary attention to language will invariably overlook Aquinas' reminder that the "mode proper to metaphysical inquiry is logical" and so unwittingly resolve to the imagination.[2] This animadversion captures the point of McInerny's most mature reflections on these matters:

> if the "analogy of being" refers to real relations, so that what is first is the cause of what is secondary, and if "analogous names" involve an ordered plurality of meanings of a common name in which the first, controlling meaning, the *ratio propria*, is not the cause of the rest, the difference is as important as the difference between logical and real orders. Thomas Aquinas took this difference between the order of our knowledge and the order of

---

[1] Ralph McInerny, *The Logic of Analogy* (The Hague: Martinus Nijhoff, 1961), *Studies in Analogy* (The Hague: Martinus Nijhoff, 1968), and *Aquinas and Analogy* (Washington DC: Catholic University of America Press, 1996).
[2] In Aquinas, *Metaphysica* 4, 574.

being to be decisive as between Plato and Aristotle. He accuses Plato of confusing these two orders and assuming that what is first in our knowing is first in being. Any confusion of the logical and real orders comes under the same criticism. A correct understanding of Thomas on analogy saves him from the grievous mistake he attributed to Plato.[3]

The Plato whom Aquinas knew, of course, was the one whom Aristotle criticized and the one filtered through Proclus in the *Liber de Causis*, on which Aquinas commented.[4] So McInerny's criticism is not of Plato but of Thomists who either confused these two orders or presumed a ready parallel between them, thereby constructing an "analogy of being" which was touted as the keystone of Aquinas' metaphysical "system."

Yet of course there is a parallel between real and logical orders for Aquinas, assured by the originating fact of creation. Its apprehension by us, however, will always be inverted, as "we are aware that what we last name is what is ontologically first," so that "knowledge of the source of all being of whom finally we know what he is not rather than what he is, . . . is the ultimate point of philosophizing"[5] – not its beginning. Words like these would have warmed Karl Barth's heart, for the *analogia entis* which he found anathema to authentic Christian theology claimed that sort of parallelism between real and logical orders which McInerny is anxious to subvert by inverting. Moreover, they claimed it in the name of the real Aquinas, to whom it had been unwarrantedly attributed. Yet these summary remarks are dense, offered by McInerny as a valedictory to his latest clarifications of Aquinas' teaching regarding analogous uses of language. The standard set by these clarifications is exceedingly high, representing as they do some 35 years of sifting and of simplifying by a mind as subtle as it is witty; and subtlety and wit are the very stuff of recognizing and employing the analogous reaches of language. I shall be arguing that McInerny's reflections have as much to do with doing philosophy as they have with Thomas Aquinas' teaching; indeed, that analogy is at the very heart of doing philosophy, especially of a philosophy which seeks to integrate the Jewish, Christian, and Muslim conviction that the universe is freely created by one God. If it is that belief which assured Aquinas that the order of logic and of reality are indeed isomorphic, it is the same teaching which reminds us that <u>we know God better the more we realize</u>

---

[3] McInerny, 1996 (note 1), pp. 162–3.
[4] See the recent English translation of Aquinas' *Commentary of the Book of Causes* by Vincent Guagliardo, O.P., Charles Hess, O.P., and Richard Taylor (Washington DC: Catholic University of America Press, 1996).
[5] McInerny, 1996 (note 1), pp. 160–6.

that we do not know our creator, as Aquinas frequently put it. So the two orders, of logic and of reality, will be the inverse image of each other in these reaches.

Creation and Participation

The remarks we have identified as valedictory to McInerny's treatment of analogy represent a fine specimen of philosophy serving as handmaid to faith, for the philosophizing in this book stops short of what is identified as philosophy's "ultimate point: knowledge of the source of all being of whom finally we know what he is not rather than what he is."[6] One explicit point of McInerny's book is to show that identifying the activity of analogous naming with "the causal dependence in a hierarchical descent of all things from God"[7] could mislead others about that source of all being. How so? It could, for example, lead one to suspect that we could know the character of that hierarchical descent, or that such a descent might already be inscribed in our language, so that we would feel no need to learn the specific practices associated with using terms of God which we have learned to use in our context. In other words, we might be tempted to turn philosophy into a proto-theology which could give us an adequate understanding of God – exactly Barth's complaint about *analogia entis* as it had been presented to him. Indeed, philosophy's preferred way of accounting for the origination of all things, the necessary emanation scheme of al-Farabi, which Aquinas came to know in Avicenna's amended version, promises just such a knowledge. Moreover, Aquinas was sufficiently taken with it to have recourse to it as an image for the unimaginable act of creating, yet only after he had shown it to be both false and redundant as an explanatory scheme.[8] False, because the model of logical deduction which animated the scheme assured that the First in such a scheme could not adequately be distinguished from the premises which followed from it; redundant, because the act of creation must be the act of a cause of being whose effect follows immediately from it, absent any motion or mediation. Indeed, this is a paradigmatic instance of Aquinas' philosophical inquiry being shaped by premises from faith. The telling text is imbedded in a question regarding God's triunity, where it

[6]   *Ibid.*, p. 161.
[7]   *Ibid.*, p. 162.
[8]   This is the burden of my comparative study: *Knowing the Unknowable God: Ibn Sina, Maimonides, Aquinas* (Notre Dame IN: University of Notre Dame Press, 1986).

is asked whether the trinity of the divine persons can be known by natural reason. Aquinas captures the opportunity offered by a sophistical objection – that knowledge of the trinity must be accessible to reason since it would be superfluous to teach what cannot be known by natural reason, yet it would hardly be becoming to say that the divine tradition of the trinity was superfluous – to offer "two reasons why the knowledge of the divine persons was necessary for us," and the first envisages "the right idea of creation: the fact of saying that God made all things by His Word excludes the error of those who say that God produced things by necessity, [a corollary of the emanation scheme]. Moreover, when we say that in Him there is a procession of love, we show that God produced creatures not because He needed them, nor because of any other extrinsic reason, but on account of the love of His own goodness."[9]

Philosophy could lead one, Aquinas thought, to understand that the universe must have been originated, but the prevailing schemes for elucidating that origination had dire consequences for a proper conception of the First as well as for human freedom, so the findings of faith will be required – "necessary," as he puts it – to have the "right idea of" this origination, as an utterly free creation. As Josef Pieper has remarked, creation is the "hidden element in the philosophy of St. Thomas" – perhaps hidden because, correctly understood, it requires a theological premise if it is to be properly understood.[10] This example offers us a tangible instance where philosophy can serve the faith yet cannot pretend to elucidate the entire story by its own resources. It bears on McInerny's treatment of analogy, for whatever exiguous knowledge we might have of God would be severely threatened without the resources of analogous language. The medieval witness to such a state of affairs was Moses Maimonides, who argued strenuously that no terms could be employed of both God and creatures, given the crucial "distinction" between creator and creatures.[11] His arguments did not turn on the immense "distance" between God and creatures so much as on what Kierkegaard would call "the infinite qualitative difference." It is not that God's justice far outstrips ours, but rather

[9]   ST 1.32.1.3.
[10]   Josef Pieper, *The Silence of St. Thomas: Three Essays* (New York: Pantheon, 1957): "The Negative Element in the Philosophy of St. Thomas," pp. 47–67.
[11]   See Maimonides, *Guide for the Perplexed* 1.51–60; for this use of "the distinction" see Robert Sokolowski, *The God of Faith and Reason* (Notre Dame IN: University of Notre Dame Press, 1981/Washington DC: Catholic University of America Press, 1995) and my interfaith commentary: "The Christian Distinction Celebrated and Expanded," in John Drummond and James Hart, eds, *The Truthful and the Good* (Boston: Kluwer, 1996), pp. 191–206, and chapter 14 in this vol.

that any statement made about God's being just would be ill-formed, since it would presume by its very structure that justice is an attribute of God, whereas God – to be God – must be utterly simple.[12] So there can be, "in no way or sense, anything common to the attributes predicated of God, and those used in reference to ourselves; they have only the same names, and nothing else is common to them." Otherwise, one might believe "that there is in God something additional to His essence, in the same way as attributes are joined to our essence."[13] So the radical difference between the creator and creatures precludes any use of the same terms, since the very form of predication belies the manner in which God is just. This chapter (56) contains a passing reference to a set of terms which might so function, called "amphibolous" by Harry Wolfson, and ill-defined by Maimonides as "applied to two things which have a similarity to each other in respect to a certain property which is in both of them an accident, not an essential, constituent element."[14] Maimonides rejects such a suggestion, since "the attributes of God are not considered as accidental by any intelligent person." The idea seems to be that such terms could not be predicated properly of either creatures or creator, since the shared accidental feature would be extrinsic to both.

Prescinding from his inadequate characterization of a usage which might have been identified as *analogous*, this observation of Maimonides is telling for our reflections on Cajetan and Aquinas, since Cajetan's insistence on *proportionality* as the normal form for properly analogous usage turns on whether or not the *ratio* can be predicated intrinsically of both subjects. Recalling Aquinas' favorite example of "health," it is easy to see that "healthy" can be attributed properly only to an organism, so there is no *something* which healthy medicine shares with a healthy organism. Rather, medicine is called "healthy" by virtue of its role in helping to cure a diseased organism. Yet Aquinas does not hesitate to offer this form of analogous usage as the model for our speaking of a just God. Note how Aquinas accepts Maimonides' criteria here: there is no *something*, no shared feature by which Socrates and God might each be said to be just.[15] As if to echo the Rambam, Aquinas eschews any similarity between God

---

[12]   *Guide*, 1.57.
[13]   *Ibid.*, 1.56.
[14]   The Arabic term is *b'ishtarâk*; I tend to use Friedlander's translation (New York: Dover, 1956), corrected from the Arabic where needed, since his use of philosophical terminology is more predictable than Pines (Chicago: University of Chicago Press, 1963), whose translations are lexically correct but often oblivious to philosophical terminology.
[15]   See my *Knowing the Unknowable God* (note 8) and Alexander Broadie, "Maimonides and Aquinas on the Names of God," *Religious Studies* 23 (1987), pp. 157–70.

and creatures except for "the sort of analogy that holds between all things because they have existence in common."[16] Yet *existence* [*esse*] cannot be a feature, so he goes on to specify: "this is how things receiving existence from God [*illa quae sunt a Deo*] resemble him; for precisely as things possessing existence [*inquantum sunt entia*] they resemble the primary and universal source of all existence [*esse*]." I have inserted the Latin here to illustrate how the Blackfriars translator, Timothy McDermott, has brought what Pieper called the "hidden element" in Aquinas' philosophical treatment into the clear light of day. There need not be any feature intrinsic to creator and creature to use the same term of both; indeed, there could be none such *a priori* if we are to respect "the distinction" between them; indeed, their "infinite qualitative difference." We are required, however, to advert to the foundational fact that whatever perfections creatures possess "must pre-exist in God in a higher manner, . . . since God is the primary operative cause of all things."[17] Without the offices of a creator, analogous predication would have to be assured by an inherent proportionality between the related uses of a term. Yet as we shall see, it is precisely recognition of God as the cause of being which allows that the same terms may be predicated of creator and of creatures, without thereby implying that there be *something* they both hold in common. Whatever *analogia entis* there may be has to be governed by the rules which Maimonides discerned, the "distinction" which Sokolowski has articulated, as well as the negation which "dialectical theology" demands – all of which is already present in Aquinas' insistence that "we cannot know what God is, but only what he is not,"[18] articulated in McInerny's trenchant reminder of what knowledge we can expect to have of the "source of all being."

These summary remarks (of McInerny's) which we have been probing are contained in a chapter entitled "Analogy and Participation," as if to remind us that if Aquinas "does not call the real hierarchy of being an analogy of being,"[19] he does structure it according to the Platonic notion of *participation*.[20] But that notion too is imported in an attempt to characterize the relation of creatures to the creator, once one has so accentuated their difference. So once again, *creation* emerges as the central, if unaccented, reality. It is as though we need to have a subset of terms –

[16] ST 1.4.3.
[17] ST 1.4.2.
[18] ST 1.3.Prol.
[19] McInerny, 1996 (note 1), p. 156.
[20] For a sterling treatment of this topic, see Rudi te Velde, *Participation and Substantiality in Thomas Aquinas* (Leiden: Brill, 1995); see my review in *International Philosophical Quarterly* 37 (1997), pp. 101–4.

those intending *perfections* – which may be used of both creatures and creator, but we will use them properly only when "we are aware that what we last name is ontologically first."[21] That there be such a set of terms is, then, a necessary condition for their being used of both creator and of creature. What must be added to the terms (*parole*), however, is their use (*langue*) according to a heightened operative awareness that we are employing them here of beings as well as of the cause of being, of the One in whom they exist pre-eminently. Moreover, when said of the cause of being, they cannot be predicated as attributes, strictly speaking, but as part of what it is to be the One whose essence is simply to be. The role of *participation*, then, is to remind us that there could be no such set of terms were the universe not itself derived from a source from which all that is, and notably what is perfect about what-is, flows. So the ontological ground of the set of terms lies in the fact that all-that-is participates in the One from whom everything derives, and their proper use demands that we bring this grounding fact to awareness. Yet we can only assert it, knowing as little as we do how to express this all-important "distinction" and the consequent relations obtaining between creator and creatures.

What *participation* clarifies, however, is a crucial ambiguity in Cajetan's criterion that properly analogous usage demands that the feature in question be possessed inherently by each party of which it is predicated, albeit in a proportional manner. For if we fail to avert to creation, understood precisely as participation, then such a criterion will be read to imply that there can be no properly analogical predication unless there be a common feature, justice, itself predicable of both God and Socrates. But the presence of such a common feature would effectively deny "the distinction" of creator from creature, as Maimonides articulates so well: to treat the creator as an item in the universe, which a shared feature would imply, is to deny the basis of Jewish, Christian, and Muslim faith in the free creation of the universe by one God. Indeed, what the device of *participation* is designed to do is to show us how "just" can be attributed to creatures as well as to the creator *without* there being a feature, justice, common to both. *Pari passu*, the *res significata* of the analogous term, justice, need not be accessible to our understanding for us to use the term properly. We need only be aware that it is a perfection, and so will outstrip any realization that we come across of it – indeed, it must do so if it is to function as it should, lest we have nothing but a conventional ethics, that is to say, no ethics at all! We will be more inclined to acknowl-

---

[21]   McInerny, 1996 (note 1), pp. 160–1.

edge that feature in practice the more we recognize that all such perfections have their pre-eminent source in a creator.

So here too, a properly analogous use of analogous terms demands an awareness that we are functioning as creatures ourselves in a created *order* whose principles remain unknown to us, yet whose lineaments can be glimpsed from time to time. Creatures can be just in their fashion, and hence properly be said to be so: the term "just" can be predicated of them inherently, without there being a proportional similarity between God's justice and theirs. For as the cause of being, the creator is not an extrinsic cause of creatures, since their very to-be is to-be-in-relation to the creator. That is why Aquinas can say that to-be [*esse*] is "more intimately and profoundly interior to things than anything else,"[22] and it is precisely this *esse* which accounts for whatever similarity can be had between creator and creature. Indeed, created *esse* brings them so close that the non-reciprocal relation of dependence, which is participated being, can be likened to Sankara's notion of *nonduality*: the distinction does not amount to a separation, as though God could be pictured as one more being over against the universe.[23] Ralph McInerny may never have suspected how his careful work in the semantics of analogous terms could facilitate moves so apparently radical as these; or again he may well have done so, but forbore drawing such conclusions, for they smack more of philosophical theology while he wished to underscore philosophy's ancillary role. Yet without such astute servants the fare which theology serves can be ill-chosen and underdone.

Practices to Heighten Awareness: *Langue* and *Parole*

Keeping the orders of discourse and of being distinct is a taxing job, notably for philosophers whose very trade involves using discourse to articulate what-is by showing the way it must be! Here is where Etienne Gilson's observations that "'analogy' for Aquinas refers to our capacity to make the kind of judgments we do" can illuminate McInerny's strategy as well as help us spell out its implications for our practice in doing philo-

---

[22]   ST 1.8.1.
[23]   On this comparison, see Sara Grant, RSCJ, *Toward and Alternative Theology*: "Confessions of a Nondualist Christian" (Bangalore: Asian Trading Corporation, 1991), new edition edited by Bradley Malkovsky (Notre Dame IN: University of Notre Dame Press, 2002), and Kathryn Tanner, *God and Creation in Christian Theology* (Oxford: Blackwell, 1988).

sophical theology especially.[24] Whoever understands that analogy is to be explicated "on the level of judgment" and not of concepts, Gilson contends, has also grasped the real divergence between Aquinas and Scotus.[25] He corroborates his point by noting, as does McInerny, that all discussion of "analogy of being" or of "analogous concepts" is utterly foreign to Aquinas, who speaks rather of "terms used analogously." Judgment is indispensable precisely because responsible analogous usage requires that we assess the way in which a term is being used in relation to its primary analogate. Yet such an assessment demands both that we identify the primary analogate as well as grasp how the use in question relates to it, and each of these apperceptions involves judgment. In practice, this comes to adducing appropriate examples, like the ones needed to make this very point. If we think of a relatively neutral but highly analogous term like "order," we can imagine any number of situations in which the term may be properly used, while each varies widely from the other. A compulsive personality may need a clean desk at work yet learn to tolerate a great deal of mess at home, especially when children are young. She could still find herself spontaneously "cleaning up" when she comes home, however, especially if she brings a colleague who has no children into her home. Yet if she relates appropriately to each environment, she knows that her own sanity demands that she respect the order proper to each. In such cases, the term is properly context-dependent, so there is no set "primary analogate"; each case establishes a base line for proper use, which can be formulated functionally: an environment is "in order" when we can interact appropriately in it.

When such a term is attributed to the creator, however, the issue of a prime analogate quickly becomes problematic. Consider Aquinas' insistence that "the order of the universe as a whole is the object proper to God's intention, . . . the direct object of God's creating act and intended by God."[26] Whatever uses of the term "order" may be functionally proper to environments in which we have come to be at home will doubtless fail when speaking of the "order of the universe," yet we do know that *order* must accompany intelligent agency. Here one's adeptness at shifting

[24] Etienne Gilson, *Christian Philosophy of Saint Thomas* (New York: Random House, 1956), pp. 105–7; *Jean Duns Scot* (Paris: Vrin, 1952), p. 101; the relevant texts he cites in Aquinas can be found in ST 1.13.5–6, 1.13.10.4, *Contra Gentiles* 1.34, 2.15.
[25] See my "Aquinas and Scotus: Contrary Patterns for Philosophical Theology," in Bruce D. Marshall, ed., *Theology and Dialogue* (Notre Dame IN: University of Notre Dame Press, 1990), pp. 105–29.
[26] ST 1.15.2.

contexts in which the term can properly be used will doubtless help in assessing how little we can expect to understand the order God intends in a universe we apprehend so minimally. Our emerging consciousness of ecological realities, contrasted with the way in which we have proceeded to "improve" a natural order in the direction of serving human needs, yet quite oblivious to the complexities of that order itself, offer some salutary reminders of the difficulty of identifying the "order of creation." What we have discovered here is our endemic tendency to align the primary analogate with human needs as we perceive them; and a similar predilection clearly operates in the usual conundra spelled out with regard to human suffering or so-called "natural evil." Where these become ludicrous, indeed, is when any one of us attempts to "explain" to someone else the place their suffering holds in "God's plan." Indeed, the very use of the term "plan" to introduce the order the creator bestows in creating begs the question, since plans and planning must be part of our ordering process (and so belong to our *mode of signifying*) but need not characterize the way divine wisdom is operative in creating at all. So what we "intend to mean" (the *res significata*) in speaking of "the order of the universe [which] is the direct object of God's creating act" lies utterly beyond our conceptual capacities. We can at best use our practiced judgment to recognize that we do not and cannot know it, all the while trusting that the universe be ordered. So analogous usage, especially in such domains, demands that we eschew any straightforward grasp of the *res significata*, relying on an astute judgment regarding the direction of the pointers which we can articulate, much as Aristotle observed that properly metaphorical discourse required a deftness of judgment.[27]

Here is where we may have recourse to the work of Pierre Hadot to remind us that doing philosophy is ever a matter of the proper *exercises*, and in executing philosophical theology, of properly "spiritual exercises."[28] Indeed, it is questionable whether the reaches of analogical language can ever be appreciated so long as one identifies "philosophy" with a "set of propositional attitudes," effectively restricting philosophical inquiry to analyzing what can be formulated, abstracted from the form of life required to carry it out. Yet expressing the relationship between formulations and forms of life remains strangely elusive. Trying to do so, however, should

---

[27] Aristotle contends that being a "master of metaphor . . . is a sign of genius since a good metaphor implies an intuitive perception of the similarity in dissimilars" (1459a5).

[28] For an illuminating introduction to the work of Pierre Hadot in English, see *Philosophy as a Way of Life*, ed. Arnold Davidson (Cambridge MA: Blackwell, 1995); for a synopsis, see his *Qu'est-ce que la philosophie antique?* (Paris: Gallimard, 1995).

illuminate Gilson's insistence that analogical usage involves exercising judgments regarding our use of the key terms in question, while identifying the character of those judgments will help us see how deeply faith is intertwined with carrying out philosophical inquiry. Trying to grasp this inner relation of formulation to practices may also clarify the way in which we are able to appreciate something about medieval philosophy which medievals themselves could not be expected to see, since they were immersed in it: the formative character of their particular world of faith, be it Jewish, Muslim, or Christian. When such forms of life take on the shape of intentional choices, as they must for us, their formative function is cast more clearly into relief, whereas so long as they remain the air one breathes, that crucial role will remain quite indiscernible.

Robert Sokolowski supplied me with the clue to this observation in his genial monograph, *The God of Faith and Reason*, where he introduces "the distinction" of God from creation as a decisively Christian achievement, "glimpsed on the margins of reason, . . . at the intersection of reason and faith."[29] By focusing on the key role which making *distinctions* plays in philosophical inquiry, and then turning the very notion of a *distinction* into a conceit or trope, he proceeds to identify just how unique is the relation of the creator-of-all with all that is created, something which Jewish and Muslim philosophers were also taxed to articulate.[30] "The distinction" then becomes a way of gesturing towards what indeed distinguishes those who believe the universe to be freely created by one God from anyone else. For the God in question would be God without creating all-that-is, so much so that everything-that-is adds nothing to the perfection of being of such a One. (To use a familiar abstract descriptor, that is what "monotheism" entails; not a simple reduction of the number of gods to one.) What makes this so significant philosophically is that it forbids any ordinary brand of "onto-theology" wherein a notion of *being* can be stretched to include the creator as well as creation.[31] Yet that is what philosophers seem to need: a univocal notion whereby we can find some sameness between creator and creatures, in order to predicate terms of God. That is what Scotus promised, in conjunction with his rejection of analogical character of "being." And while it can be argued that the

[29]   See "Christian Distinction" (note 11), citation at p. 39.
[30]   See my "The Christian Distinction Celebrated and Expanded" in chapter 14 of this volume (and note 11).
[31]   See J.-L. Marion, "Saint Thomas d'Aquin et l'onto-théo-logie," in *Révue Thomist* 95 (1995), pp. 31–66, where he expands on his Preface to the English edition of *God without Being* (Chicago: University of Chicago Press, 1991).

account of analogy which he rejected was that of Henry of Ghent and not that of Aquinas, the legacy stands, presumably because it answers so well to a standing predilection of philosophers.[32] What seems to defeat philosophers, ironically enough, is the practice of "Socratic unknowing." This practice of Plato's Socrates is linked with displaying a mode of discourse beyond the theoretical (Plato's *dianoia*), which Plato called "dialectic" and usually articulated in a mythic manner. What philosophical discourse could not realize had to be displayed in another idiom, gesturing towards something which language could only intimate.[33] Yet as Pierre Hadot reminds us, the intellectual exercise of dialogue itself could also be summed up as "dialectical," so the virtues which Socrates' interlocutors had to develop would have prepared them to respect the limits of the univocal discourse which theory [*dianoia*] requires, yet do so in such a way as to recognize that the very *élan* of their inquiry pointed beyond such language.

So philosophical dialogue, as exercised by Socrates, represents a mode of doing philosophy which is also a spiritual exercise, and which calls forth from its participants a palpable sense of "something more," something towards which the inquiry is directed and which can be said to guide it to the outcomes which it can attain. Plato called this lure "the Good," and the tradition which traced itself to Plato demanded of its adherents a way of living in relation to that Good which could not but affect the way in which they carried out intellectual inquiry. Medieval philosophers were often themselves participants in a vowed community life which made similar demands on them, demands which have also been called "spiritual exercises." How can we identify the connection between these ways of life and their use of philosophical discourse? In approaching Aquinas for an answer to this question, I have found it useful to attend to the matter-of-fact way in which he will put things which we find arresting. Consider, for example, the straightforward introduction to questions 3–11 at the outset of the *Summa Theologiae*, where he announces that "we cannot know what God is, but only what he is not, so we must consider the ways in which God does not exist, rather than the way in which he does." One could not, it seems, engage in "negative theology" so gracefully without having some other access to the One whose nature remains

---

[32] See my *Analogy and Philosophical Language* (New Haven CN: Yale University Press, 1973), p. 96, and on the larger point, Eric Alliez, *Capital Times*, trans. Georges Van Den Abbeele (Minneapolis MN: University of Minnesota Press, 1996).

[33] For a telling example, consider the words of Socrates which form a transition to the closing myth in the Phaedo: "if you analyze [the initial hypotheses] adequately, you will, I believe, follow the argument to the furthest point to which a human being can follow it up; and if you get that clear, you'll seek nothing further" (107b5–10).

unknown to us, for philosophers trained in a modern idiom invariably find such statements utterly disconcerting. And that other access must be such that it does not reduce the "unknowing" but rather offers a way of living with it. In the terms which we have been using from Aquinas' treatment of discourse *in divinis*, we need not be able to articulate the *res significata* to assure ourselves that there is such. What we need to be able to do, however, is to recognize that the very terms we use have a reach beyond the *modus significandi* that is accessible to us. Indeed, their proper use in human contexts demands just that, as my allusion earlier to conventional morality suggested. Normative language needs to have a purchase on us which carries us beyond the descriptive domain of "everybody does it," and that must be inscribed in the key terms themselves, without our possessing a firm criterion for their transcendent use.[34] For that demand readily translates into asking one to articulate the *res significandi*, the prime analogate proper to the creator, rather than the ones accessible to creatures.

Aquinas had explicit recourse to the creature/creator relation to respond to Maimonides' objections to our using our perfection terms of God: "any creature, in so far as it possesses any perfection, represents God and is like to him, for he, being simply and universally perfect, has pre-existing in himself the perfections of all his creatures. But a creature is not like to God as it is like to another member of its species or genus, ... thus words like 'good' or 'wise' when used of God do signify something that God really is [*divinam substantiam*], but they signify it imperfectly because creatures represent God imperfectly."[35] All of the semantic markers are here: the terms must be "perfection-terms," they cannot be univocal (pertaining to the same genus), and therefore they can "signify imperfectly" what they "intend to signify." Our capacity to do just that – intend to signify by the terms we employ – responds to the deeper objection of Maimonides, which Aquinas acknowledges: "when we say that a man is wise, we signify his wisdom as something distinct from other things about him – his essence, for example, his powers or his existence. But when we use this word about God we do not intend to signify something distinct from this essence, power or existence."[36] How can we do something like that? By the power of judgment which directs our use of the discourse we employ; Aquinas has recourse to this power in his final assessment of our ability to "name" the God we cannot know, a capacity that is dis-

---

[34]   The work of Julius Kovesi, *Moral Notions* (New York: Humanities Press, 1967), continues to be fruitful here.
[35]   ST 1.13.2.
[36]   ST 1.13.5.

played in the way we make statements: "God considered in himself is altogether one and simple, yet we think of him through a number of different concepts because we cannot see him as he is in himself. But although
we think of him in these different ways we also know that to each corresponds a single simplicity that is one and the same for all. The different ways of thinking of him are represented in the difference of subject
and predicate; his unity we represent by bringing them together in an
affirmative statement."[37] The translator (Herbert McCabe, O.P.) supplies
"statement" here, but its addition is crucial for us to grasp how judgment
enters in at this very point. Aquinas' term is *compositio*, which is the task
he reserves to judgment, reminding us how for Aristotle, propositions or
sentences are parasitic upon the act of stating something to be the case,
as *langue* is posterior to *parole*, to language in use.

So it is never enough to identify a subset of terms which are susceptible of analogous usage; one must always display them in use. And to do
so will exhibit a judgment in operation; in this case, a judgment informed
by "knowing that" in God a "single simplicity" corresponds to these distinct terms. It is this judgment which reminds us that the compositional
form of the statements made is improper when used of God, so it belongs
to judgment to factor such a "knowing that" into one's use, thereby off-
setting the inherently misleading form of the statement itself. This will
sound complicated to one who expects language to reflect on its face all
that we accomplish when we use it properly; yet a bit of reflection shows
that we make such subtle judgments all the time. In fact, when we cannot
do so, our speech is justly described as "wooden." So analogous usage
need not be justified; it only needs to be pointed out. Yet justifying using
it with respect to God does require the explicit premise of creation. And
Aquinas insists that we need a Trinitarian revelation if we are going to
get that relation right, so Pierre Hadot's observations about the need to
understand philosophical inquiry in terms of the modes of life consonant
with it are vindicated in Aquinas' case. For revelation can never be a
simple fact; it always requires our commensurate response. Such at least is
the testimony of any faith-tradition, to which we must have recourse to
learn the proper use of a term like "revelation." Yet it should not appear
all that strange that a thesis like Ralph McInerny's – that "analogy" is a
linguistic doctrine – should lead to such consequences, for language in
use can take many forms, and respecting them, as Aristotle and McInerny
note, is the mark of a wise person.

---

[37]   ST 1.13.12.

Part II

DIVINE FREEDOM AND HUMAN FREEDOM

Chapter 9

THE CHALLENGE TO MEDIEVAL CHRISTIAN PHILOSOPHY: RELATING CREATOR TO CREATURES

Moses as protagonist in the dramatic shift from ancient to medieval philosophy

In leading students into the vortex of the debate which the Hebrew scriptures were to engender in philosophical circles, it has proven beneficial to pursue closely Aristotle's inquiry in the *Metaphysics*, showing how his attempt to respond to a legacy of questions, notably from Plato, virtually set the agenda for subsequent philosophical reflection on these comprehensive issues. Yet the encounter with Moses (as the putative author of Genesis) displays a lacuna which earnest students of Aristotle might well miss: how effectively he steers clear of the issue of the origin of the universe.[1] Edward Booth has traced the effects of this lacuna through the subsequent commentaries, notably as it was displayed in a lingering *aporia* which bedeviled that tradition: does Aristotle give primacy to the individual existing thing, as his critique of Plato leads us to believe he will, or rather to *essence* as its intelligible component?[2] It remains a nice question whether the inner dynamic of the inquiry called "metaphysics" would

---

[1] A little book on this very topic makes its point extremely well: Patrick Madigan, *Christian Revolution and the Completion of the Aristotelian Revolution* (Lanham MD: University Press of America, 1988).

[2] *Aristotelian Aporetic Ontology in Islamic and Christian Writers* (Cambridge: Cambridge University Press, 1985).

have insisted on addressing the issue of origins without encountering Genesis. Plotinus makes one believe that it would, yet might his resolute orientation to the One not be an assertive answer to the advent of revelation? However we may assess that, it is clear that Moses' joining the conversation puts the issue of origins firmly on the table. Yet once there, the issue is joined in the precise manner in which Plotinus poses it: must the origin of the universe be construed as a necessary consequence of the One in its inner fecundity, or does the universe come forth freely from that One?[3] What is at stake, as we shall see, is at once the conception we might be able to have of the One, as well as of the universe itself.

When I began tracing the interaction among the Abrahamic traditions regarding this question, I allowed the classical problematic of *necessary vs free* to set the agenda for exposition and for inquiry. In retrospect, however, I now see that each of these terms functions ambiguously in these reaches, so the issue cannot simply be one of stark opposition.[4] For the *necessity* operative in the prevailing necessary emanation scheme was that of logical deduction, on which the scheme was modeled. That sort of necessity is perforce impersonal, of course, so hardly befits a free creator. Yet the One who creates without any presuppositions whatsoever (i.e., *ex nihilo*) cannot be said coherently to choose among alternatives, for such a One is quite literally faced with nothing at all from which to choose. So the freedom associated with creating will have to be a freedom closer to accepting the determinations of divine wisdom than choosing among alternatives. The radical alternative not to create anything at all would always remain, of course, yet that freedom is better described as consenting to the inherent tendency of *good* to overflow and diffuse itself than it is a "free choice." In Plotinus' scheme, of course, refusing that consent would be impossible to "the One" (in the measure that this One is also "the Good"), so even that radical freedom would be counter-factual, in the sense of running counter to the very nature of the One as the Good.

So the precise sense in which the one God is free to create must indeed escape us, as Aquinas implicitly affirms in insisting – employing another sense of "necessary" – that knowledge of divine triunity is "'necessary' for us to have the right idea of creation, to wit, that God did not produce things of necessity, [for] when we say that in God there is a procession of

---

[3]   See Lloyd Gerson's magisterial study: *Plotinus* (New York: Routledge, 1994).

[4]   It was Bernard McGinn, in the course of our conference published as *God and Creation* (Notre Dame IN: University of Notre Dame Press, 1990), who first raised this possibility with me; given how long it has lingered, this exploration is dedicated in gratitude to him and his work. Most recently, Louis Dupré made a similar observation, and I realized how much the issue needed to be nuanced.

love, we show that God produced creatures not out of need, nor for any other extrinsic reason, but on account of the love of God's own goodness."[5] Not even for the intrinsic reason of "God's own goodness," but out of God's love for that very goodness, where the reduplication gestures at an "interpersonal" life within the One which philosophy could never have conceived. So "the right idea of creation" will elude reason operating unilluminated by revelation – indeed, by the Christian revelation – since reason itself could never conclude to the divine triunity which we need to direct our thinking about intentional origination. And by a similar reasoning, the precise sense in which God's creating can be said to be free will escape us as well. For if we would be unable confidently to affirm it without having been informed of the divine triunity, which itself escapes our comprehension, then so will the freedom which that triunity announces and protects.[6] We have, of course, moved well beyond logical necessity here, yet the generation of the Son (Word) and the procession of the Holy Spirit (Love) in God, which in Aquinas' thought alone secures the freedom of creation, cannot itself be a free act of God, but is presented as God's own revelation displaying for creatures the inner life (or complete "nature") of the creator.[7] Once that life is revealed, then, it will be *necessary* that such a One act freely, out of love, yet the manner whereby that loving free consent to the divine goodness allows it to overflow into creation will utterly escape us. So just how God is free in creating is not for us to know.

Once we are invited by a revelatory tradition, however, to assert that the universe is freely created, we will be constrained to find a metaphysical way of expressing this relation of the universe to its source. If the model of logical deduction failed to distinguish the One adequately from the universe by having all-that-is emanate from the One as premises from a single axiom, what possible connection can there be to this One who now freely speaks it? For free origination does not answer to any explanatory mode, yet whatever exists does exist by being freely spoken.[8] So we

---

[5]   ST 1.32.1.3.

[6]   Norman Kretzmann's struggles with this issue offer oblique testimony to Aquinas' point: "A General Problem of Creation: Why Would God Create Anything at All?," in Scott MacDonald, ed., *Being and Goodness* (Ithaca NY: Cornell University Press, 1991), while James Ross' attempts to offer a positive characterization help to confirm ours: "Real Freedom," in Jeff Jordan and Daniel Howard-Snyder, eds, *Faith, Freedom and Rationality: Philosophy of Religion Today* (New York: Rowan and Littlefield, 1996), pp. 89–117.

[7]   For a constructive treatment, see Gilles Emery's magisterial study of Aquinas' commentary on Lombard's *Sentences*: *La Trinité Créatrice* (Paris: Vrin, 1995).

[8]   See Nicholas Lash in MacKinnon festschrift: "Ideology, metaphor and analogy," in Brian Hebblethwaite and Stewart Sutherland, eds, *The Philosophical Frontiers of Christian Theology*

are pressed to ask: *what* is it that God speaks? What is the proper effect of creation in the universe? The response natural to those traditions which insist on God's creating by speaking would be the one found in the wisdom literature of the Hebrew scriptures and elaborated by Philo: the trace of the creator in creation is God's ordering wisdom. Continuing his insistence on the appositeness of the Christian revelation of God's triunity, Aquinas will identify that wisdom with the Word "through whom the universe is made," yet locate its operation in the act of bestowing things' very existence: "the proper effect of the first and most universal cause, which is God, is existing itself [*ipsum esse*]."[9] Beholden to Avicenna's celebrated distinction of *essence* from *existing*, Aquinas will nonetheless transform it by rendering *esse* as an *act* rather than an *accident*, thereby removing any suspicion that there might already be "things" which then receive their existence, as well as any hint of the creator being *essentially* related to the universe. Indeed, the role which *esse* plays will allow the creator to constitute the universe yet more intimately. It is that drama which we need now to allow to unfold.

The Primacy of *Esse*

What the revelatory traditions of Bible and Qur'an alike insist upon is "the distinction" of creator from creation: nothing uncreated can be "associated with" the creator, as Islam prefers to put it in celebrating the radical oneness of God [*tawhîd*]. The rabbis were equally insistent, of course, in distinguishing God's revelation to Israel from the surrounding polytheisms, for the revelation of there being but one God cannot simply mean that one out of the current pantheon wins out. Once this one God is identified as the One from whom all-that-is comes forth, such a One cannot be part of the universe God originates, nor have any rivals. That is the simple logic of asserting the oneness of the creator. Robert Sokolowski has detailed the implications of this logic, introducing it by a philosophical conceit which he calls "the distinction."[10] He insists, of course, that it

---

(Cambridge: Cambridge University Press, 1982), pp. 68–94; both the Bible and the Qur'an offer the model of speech to underscore the creator's free involvement.

[9]   ST 1.45.5.

[10]   See Robert Sokolowski, *The God of Faith and Reason: Foundations of Christian Theology* (Notre Dame IN: University of Notre Dame Press, 1982/Washington DC: Catholic University of America Press, 1995), where he gives cogent reasons for further identifying it as "the Christian distinction"; but see my contribution to the Sokolowski festschrift which is included in the current volume as chapter 14: "The Christian Distinction Celebrated and Expanded."

cannot be a distinction like the ones we routinely make, for creator and creatures do not share a common domain; indeed, this *distinction* is utterly unique in that "one of the terms of the distinction, God, is more fundamental than the distinction itself [once it] is appreciated as a distinction that did not have to be, even though it in fact is." For in this *distinction* "God is understood as 'being' God entirely apart from any relation of otherness to the world or to the whole. God could and would be God even if there were no world, [since] God is understood not only to have created the world, but to have permitted the distinction between himself and world to occur."[11] As Aquinas, the metaphysician, will identify existing [*esse*] with Aristotle's premier analytic category of *act*, thereby transforming Aristotle's metaphysics to meet the demands of a universe revealed to be created; so Sokolowski, the phenomenologist, will exploit what he has already identified as the premier activity of philosophers – making distinctions – to show how a central feature of the faith-life of Christians carries profound philosophical implications.[12]

The first of these is the way in which "Christian belief in creation makes the world or the whole explicitly thematic because it urges a special kind of negation of the world or the whole; it urges a distinction between the whole and God."[13] Yet a distinction of a unique sort, for:

> one danger in this is that the world might lose its character as a matrix and ultimate setting and begin to look like a large thing, a global object, instead of being taken as a setting for things and objects; this would occur if the distinction between God and the world is misread as one of the distinctions we make naturally and spontaneously between things within the world. This misunderstanding of both the world and God, this taking of both of them as new kinds of objects, can be prevented by a proper emphasis on the philosophical inquiry into the whole and its necessities; by an awareness of the special sense of God as *ipsum esse subsistens* and the special transformation of language that occurs when we begin to speak, religiously and theologically about God; and by an explicit study of the unusual character of the distinction between the whole and God.[14]

A challenging agenda, any one of whose demands has often been neglected in much that passes for "philosophy of religion," yet the focus

---

[11] Sokolowski 1995 (note 10), pp. 32–3.
[12] See Robert Sokolowski, "Making Distinctions," *Review of Metaphysics* 32 (1979), pp. 3–28.
[13] Sokolowski 1995 (note 10), p. 46.
[14] *Ibid.*, p. 46.

of our exposition will be the way in which Aquinas' ability to characterize the creator as *ipsum esse subsistens* allows him to offer a way of articulating the singularity of the *relation* of creator to creation.[15] And since
the relation in question only emerges with the revelation of a free creator,
one could hardly expect the philosophical tools needed to articulate it to
be found ready to hand in Greek philosophy. Like "the distinction," this
relation will be unlike any that we can know between items in the universe. How then does Aquinas' strategic use of *esse* [existing] as *act* serve
to transform the metaphysical matrix which he had inherited, and had
determined to make available to Christian theology, thereby allowing him
to set at the center of his work something they had managed to overlook? And what does the ensuing *relation* look like?

To characterize creation in a manner faithful to the whole of the scriptures, creator and creatures must be related by a "non-reciprocal relation
of dependence."[16] Aquinas' reasoning to this special status for the
creator/creature relation coheres neatly with the uniqueness of
Sokolowski's "distinction":

> since God is altogether outside the order of creatures, since they are ordered
> to him but not he to them, it is clear that being related to God is a reality
> in creatures, but being related to creatures is not a reality in God; we say
> it about him because of the real relation in creatures.[17]

Those untutored in "the distinction" have misread this passage as stating
that the creator is "unrelated to the world" in the sense of being indifferent to it. But what Aquinas means by the "real relation" which he is
careful to deny of the creator is a reciprocal one which obtains between
two items in the universe, so denying reciprocity is but another way of
calling our attention to the fact that creatures have their very being from
the One who is, while that One's being in no way depends on creating.
Yet were one to think of God and creatures simply as two things, quite
naturally presuming them both to be items in the universe, to deny any
real relation between them would indeed be to separate one radically from

---

[15] Kathryn Tanner's way of articulating the relation as "non-contrastive" will also prove
useful in identifying its unique features: *God and Creation in Christian Theology* (Oxford:
Blackwell, 1988).

[16] The phrase is Sara Grant's, in her Teape lectures: *Toward an Alternative Theology: Confessions of a Non-Dualist Christian* (Bangalore: Asian Trading Corporation, 1991), p. 35, new
edition edited by Bradley Malkovsky (Notre Dame IN: University of Notre Dame Press,
2002), p. 40.

[17] ST 1.13.7.

the other. In the light of "the distinction," however, we shall see how denying that sort of reciprocal relation amounts rather to affirming an inexpressible intimacy of creature to creator which Sara Grant suggests is best expressed by Sankara's term "nonduality." Yet the metaphysical device needed to bridge the ostensible gap (or "infinite qualitative difference") between creator and creature will be *esse* as the "act of being" proper to each existing thing, with creatures participating in the *esse* which God is.[18]

Both *esse* and *participation*, however, are ways of attempting to express the inexpressible, for just as "the distinction" must be unlike any one we know, so a "nonreciprocal relation of dependence" cannot obtain between items within the universe. Metaphysics is being stretched to serve a revelation whose affirmations exceed its proper reach. As Sokolowski puts it: "the distinction is glimpsed on the margin of reason, [indeed] at the intersection of reason and faith."[19] This fact brings out better than any other a characteristic peculiar to thirteenth-century thought, notably that of Aquinas, and helps to account for the fragility of his synthesis. For reason and revelation need to function together as interlocking criteria, and do so in the face of conventional ways of distinguishing them which tend to separate their respective contributions, with reason ideally leading to knowledge in such a way that once something is known it need no longer be believed. Aquinas' deft recasting of Avicenna's distinction between essence [*mahiyya*] and existence [*wujûd*] to make *esse* to be *act* rather than *accident* already gestured towards an ineffable aspect of *esse*, since Aristotle had already remarked that we cannot define *act* so much as discover its presence by a string of examples marking the difference of waking from sleeping, seeing from looking, understanding from thinking. Since there is no potentiality at all (like that of thinking prior to understanding) to lead one into *ipsum esse subsistens*, however, it will utterly defy conceptualization; and the participated *esse* which creatures enjoy will share in that ineffability, given the fact that essences are what we can understand and classify.

That something we have thought of in fact exists can hardly follow from our thinking about it, nor can it be simply a "fact," in our sense of the term, either. There is an irruption to existing, signaled by Aquinas' using Aristotle's *energeia* to identify it, yet recognizing this singularity may

---

[18] "Infinite qualitative difference" is Kierkegaard's phrase, invoked simply to show how "the distinction" keeps re-appearing in different keys. For participation, see Rudi te velde, *Participation and Substantiality in Thomas Aquinas* (Leiden: Brill, 1995).
[19] Sokolowski 1995 (note 10), p. 39.

well require prior attention to the originating activity of the creator.[20] To bracket the origination of the universe, as modernity felt impelled to do, has the effect of dulling our sensibilities to the novelty of existing, inclining us to regard it a mere *given* rather than an undeserved *gift*, thereby allowing philosophers to move in accustomed conceptual paths which quite naturally privilege essence.[21]

Esse Freely Bestowed

That existing is "undeserved" is a logical (or "grammatical") point, of course, reminding us that there is nothing there to claim or even be given existence. So any talk of "possible worlds" being "actualized" can be nothing more than a *façon de parler*, and to my mind a grossly misleading one.[22] For as Aquinas had to remind Avicenna, the only possibility there can be prior to creation *ex nihilo* lies not "in the passive potentiality of matter, but [in] the active power of God" to create without presupposing anything at all.[23] What we can feel of that gratuity is the irruption, the utter novelty of something's existing. From the side of the agent, however, the action will have to be thoroughly intentional, both that the creator be a full-blooded agent, and that creation itself be pure gift.

That is the key to understanding the metaphysical challenge to Muslim, Jewish, and Christian thinkers: how to conceive the One from whom all-that-is freely emanates. Indeed, *emanation* remains the best corrective to the master metaphor of *artisan* in our attempt to capture the *sui generis* activity of creating.[24] Hence Aquinas will not hesitate to characterize creation as the "emanation of all of being from the universal principle of all being,"[25] even after he has taken pains to follow Moses Maimonides' lead

---

[20] David Braine remarks on the novelty characteristic of existing in his *Reality of Time and the Existence of God* (Oxford: Oxford University Press, 1988); Emilie Zum Brunn notes the intertwined character of revelation and reason in discovering the singularity of *esse* in her essay in *Dieu et l'Etre* (Paris: Etudes Augustiniennes, 1978), as well as the subsequent volume edited with Alain de Libera: *Celui qui est* (*Exodus 3:14*) (Paris: Cerf, 1986).

[21] For a characteristic "modern" take on Aquinas, which misses the primacy of *esse* even in his work, see Christopher Hughes, *On a Complex Theory of a Simple God* (Ithaca NY: Cornell University Press, 1989); for substantive reflections on overlooking origination, see George Steiner, *Real Presences* (London: Faber and Faber, 1989).

[22] See Barry Miller's treatment of this issue in *A Most Unlikely God* (Notre Dame IN: University of Notre Dame Press, 1998).

[23] ST 1.46.1.1.

[24] See my *Knowing the Unknowable God: Ibn Sina, Maimonides, Aquinas* (Notre Dame IN: University of Notre Dame Press, 1986).

[25] ST 1.45.1.

in eviscerating any hint of logical necessity associated with *emanation*. In fact, by following the scriptures to rehabilitate the master metaphor of artisan, he prepared the way for depicting the act of creation as a free act of practical reason, so implicitly upsetting the predilection for speculative reason endemic to Hellenic thought.[26] But how can we possibly understand the freedom peculiar to the One who creates without having to do so?

Our temptation, of course, will be to model it after a *decision*, or what is even more banal, a *choice* among "possible worlds." Decisions are normally more weighty than mere choices; it may even trivialize crucial decisions, like those involving a spouse or a vocation in life, to speak of them as "choices." Can we honestly say that we *choose* our spouse, out of a field of contenders; or that we reached out to grasp a vocation in life? Indeed, for the latter as well as the former, Jesus' words in the gospel of John sound far more fitting: "You did not choose me; I chose you" (John 15:16). There is a fittingness to our *accepting* our spouse or our vocation in life that moves the action closer to a kind of "necessity," to recognizing the truth of the path which opens before us. It is this experience which should lead us to question the current proclivity to identify human freedom with choosing, which "libertarians" simply presume, and then proceed to develop the intellectual apparatus to endorse.[27] As Aquinas implied, in his pithy resume of the Trinitarian structure inherent in creation properly conceived, the gracious move to creating a universe in the absence of any need whatsoever is best conceived as the One's acquiescing to the One's own inner constitution. What constitutes free creation, then, would be that gratuitous act of acquiescing, much as we consent to what we discern to be the good held out before us – whether it be spouse or vocation – in an act which is the very source of freedom without itself being a *choice* at all.[28]

Our freedom, of course, includes the possibility of refusing to acknowledge and to pursue that discerned good, and to that extent answers to a "libertarian" paradigm. But to refuse is to fail, and it should count deci-

---

[26] See my article which is included in the present volume as chapter 3: "Why not Pursue the Metaphor of Artisan and View God's Knowledge as Practical?"

[27] See Luis de Molina, *On Divine Foreknowledge* (Part IV of the "Concordia"), translated, with an introduction and notes, by Alfred J. Freddoso (Ithaca NY: Cornell University Press, 1988), xiv + 286 pp., Introduction, pp. 1–81; and Thomas P. Flint, *Divine Providence: The Molinist Account* (Cornell Studies in the Philosophy of Religion) (Ithaca NY: Cornell University Press, 1998).

[28] A clear rendition of this apparently paradoxical account can be found in Yves Simon, *Freedom of Choice* (New York: Fordham University Press, 1969).

sively against a libertarian account of freedom that it would propose a failure as the very paradigm of a free act. Again, what Aquinas' cryptic reference to the creator's inner Trinitarian life suggests is that creating is a fully gratuitous act, operating out of a fullness that needs no further completion. But of course, our experience could at best intimate such a state, since we are always in need of being fulfilled, even by what appear to be gracious acts of kindness. Only at our best, it seems, and then only in ecstatic moments, can we even imagine, must less execute, purely gratuitous acts. So an adequate account of God's freedom in creating will escape us in principle; hence Aquinas' prescient reference to a dimension of divinity which we could never reason to ourselves, but could only be revealed to us.

What proves significant here is the way in which this presumption is shared by Jewish and Muslim thinkers as well. Without the benefit of an explicitly Trinitarian revelation, both Moses Maimonides and al-Ghazali perceive clearly how the issue of free creation implies and is implied by the unanticipated and undeserved bestowal of the Torah and of the Qur'an, respectively. Indeed, it belongs to the ethos of Islam to insist that humankind needs to be alerted to the traces [ayât] of divine wisdom in the world by pondering the verses [ayât] of the Qur'an. One might indeed reason to the universe's origination, after the fashion of the Muslim falâsifa and in the spirit of Plotinus, but to see all that is as the "best possible" effect of divine wisdom requires God's revelatory initiative.[29] Yet once averred, the word of divine creative wisdom assumes center stage in creation. Here the testimony of revelation, as in the Qur'an's repeated avowal: "God said 'be' and it is," confirms the inference from metaphysics that creation involves no change at all![30] In literary terms shared by both Bible and Qur'an, everything is accomplished by God's merely speaking the creative word, the Word which is made Arabic in the Qur'an and human in Jesus. And that same Word, "by whom the universe is made" (John 1:10), structures the very order of the universe, which discloses traces of divine wisdom to those attuned to it.

Here is where the metaphysical theorem enunciating creation by identifying created esse as a participation in the esse subsistens of God joins the intentional discourse of word and wisdom to remind us just how elusive is the relation of creation to its creator. Kathryn Tanner has elaborated a set

[29]   Eric Ormsby, *Theodicy in Islamic Thought: The Dispute over al-Ghazali's "Best of all Possible Worlds"* (Princeton NJ: Princeton University Press, 1984), further explicated in his "Creation in Time in Islamic Thought with Special Reference to al-Ghazali," in David Burrell and Bernard McGinn, eds, *God and Creation* (Notre Dame IN: University of Notre Dame Press, 1990).
[30]   The classic statement is Aquinas' in ST 1.45.2.

of semantic rules to articulate properly what she calls a "non-contrastive" relation of creatures to their intentional creator.[31] The effort dovetails with Sokolowski's "distinction," as each reminds us that the creator cannot be "other than" creatures in the way in which one creature is other than another. Sara Grant carries this mode of thought a step further to make a highly suggestive connection with Sankara's *advaita*, proposing that we read Aquinas' determination that creation consists in a "non-reciprocal relation of dependence" in creatures as a western attempt to articulate what Sankara calls "non-duality."[32] For is that not what the "non-contrastive" relation between creator and creatures comes to, in our terms: not *other*, yet not the *same* either? What has long been regarded as sharply differentiating western from eastern thought turns out to be a conceptual illusion on our part: we did think that we could adequately distinguish God from creatures and readily accused Hindu thought of failing to do so. Charges of "monism" used to abound; can they be sustained? We must also revise, as I have suggested, any sharp difference between emanation properly understood (that is, no longer identified with its model of logical inference) and free creation, perhaps coming to regard these two schemes as complementary ways of articulating what defies proper conceptualization. Here a study of Aquinas' dicta would have to be complemented by an examination of Meister Eckhart's assertions regarding these matters, allowing for a signal difference in the genre of their writings as well as the goal of their respective inquiries.[33] Aquinas' goal was to show how and in what respect *theologia* could be a *scientia* (where both terms become ambiguous for modern readers when translated), while Eckhart, presuming that work had been accomplished, could focus on plumbing the implications of the teaching itself.

Whatever may be the results of such an inquiry, which I shall do little more than sketch here, they would reveal a dimension of Christian philosophical theology in the creative medieval period that is closer in spirit to the mode of inquiry which Pierre Hadot finds in ancient philosophy, one replete with "spiritual exercises," than to the "scholasticism" which emerged from the fourteenth century.[34] I have repeatedly tried to show

---

[31] Cf. note 15.

[32] Cf. note 16.

[33] I am indebted to a conversation with Stacey Wendlinder, currently a doctoral candidate at Notre Dame working on Eckhart, for proposing this way of suggesting the difference between them.

[34] Pierre Hadot's original work, *Exercises spirituels et philosophie antique* (2nd edn 1987) is now out of print, but an excellent summary of his thought is available in his *Qu'est-ce que la philosophie antique?* (Paris: Gallimard, 1995) and a superb collection of his articles has been translated and presented by Arnold Davidson: *Philosophy as a Way of Life* (Oxford: Blackwell, 1995).

how reading Aquinas in this way can open us to some crucial turns in his thought which a merely propositional assimilation can easily overlook.[35] Perhaps our reflections on the difficulty of articulating the relation of creatures to their creator can help us identify the point here: something must *show* the inadequacy of discourse, especially when the aim of the writer – in this case, Aquinas – is to articulate the realities of *theologia* as adequately as is humanly possible by showing how the study of "God and the things of God" can be fashioned into a kind of *scientia*.[36] Yet like Eckhart, once we have apprenticed ourselves to that inquiry, we are brought to regard the differences between this inquiry and *scientia* as even more relevant than the ways in which one can be assimilated to the other; or better still, we become aware of the multiple ways in which Aquinas himself stretched and even transformed the shape of *scientia* as well as many of its key categories, to make his point. It is worth noting how this recognition differs from that of many Thomists in the early twentieth century, who were intent on showing how adequately Aquinas rendered Christian thought as a coherent *philosophy*, that is, as the modern analogue of *scientia*. Current reflections on Aquinas as theologian, albeit as philosophical theologian, point in the other direction: towards reason and faith as mutually normative in any profound human inquiry into the origins or goals of existence.[37]

Faith as a Mode of Knowing

Even to suggest that faith and reason might complement one another in executing human inquiry is to move beyond the thought categories of modernism, where speaking of faith as a mode of knowing would have displayed a severe breach of etiquette, if not constituted an oxymoron. Alasdair MacIntyre's trenchant argumentation designed to show how any human inquiry must be tradition-directed recalls John Henry Newman's *Grammar of Assent*, composed to counter a set of Cartesian presumptions regarding paradigmatic rational inquiry in the heyday of modernity, the

[35] First in *Exercises in Religious Understanding* (Notre Dame IN: University of Notre Dame Press, 1974) and more extensively in *Aquinas: God and Action* (Notre Dame IN: University of Notre Dame Press, 1979).
[36] The title of M.-D. Chenu's masterpiece, *Théologie comme science dans la treizième siècle*, says it all with that delicate "*comme.*"
[37] See my "Theology and Philosophy," in Gareth Jones, ed., Blackwell *Companion to Modern Theology* (Oxford: Blackwell, 2004).

latter half of the nineteenth century.[38] The relevance of his reflective study today aptly confirms his observation that ideas have their time. Yet if the mutual normativity of faith and reason exemplifies the thirteenth century, while cleanly separating (if not opposing) them characterizes modernity, the move to postmodernity — however that protean term be construed — is intent (in its constructive mode) on seeking proper contexts for the exercise of reason. Indeed, the mood has shifted so palpably that we need to remind ourselves just how self-sufficient rationalist reason claimed to be, as it would have found the current cliché — that we have lost our faith in reason — a clear oxymoron. Nor should we be surprised to find affinities between medieval and contemporary thought; only the inevitably Hegelian overtones of the expression "premodern" make it paradoxical to link pre- with postmodern. Overtones of the Hegel, that is, who taught us to think in terms of linear development, yet if, as I am suggesting, the relationship between the thought forms at issue here is more properly dialectical, another Hegel will remain our guide.

If we can succeed in bracketing, or better yet, excoriating the model of progressive development, the connection between medieval and some forms of postmodern discourse will emerge more clearly. We might think of it in the following dialectical manner. Modernity was fairly constituted by a quite specific opposition to medieval thought, as we have noted, so could be called "post" or even "antimedieval." I have noted how this mode of thinking proceeded by avoiding, if not aggressively removing, any reference to creation and the creator/creature relation. It would follow from that characterization that some forms of "postmodern," in the sense of "antimodern," discourse would display affinities with medieval inquiry, since "postmodern" could be translated as "anti-antimedieval." These observations operate at a level of excessive generality, of course, and the overlap will always be imperfect, since it is never the same things that are denied, nor in the same way; yet displaying the dialectics of the matter in this way should allow us to expect the affinities which have in fact emerged. John Paul II's recent encyclical, *Fides et Ratio* [*Faith and Reason*], illustrates this dynamic, as does a friend's remark that the Pope's offering faith as the fruitful context within which reason can flourish would have left Voltaire speechless. Yet the fact remains that we have "lost our faith in reason," and that the mode of reflection characteristic of Aquinas and other medieval luminaries may well be poised to show us a way in which these two — faith and reason — are inextricably in need of one another.

---

[38] See Nicholas Lash's introduction to his edition of the *Essay in Aid of a Grammar of Assent* (Notre Dame IN: University of Notre Dame Press, 1979).

For that conviction suffuses their writings, while many realities conspire to bring us to it in the wake of the failure of modernism to sustain itself.

One further dimension, especially relevant to this colloquium, will display affinities between our period and the medievals which historical scholarship mostly managed to avoid until recently; that is the interfaith dimension. It is significant that Aquinas turned to "Rabbi Moses" as a key interlocutor in developing his project of enlisting reason to elucidate faith, and that Avicenna's distinction of *esse* from *essence*, suitably transformed, offered Aquinas just the tool he needed to appropriate Hellenic philosophy to his purposes. In that sense, the classical Christian synthesis wrought largely at the hands of Aquinas can be seen to have already been an intercultural, interfaith achievement. The relationship is more inherent and dialectical than it is one of traceable "influence," though Aquinas did read Maimonides' *Guide of the Perplexed* as soon as it was translated into Latin, and we can easily trace at least five central strategies which Aquinas adopted from him.[39] In the endeavor which Maimonides and Aquinas shared, al-Ghazali would have been a more relevant Islamic interlocutor than Ibn Sina, but the only work of his which Aquinas knew was the *Aims of the Philosophers*, which is little more than a recasting of Avicenna's summary of "philosophy" composed in Persian, the *Danesh Nameh*.[40] So Aquinas never encountered his Islamic counterpart struggling with faith/reason issues as Maimonides had, yet we can do so, and with great profit. In sum, the capacity to find analogies in the ways that thinkers from other faiths utilize reason to illuminate and critically appropriate their tradition can offer us a strategy for comparative understanding whose results are not unlike those claimed for "natural law"-type inquiries, with the decided advantage that we need not claim anything more for "natural law" than the fact that the key notions in such questions prove to be inter-translatable in the minimal sense of providing fruitful comparisons.

[39] See my "Aquinas' Debt to Maimonides" included in the present volume as chapter 5.
[40] An English translation of this work by David Burrell and Tony Street will be published by Brigham young University Press. For the text history, see J. Janssens, "Le *Dánesh-Námeh* d'Ibn Sina: un texte a revoir?," in *Bulletin de philosophie mediévale* 28 (1986), pp. 173–7, followed by a more extensive study of "Al-Ghazâlî, and his use of Avicennian texts" published in the acts of the 1996 Budapest symposium on "Problems in Arabic Philosophy."

Chapter 10

FREEDOM AND CREATION IN THE ABRAHAMIC TRADITIONS

It may seem redundant to remind ourselves how much intellectual explorations are stimulated and guided by cultural factors attending the lives of the inquirers, but philosophers especially need to be reminded of such obvious things. It was John Henry Newman, who found himself having to remind philosophers of many such things, who remarked that ideas have their time. And the living proof of that contention is the current relevance of his *Grammar of Assent,* composed (in 1867?) as a powerful corrective to rationalistic accounts of human reasoning in the teeth of an overweening confidence in human progress attributed to contextless reason.[1] A little more than a century later, when we find ourselves having lost faith both in progress and in reason, his argument proves more compelling than ever. Moreover, a variant of his argument has just been put forward by John Paul II (in *Fides et Ratio*), contending that the proper exercise of reason requires a context of trust or faith, so that it makes sense to speak of "our having lost faith in reason," as "postmodernists" are wont to do and to display, whereas such an expression must have sounded oxymoronic to enlightenment thinkers in Newman's time.[2] (To grasp just how bizarre a shift that has been, think of Voltaire hearing that

---

[1] Consult preferably Nicholas Lash's edition of Newman's *An Essay in Aid of a Grammar of Assent* (Notre Dame IN: University of Notre Dame Press, 1979) for its illuminating introduction, yet also note the way in which Joseph Dunne utilizes Newman to initiate his recovery of Aristotle's *phronesis* in his *Back to the Rough Ground* (Notre Dame IN: University of Notre Dame Press, 1993).

[2] An English translation of the encyclical letter of John Paul II, *Faith and Reason,* can be obtained from the Publication Service of the National Conference of Catholic

the "Pope of Rome" had just issued a screed in defense of reason!) It is
in this context that I propose to explore issues which we Americans
thought we had resolved at our inception, and have indeed been busy
promoting throughout the world ever since: issues of freedom.[3]

I shall argue that *freedom* — and notably the tendency we have to identify the notion itself with our cherished set of views regarding human
freedom — will prove to be as contentious as *reason*; indeed, that we may
soon find ourselves losing faith in that conception of freedom (if we have
not already) and rather than busy ourselves promoting it with missionary
zeal, should begin to inquire what we might learn from others regarding
freedom itself. Moreover, the task of bringing these unconscious presumptions to the surface will prove to be an appropriately philosophical
one, as well as one which will find itself learning a great deal from historical as well as comparative inquiries. Finally, in that curious reversal of
Hegel by which postmodern thought finds itself learning from modes of
reflection which we had been taught to call "premodern," I shall argue
that those very religious worldviews which the Enlightenment explicitly
rejected for averring the universe to be freely created by one God will
prove to be the ones which offer us a yet more coherent view of human
freedom than the prevailing one of "autonomy," traceable initially to John
Duns Scotus only to be elaborated by Kant.[4] Again, modernist thinkers
confirmed in their progressive view of human understanding by Hegel,
must find this proposal as unwelcome as Voltaire would find the Pope's
defense of reason! So we shall have to proceed gingerly, contending as we
shall be with so many presumptions — at once modern and American —
which may well seem axiomatic to "our way of life."

The century which separates John Paul II's *Fides et Ratio* from Leo
XIII's *Veterum Sapientiae*, however, will allow us properly to distinguish
these reflections intent on retrieving some medieval wisdom from a project

---

Bishops, Washington DC. For a complementary treatment of these issues, see my "Theology and Philosophy," in Gareth Jones, ed., *Cambridge Companion to Modern Theology*
(Cambridge: Cambridge University Press, 2004).
[3] The current contentious debate surrounding the work of John Courtney Murray is a
vivid illustration of the dimensions of *freedom* which have emerged even since his writings
on the subject. See Todd David Whitmore and J. Leon Cooper, S.J., eds., *John Courtney
Murray and the Growth of Tradition* (Kansas City MO: Sheed and Ward, 1996), especially the
contributions by David Hollenbach and Todd Whitmore.
[4] For an anti-Hegelian argument exposing the manifest affinities one finds between
"postmodern" and "premodern" modes of thought, see my "The Challenge to Medieval
Christian Philosophy: Relating Creator to Creatures" included in this volume as chapter 9
and to signal my continuing debt to John Milbank, see his set of essays: *The Word made
Strange: Theology, Language, Culture* (Oxford: Blackwell, 1997), especially "The Second Difference," pp. 171–93.

called to formulate a *philosophia perennis*. What intervenes is a critical appropriation of a view of human history which can appreciate the processes of development inherent in human thought, while rejecting the Hegelian corollaries which deem those processes unilinear and progressive, effectively rendering the past irremediably *past*. Yet once the past has been rendered *past*, any effort to learn from it will parallel that needed to learn from other traditions, so both enterprises will involve encountering what is or has been made to be "other." Engaging in a retrieval of our own past may indeed prove to be more of a homecoming, since (as Michel Foucault's inquiries constantly remind us) the inescapable archaeology of thought will find traces of earlier strata reflected in the rejections which have marked its historical stages. Yet the homecoming will also prove to be enlightening, and more so for the effort expended in retrieving the origins of one's thought, so there can be no hope of such efforts issuing in a *philosophia perennis*. (Note that the very project of retrieving, and especially of learning from, what has gone before us counters so directly the presumptions governing "historicism" that the tendency of some to label anything critical of the project of "perennial philosophy" *historicist* will miss the way our proposal represents more of a *via media*, at once beholden to and critical of modern "historical consciousness.")[5] Let us then proceed to delineate those dimensions of medieval thought – Jewish, Christian, and Muslim – which may prove illuminating to us.

Introducing Medieval Conceptions of Freedom by Sharpening the Differences

We will only be able to recognize the crucial role which creation plays for medieval Jewish, Christian, and Muslim thinkers if we begin by contrasting the free creation which they propound with then current Hellenic schemes of necessary emanation (which philosophers of the time thought to be the only respectable strategies), and then proceed to recall

---

[5]   In this respect, we are all grateful to Alasdair MacIntyre for blazing this "middle" trail, especially in the work which culminates his extended argument: *Three Rival Versions of Moral Enquiry* (Notre Dame IN: University of Notre Dame Press, 1990). Indeed, the failure to appreciate this properly dialectical dimension of his presentation mars the otherwise illuminating essay of Thomas F. O'Meara, O.P.: "Virtues in the Theology of Thomas Aquinas," in *Theological Studies* 58 (1997), pp. 254–85. Perhaps my own involvement in the parallel project of finding "mutual illumination" from other traditions, however, inclines me to favor John Milbank's contention (over against MacIntyre) that the arguments we propose to assess other traditions can at best be rhetorical and not demonstrative in nature. See his discussion with MacIntyre in *Theology and Social Theory* (Oxford: Blackwell, 1993).

how a concerted attempt to circumvent creation stamped modernity. And in the spirit of this inquiry, we must regard these two poles as quite distinct, for though many moderns tried simply to return to the Greeks, they could only do so by deliberately side-stepping creation, and so in effect denying it. For while Aristotle could simply presume that the universe always was, and the Neoplatonic emanation schemes disallowed any personal agency, medieval efforts to transform both by relating the universe explicitly to a free creator represented an achievement which could hardly be ignored. It would have to be repudiated, at least in practice, in order to be circumvented. Indeed, the motivation to replace symbolic or metaphorical thinking with literal assertion, which so marked philosophy after Descartes and has been credited with setting the stage for the development of modern science, can be seen as part of this attempt no longer to view the universe as created, as an effect with traces of its agent, but as itself autonomous and so open to the probing inquiry of human intelligence. Yet as we shall see, especially in relation to articulating human freedom, the faith-assertion of free creation by an intentional agent whose wisdom then suffused the universe will prove to be a more plausible grounding for sustaining scientific inquiry, yet the denials which modernity deemed essential to its project will force it to operate in a less metaphysical and more pragmatic vein, whereby science will come to be justified by its technological achievements.

But what was really lost by this denial, whether implicit or explicit, since even the medievals never claimed that this unique relation could be formulated? What difference would the universe exhibit when the creator is removed from consideration, when never a trace of it could be found when it was averred? (Aquinas was clear about this: the only *similarity* one can assert between creator and creatures is that each can be said to exist, but besides God's existing *in se* while creatures exist by virtue of the creator, so that their "qualitative difference" is, as Kierkegaard would say, "infinite," *existing* cannot be a discernible feature of anything.)[6] Furthermore, it seems that the laws of nature would be no different, since "the distinction" between creatures and creator does not derogate from natural necessities; in fact, it confirms them.[7] Perhaps, however, a difference would show in that portion of the universe said to be able to relate to all-that-is, and hence deserving of the name "spiritual." That will be my con-

[6] ST 1.4.3; Soren Kierkegaard, *Sickness unto Death*, Part 2, Ch. 1 (London: Penguin, 1989), pp. 111–20.
[7] Robert Sokolowski, *The God of Faith and Reason* (Notre Dame IN: University of Notre Dame Press, 1982/Washington DC: Catholic University of America Press, 1995).

tention: that human freedom best displays the difference which modernity deliberately wrought over against medieval thought, and that this difference turns uniquely on affirming or overlooking (and in effect denying) creation as a constitutive relation structuring whatever exists. As a result, postmedieval thought had no choice but to construe free agents as self-starters. Yet while this view bore a *prima facie* resemblance to Aristotle's contention – constitutive of our legal fabric – that human agency must be uncaused if we humans are to be deemed responsible for our actions, exposing the differences will help us to see why what we spontaneously regard as problematic will prove to offer a more coherent alternative to our quite incoherent view of human freedom.

Roderick Chisholm led me to this insight about the modernist conception of freedom when he noted, in a 1964 lecture, that libertarian freedom demands that the free agent be, as it were, an Aristotelian prime mover.[8] The allusion to Aristotle is inaccurate, of course, since Aristotle's "prime mover" moves all there is by "being desired," so is an agent in a very special sense. What Chisholm meant, however, was that free agents would have to be themselves uncaused in their actions, and so have to initiate things *de novo*, as it were. So he was really suggesting that human persons thought to be free, in this sense, would each have to be creators in their own right. A great deal could be presupposed, of course, so free actions would not have to emerge *ex nihilo*; but with respect to their freedom, no other agents could be so decisively within range as to dilute individuals' taking responsibility for what they have done. And least of all, God who to many philosophers, seems to be the "biggest thing around." (We shall see that an early Islamic attempt to account for human freedom would take just such a tack, but for the moment let us follow the dialectic train suggested by Chisholm.) In characteristic "libertarian" fashion, freedom is equated with choosing, and the initiative must come from the agents themselves, or more specifically, from their individual wills. So absent a creator, we must each be creators, and as Nietszche would insist, of ourselves first of all.

Let us preview the medieval alternative to such a view by introducing three protagonists, each representing an Abrahamic tradition, presented in the actual order of their historical appearance: al-Ghazali, Moses Maimonides, and Thomas Aquinas.[9] Each of their traditions is deeply com-

---

[8]   Published in Gary Watson, ed., *Free Will* (New York: Oxford University Press, 1982) as "Human Freedom and the Self," pp. 24–35, citation at p. 26.
[9]   For a more detailed treatment of these three, see my *Freedom and Creation in Three Traditions* (Notre Dame IN: University of Notre Dame Press, 1993).

mitted to human freedom in the sense of attributing responsibility to individuals, so differences will reflect the ways that is formulated, especially in the face of asserting that everything is created by one God, and freely so. Al-Ghazali profited by the way his guide in such matters, al-Ash'ari, had already criticized the earlier Mu'tazilite view. For they had presumed that free actions were tantamount to creations, so restricted God's creative activity to the world of nature, with humans creating and thus responsible for everything in their domain. Yet however effective that solution may have been to save God from perpetrating evil, it removed a vast domain from the sovereignty of the creator-of-all, clearly offending the plain sense of the Qur'an. So Ghazali signed on to the solution proposed by al-Ash'ari: indeed, everything is created by God, including evil actions, yet created agents are themselves responsible for performing them. Maimonides' formulations go into less detail, although he insists that the Torah is explicit on the fact of human freedom (notably in Deuteronomy), and since observance is primary for Jews, action needs to be underscored. Maimonides, however, was far more interested in knowing than doing, so he rests content to explicate freedom as practical reason, following the lead of Aristotle. Aquinas' treatment is the most sophisticated, coming as he did in his tradition after Augustine's decisive explorations of the language of *will*. Yet intellect and will are hardly separate for Aquinas, and his treatment of *will* itself as "intellectual hunger" is thoroughly Aristotelian, incorporating (as Aristotle himself does) Plato's legacy of will as hunger for "the good."

We shall soon consider these treatments in greater detail, to show illuminating similarities and differences, yet one thing is already clear for all of them: *will* names the appetitive dimension of human beings, the affective dimension of our inquiring selves. So it cannot simply be what motivates externally, as it were, like profit! It must rather be what allows us joy in discovery, and so lets us be drawn on to more, as we can recognize in ourselves undertaking an intellectual inquiry for the sheer delight of understanding. We need only recall how Plato's *Phaedrus* explicitly elaborates the *eros* required to answer the leading question of the *Republic*: why lead an exemplary life? Goals of that sort are not extrinsic to the activities themselves, but inherent in their undertaking. Such is Aquinas' portrayal of intellect-cum-will as we pursue our goals, and it is a picture shared by Maimonides and Ghazali as well, though less explicitly developed. The essential ingredients remain Aristotle's account of practical reason and Plato's *eros* for "the Good."[10] The goals we actually pursue may

---

[10]   Alasdair MacIntyre's treatment in *After Virtue* (Notre Dame IN: University of Notre Dame Press, 1981) remains the best contemporary presentation of these issues.

be quite unethical, of course, yet we are constrained to regard them as good. Yet not for long, Plato hopes, as our discerning intellect will begin to recognize what dissonance there may be between our putative goods and "the good." Or as Aristotle would put it, we are constantly assessing whether our goals are indeed *good*. We need to remind ourselves of this central point, since it entails that the will cannot be entirely "free" (in our accustomed sense) if we are to act freely! For it has no *choice* – which we spontaneously identify with freedom – about its orientation to "the good;" that belongs to it *naturally*. One can see, then, why Jean-Paul Sartre had to insist that human beings have no "nature," and why Sartrean freedom is incoherent from this classical perspective – nor does it seem to be any more feasible in practice!

All this implies that we cannot *do* anything about our primordial orientation to "the good;" whatever we undertake we must regard as *good*, though we can and indeed must continually assess whether these undertakings contribute to or detract from "the good." But is that not in fact what we are always doing? Indeed, wondering about the relation of short- to long-term goals is thoroughly Aristotelian. So freedom as we exercise it and normally think about it fits quite nicely with a classical view. Difficulties rather arise in the face of an intervening philosophical construction, called "libertarian." My extended argument is designed to show that view to be both incoherent and ill-fitting our practice. As we shall see, everything turns on whether we equate freedom with choice, as libertarians must; or see choosing as imbedded in a larger venture called "freedom." If freedom is identified with choosing, then the goal will be irrelevant; all we need to do to be free is to choose. If freedom is more than choosing, however, then the goal will be ingredient to our exercising our freedom. Yet liberal political theory asserts that freedom is equivalent to choice, while coherent political practice demands that freedom be more than choice, that the goals be ingredient in the practice of freedom.[11] No wonder we are so confused about freedom!

To see whether and how these medieval Jewish, Christian, and Muslim thinkers can help bring us to greater clarity, let us try to understand how it was that modern liberal theory replaced the classical view. If our narrative is accurate in the main, it will help us to deconstruct our current presumption by playing it backwards to the sources of difference. Three monumental western thinkers quite literally stand between us and our

---

[11]   Robert Bellah and his group have been telling us this, in slightly different terms, for some time. See their *Habits of the Heart* (New York: Harper and Row, 1985) and *The Good Society* (New York: Harper and Row, 1994).

three medieval witnesses of Muslim, Jewish, and Christian views of these matter: John Duns Scotus, Francisco Suarez, and Immanuel Kant. Scotus was the first to rupture Aquinas' careful symbiosis of will with intellect by introducing the will as an agent in its own right, whose "elicited act" (*actus elicitus*) emerged spontaneously from this power, thereby identifying will as the source of agency. Scotus would insist, of course, that the will needed to be informed by the intellect, but his use of the verb *informare* was now bereft of that robust Aristotelian sense (in which Aquinas used it) according to which matter is *informed* by what gives it its proper shape and direction, form. Here it has more the sense of will consulting intellect for directions, and then operating itself.[12] However complex Scotus' thought may be to unravel, it was communicated quite successfully in the late middle ages via the highly influential works of Francisco Suarez, who taught generations of scholars to read the medievals through the distinctions and perspective of Scotus.[13] Finally, in a new context which he would help define as "modern," Immanuel Kant rendered the will more autonomous than ever by removing it from appetite. Aquinas' description of will as a "rational appetite" became an oxymoron after Kant's metaphysical confirmation of Descartes' mind/body duality by relegating appetite to the world of nature, and will to the noumenal realm, in such a way that only wills can be good.[14]

What have all of these accounts in common? That they see human beings as self-starters, which presents a decisive break with medievals who saw human beings as responders. For medievals, in concert with what Aristotle inherited from Plato, human life has a single, over-riding goal. Translating "the good" by virtue of the revelations granted to them, these thinkers would concur in the formula which is most clearly illustrated in Islam: to return everything to the One from whom we have received everything. The initiator is then the creator, with creation taking the form of an *exitus*, and human beings given the place of the vehicles through whom this *exitus* becomes a *reditus*. Bereft of this scheme, which for our thinkers was a corollary of their act of faith in an intentional creation, the special status of human beings becomes a function entirely of their freedom and its exercise. Moreover, the freedom involved is a sign of their

---

[12] See William Frank, "Duns Scotus on Autonomous Freedom and Divine Co-Causality," in *Medieval Philosophy and Theology* 2 (1992), pp. 142–64.

[13] See Jean-François Courtine, *Suarez et le système de la metaphysique* (Paris: Presses univérsitaires de France, 1990).

[14] See Bonnie Kent, *Virtues of the Will: The Transformation of Ethics in the Late Thirteenth Century* (Washington DC: Catholic University of America Press, 1995).

status as originators, so it is this characteristic which must be championed. That is what we call "modernity."

The Role *Creation* Plays in Medieval Thought

The *exitus/reditus* scheme was not itself a product of these faith-traditions; indeed, it first emerges as a competitor to them, in Plotinus.[15] Yet when Muslims first encountered Hellenic strains of thought, early Islamic philosophers simply adopted it as an altogether natural expression of the Qur'an's insistence: "God says 'be' and it is" (40.68).[16] It was al-Ghazali who first challenged this assimilation of the Qur'an to Plotinus, yet Maimonides followed suit from the perspective of the Torah, while Aquinas gave the "necessary emanation" scheme its *coup de grace* by declaring it utterly redundant in the face of a free creator, an intentional "cause of being" (*causa essendi*). Yet as we shall see, the *exitus/reditus* scheme, serving now as a powerful metaphor, remained the dominant image linking creatures with creator, with human beings serving the unique place as vehicle of the return. Ghazali had to operate on two fronts: one in theological discourse (*kalâm*), where he was fully at home yet sensed its limitations; and the other in "philosophy" (*falasifa*), which he assiduously learned, if only to clip its pretensions to offer a total explanation of the universe in its coming forth from the One.[17]

On the side of *kalâm*, as we have noted, he rejected the key presumption of the early Islamic Mut'azilite school – that a full-fledged agent must be a creator; and signed on to the resolution of al-Ash'ari, that followers of the Qur'an must acknowledge that everything is created by God, human acts included – good or bad, but these actions are freely performed by their created agents.[18] With regard to al-Farâbi and Ibn Sina, the

[15] For a sympathetic account of Plotinus, see Lloyd Gerson, *Plotinus* (London: Routledge, 1998).

[16] See David Burrell, C.S.C., *Knowing the Unknowable God: Ibn Sina, Maimonides, Aquinas* (Notre Dame IN: University of Notre Dame Press, 1986) for an account of al-Farabi and Ibn Sina's role.

[17] Ghazali is best known in the history of philosophy for his critical *Tahafut al-falasifa*, recently translated by Michael Marmura (Ogden UT: Brigham Young University Press, 1998), yet the western medievals knew only his expository treatise (largely beholden to the Persian work of Avicenna, *Danesh Nameh*), *Maqâsid al-falâsifa* ("Aims of the Philosophers"), translated by David Burrell and Tony Street, to be published by Brigham Young University Press.

[18] For an attempt to make clear sense of this contested doctrine of *kasb* (or *iktisâb*), see Richard Frank, "Moral Obligation in Classical Muslim Theology," in *Journal of Religious*

"philosophers" (*falâsifa*), Ghazali took their adherence to the scheme of necessary emanation, as a way of articulating Islamic faith in free creation, to run contrary to the Qur'an on three crucial counts: that the First would not be free to create or not, that the First could not know individuals, and that the Neoplatonic flavor of the scheme inevitably turned "resurrection of the body" into "immortality of the soul." This summary judgment, leveled in the *Tahâfût*, would render this classical form of Islamic philosophy quite useless for elucidating Muslim faith, which would have to wait for a resurgence in the Muslim heartland, triggered by the "Sheik of Islam," Ibn al-Arabi.[19]

On the part of Judaism, Moses Maimonides reinforced al-Ghazali by insisting that "necessary emanation" militated against God's giving of the Torah, thereby corroborating the inner connection between free creation and revelation that would come to characterize all three traditions. In fact, he engages in a careful hermeneutic analysis to show that Aristotle never proved an everlasting universe, but rather simply presumed that motion had always to have been, since he never managed to arrive at a "cause of being."[20] Throughout his extended argument, Maimonides simply presumes (as did Ghazali) that an everlasting universe leaves no room for free creation, in which he conflates *creatio ex nihilo* with *creatio de novo* – that is, not simply that nothing is presupposed to creation, but that it takes place such that there is an initial moment of time.[21] For both Maimonides and Ghazali, this is simply what it means to speak of a "free creator."

Aquinas declares his indebtedness to both by concurring with Maimonides that neither position – everlasting or temporal creation – admits of proof, yet he refuses to foreclose the conceptual possibility of a free creator (in the biblical or Qur'anic sense) creating everlastingly. In short, it need not be part of the meaning of "free creator" that there exists an initial moment of time. He does concede that postulating an initial

---

Ethics 11 (1983), pp. 204–23, esp. note 19; yet Daniel Gimaret's criticism of Frank's resolution should also be consulted: *La Doctrine d'al-Ash'ari* (Paris: Cerf, 1990), pp. 371–72, esp. note 1.

[19] Sayyed Hossain Nasr has reminded us of this lacuna in western scholarship; see his *Islamic Life and Thought* (SUNY, 1981).

[20] Maimonides, *The Guide for the Perplexed*, trans. Schlomo Pines (Chicago: University of Chicago Press, 1956).

[21] See William Dunphy's "Maimonides and Aquinas on Creation: A Critique of their Historians," in Lloyd Gerson's festschrift for Joseph Owens: *Graceful Reason* (Toronto: Pontifical Institute of Mediaeval Studies, 1983), pp. 361–80; also Seymour Feldman's account: "'In the Beginning God Created': A Philosophical Midrash," in David Burrell and Bernard McGinn, eds, *God and Creation* (Notre Dame IN: University of Notre Dame Press, 1990), pp. 3–26.

moment would make the case more evident, as "creationists" welcomed the "big bang" of astrophysics, but strictly speaking, the case for creation *de novo* rests solely with revelation. Nothing would prevent a free creator from originating the universe in such a way that nothing at all were presupposed (and so *ex nihilo*) yet such that it had always existed. (There is no conceptual difficulty with an eternal God creating an everlasting universe, precisely because one can clearly distinguish the *eternity* which characterizes God alone from a temporality without beginning.) So Aquinas succeeded in opening more conceptual space than either Ghazali or Maimonides had allowed, which is perhaps why he could then be more amenable to using emanation as an image or metaphor, once he had gutted it as a proper conceptual strategy. But the major fruit of his expressly counterfactual exploration of creation without a beginning (*ex nihilo* yet not *de novo*) is to have located the paradigmatic meaning of creation as dependence in existing.

Creator as Intentional "Cause of Being": Implications for Created Freedom

What united these three thinkers – working serially so that the next one could profit from whomever preceded him – was their insistence that the creator who is the cause of being is also an intentional cause, for what was at stake for each was an articulation of free creation as found in their respective revelations. How might this complex articulation of the First or the One as the free source of all contribute to our understanding of human freedom? First, as cause of being, there is no competition with the creatures whose being it causes; and as intentional agent, the creator is open to a personal relationship with created persons. Second, as cause of being it is the source of all perfections, and as intentional agent, the focus of gratitude on the part of creatures able to recognize such a One as source of their being and well-being. A cause of being is clearly not one of Aristotle's four candidates for *cause*. Of another order, its causation does not compete with a creature's causing, even if its causation must on that account be pervasive. That is, even though it is true to say that "when Muhammad threw, it was God who threw" (Qur'an 8.17), we cannot then infer that God made Muhammad throw, but rather that "God makes it to be that (Muhammad throws)."[22] Moreover, to be cause of being, it must

---

be God's nature simply to exist, yet the *existing* at issue here is not a minimal floor to which anything further must be added, but the source of all operative perfections.[23] So also to speak of the cause of being as an intentional agent effectively draws out the implications of what it means to be a "cause of being," thereby reinforcing Plotinus' powerful *exitus/reditus* scheme by rendering it in a more personal idiom.

To return to the original motivation of these articulations, the avowal of free creation by Jews, Muslims, and Christians has elicited a searching philosophical inquiry into origins – the very step which Aristotle failed to take. That inquiry has turned up a relationship which philosophy itself cannot quite articulate satisfactorily: a creator who is cause of being, together with everything else whose very existence displays a "non-reciprocal relation of dependence."[24] Robert Sokolowski celebrates this unique relation as "the distinction," arguing as well that it is a paradigmatically "Christian distinction," which turns the universe itself into a "new kind of whole" – indeed, a *gift* rather than a mere *given*, so *existing* becomes a perfection bestowed rather than a "value-neutral" precondition for all that a creature might become.[25] By calling attention to the utterly unique "distinction" which creation introduces, a phenomenologist like Sokolowski can display how revelation allows us to do what Kant eschewed doing, namely, to speak of the universe as a whole; yet at the same time show us how prescient it was of Kant to resist incorporating so unique a relation into his philosophical system. The conscious sector of that universe then become more fully agents as they respond to this gift with gratitude, which bespeaks the original shape of Jewish and Christian, as well as Muslim prayer. So the glory of a human being is to respond rather than originate; responding is the creativity proper to creatures.

All this may well seem like a come-down from Nietszchean self-assertion. It certainly did seem so to the early modernists who sought an alternative to the medieval world view long before Nietszche. Yet whatever their motivations, our "postmodern" perspective invites us to ask our-

---

[23]   For a summary of the issues at stake here, together with a list of sources for the discussion, see my "Simpleness" in Brian Davies, O.P., ed., *Philosophy of Religion* (London: Cassell, 1998), pp. 70–4.

[24]   The phrase is Sara Grant's in her *Towards an Alternative Theology: Confessions of a Non-Dualist Christian* (Bangalore: Asian Trading Corporation, 1991), with a new edition ed. Bradley Malkovsky (Notre Dame IN: University of Notre Dame Press, 2002); and while it is formulated with regard to Sankara, it is inspired by Aquinas' account in ST 1.44–6.

[25]   Sokolowski (note 7), as well as my attempt to show this "distinction" operative in each of the Abrahamic faiths: "The Christian Distinction Celebrated and Expanded," included as chapter 14 in this volume.

selves whether it makes sense to equate freedom simply with choosing, no matter what the results; or whether the proper exercise of human freedom entails situating human creativity in a larger "ecological" context? If the history of modernity has led us to this point, the medieval context of creation can offer us a powerful alternative model, if not an enticing invitation to a different form of life. When human beings are regarded primarily as responders rather than initiators, for example, "careers" become transformed into "vocations," while our unmistakably privileged place on earth cannot be considered one of domination but must rather be one of stewardship, seeking to return all that is, as best we can, to the One from whom everything freely comes.

Postlude on "Postmodernity" in the light of John Paul II's *Fides et Ratio*

We have seen how consciously "postmedieval" modernity was, as we have had to endure some of its horrific consequences in the destructive rationalisms of Marxism and fascism, each of which proposed to use reason to alter the future course of humanity. One way of appreciating a "postmodern" sensibility is to see it as an inevitable reaction to human reason pretending to operate outside any context whatsoever; or put it another way, to be its own context. (The utterly efficient face of Auschwitz should display why the form of *reason* which could plan and execute such a master plan had to be rejected by humanity.) We have also seen how, for medieval Jews, Muslims, and Christians, efforts to articulate the free creation of the universe on the part of the One who also revealed God's way in the Torah, Jesus, and the Qur'an, provide a fertile context for employing reason in a responsive fashion. The point of John Paul II's encyclical *Fides et Ratio* is that reason can only be trusted within a larger context; indeed, one of faith. Moreover, faith-traditions offer the most trustworthy vehicles for an intelligent faith, since such traditions can only perdure if they continue to be self-critical. That is a huge step to take, of course: to believe that the universe – all-that-is – comes forth freely from a single personal source. So one may, in the interim, at least recognize the power of the structural argument, and ask oneself what serves as the context for one's own rational inquiry. That is the question raised at once by John Paul II and by a postmodern sensibility!

Chapter 11

AL-GHAZALI ON
CREATED FREEDOM

This chapter intends to show the value of pursuing questions surrounding human freedom through the tradition of Islamic philosophy and
theology. Indeed, the goal is both contemporary and compelling: to mine
al-Ghazali's preoccupations to display an alternative view of freedom to
that which tends to occupy center-stage in current discussions, and thereby
show up the inadequacies of (1) current standing polarities of *libertarian*
versus *compatibilist* accounts of human freedom, especially in the face of
the creator/creature relation, as well as challenge (2) a style of philosophical inquiry which pretends to set out from "our intuitions" about such
matters – as though these were not already structured by philosophical
positions internalized in *our* culture. In other words, in doing philosophy
we dispense with the practice of hermeneutics at our own peril. The first
polemic is inspired by David Braine's detailed presentation of Aquinas'
understanding of the human person (in his recent work, *The Human
Person*), which quite effectively challenged the usefulness of the current
polarity of *dualism* versus *materialism* in philosophy of mind. The second
finds an eloquent precedent in Alasdair MacIntyre's response to William
Frankena's review of his *After Virtue*, in which he counters the criticism
that he was "doing history and not philosophy" with illustration after illustration of the ways in which neglect of historical precedents condemns us
to tilling similar ground again and again.[1] I shall try to keep these polemical perspectives secondary to the constructive alternative view of freedom,
which can be introduced by a resume of Ghazali's role in the Muslim
debate, and developed with an eye to Aquinas and Dante.[2]

---

[1] See: Alasdair MacIntyre, *After Virtue*, 2nd edn (Notre Dame IN: University of Notre
Dame Press, 1984) and David Braine, *The Human Person: Animal and Spirit* (Notre Dame
IN: University of Notre Dame Press, 1992).
[2] Here I owe a debt of gratitude to Ralph McInerny's work on human action, and more
recently to Christian Moevs' dissertation: "The Metaphysics of the *Primo Mobile*: Love,

Objections to the libertarian/compatibilist polarity abound, but I shall mention the ones I find most telling. The presumption seems to be abroad that "libertarian" accounts of freedom exhaust the field of viable analyses of genuinely free human action, so that those who subscribe to human freedom must indeed place themselves in the libertarian camp. So by an optical illusion generated by ignorance of viable alternatives, a particular analysis can come to supplant nontheoretical claims that human beings possess responsibility for their actions – like the one found in Aristotle's *Ethics*, which stands at the root of our legal system, and indeed of interpersonal relations more generally. This same complaint is echoed by "compatibilists" of course, so that the alternative I shall be developing could simply be seen as developing another compatibilist account. Hence I shall have to show how my objections to the libertarian picture of human freedom offer a genuine alternative to both of these standard poles. Here is where the creator/creature relation will figure so critically, for (as Ghazali can help us see) it is a bowdlerized version of that ineffable relation which has compelled many theists to feel they must adhere to a libertarian account of freedom. In fact, a preoccupation with keeping the creator *out of* the action has often made libertarian accounts attractive to "Christian philosophers," as witnessed by Jonathan Kvanvig's remark that "no action is free unless brought about *only* by the agent himself" (emphasis added).[3] But enough polemic; let us see how the Islamic tradition may help us understand the positions available to us in such recondite matters.

Mu'tazilite Defense of Human Freedom

Early *Kalâm* writers moved quickly to an ontological reading of things, despite the paucity of conceptual tools in their possession.[4] Reception of the Qur'an had led, understandably enough, to quite disparate views on the relation of human and divine freedom: one which underscored human responsibility for responding to the invitation proffered in the Qur'an; the

---

Mind, and Matter in Dante's *Comedy*" (Columbia University, 1994), to be published in a thorough revision by Oxford University Press in 2004 as *Love, Mind and Matter in Dante's Comedy*.

[3] *The Possibility of an All-Knowing God* (New York: St Martin's Press, 1986), p. 119, cited in Gerard F. O'Hanlon, S.J., *The Immutablity of God in the Theology of Hans Urs von Balthasar* (Cambridge: Cambridge University Press, 1990), pp. 158, 160.

[4] Richard Frank is an astute and reliable guide to these matters; see his "Moral Obligation in Classical Muslim Theology," *Journal of Religious Ethics* 11 (1983), pp. 204–23.

other which emphasized divine sovereignty.[5] Given the inherently dialectical character of such debates, it is probably unsurprising that a defense of one would utilize the perspectives of the other; those intent on reminding us of the freedom to choose which pervades the Qur'an were dubbed *qadarites* (from the Arabic *qadr* or "power") while those defending divine sovereignty over all of creation were called *jabarites* (from the Arabic *jabr* or "constraint"). Yet a defense of human empowerment to make such momentous decisions about one's destiny took its lead from the dominant picture of divine sovereignty, insisting that a space be cleared within which humans – and *not* God – would be sovereign. Their reasoning in this regard presumed that a free action must effect an absolute beginning, so free human actions were likened to God's activity in creating *ex nihilo*.

Reaction and Responses to Mu'tazilites: al-Ghazali

It is not hard to see that such a position could not prevail in a tradition which insisted that God is the free creator of all that is. To remove an entire domain from God's creating power – indeed, a domain as extensive as that of free human actions – certainly counters a primary tenet of Islam. So a Mu'tazilite thinker, al-Ash'ari, came to see the light, and played a major role in developing an alternative position which proposed to preserve both human responsibility and divine sovereignty. Yet he too was constrained by the paradigm of full-fledged free action as amounting to creation *ex nihilo*, so offered an intermediate status for human actions according to which human beings *perform* the actions which God *creates*; we play, in other words, scripted parts.[6] Al-Ghazali subscribed to the view originally proposed by al-Ash'ari, which had become the accepted position in Islam, although (as we shall see) he could not permit himself to restrict *acting* to *creating*. Nonetheless, creating remained for him as well the prime analogate for a term susceptible of different uses, so he will insist that the key to a proper stance in Islamic philosophical theology lies in affirming that "there is no agent but God most high."[7]

[5] William Montgomery Watt has canvassed this debate in *Free Will and Predestination in Early Islam* (London: Luzac, 1948).

[6] See my development of *kasb* in *Freedom and Creation in Three Traditions* (Notre Dame IN: University of Notre Dame Press, 1993), pp. 79–83; for a comprehensive view see Daniel Gimaret, *La Doctrine d'al-Ash'ari* (Paris: Cerf, 1990).

[7] Citations from al-Ghazali are taken from my translation: *Book of Faith in Divine Unity and Trust in Divine Providence* [*Kitâb at-Tawhîd wa Tawakkul*] from the *Ihya' 'Ulum ad-Dîn*

In developing this key statement in relation to human agents, Ghazali will align himself with al-Ash'ari in principle, yet refuse to rest with resolutions which seem mostly verbal, or with a merely "ontological" account of human action. His way of illustrating *tawhîd*, the central faith conviction of Islam, as "there is no agent but God most high" involves (1) reminding us that "agent" is a multivalent term, and (2) probing the convoluted path of *willing* in humans. With regard to our use of "agent" he remarks:

> if human beings are agents, how is it that God most high is an agent? Or if God most high is an agent, how is a human being an agent? There is no way of understanding "acting" as between these two agents. In response, I would say: indeed, there can be no understanding when there is but one meaning for "agent." But if it had two meanings, then the term comprehended could be attributed to each of them without contradiction, as when it is said that the emir killed someone, and also said that the executioner killed him; in one sense, the emir is the killer and in another sense, the executioner. Similarly, a human being is an agent in one sense, and God – great and glorious – is an agent in another. The sense in which God most high is agent is that He is the originator,[8] the one who brings about existence [*al-mukhtari' al-mûjid*], while the sense in which a human being is an agent is that he is the locus [*mahal*] in which power is created after will has been created after knowledge has been created, so that power depends on will, and movement is linked to power, as a conditioned to its condition.[9]

But depending on the power of God is the dependence of effect on cause, of the originated on the originator. So everything which depends on a power in such a way as it is the locus of the power is called "agent" in a manner which expresses that fact of its dependence [273], much as the executioner can be called "killer" and the emir a killer, since the killing depends on the power of both of them, yet in different respects. In that way both of them are called "killer," and similarly, the things ordained [*maqrûrât*] depend on two powers.

Ghazali's constructive view of the hidden pathways of human motivation involves an extended parable in which the pilgrim is taken on a

---

[8] This term is not Qur'anic nor is it a name of God; cf. L.P. Fitzgerald, *Creation in al-Tafsîr al-Kabîr of Fakhr ad-Din al-Râzî* (Ph.D. dissertation, Australian National University, 1992), p. 34.
[9] Cf. Richard Frank, *Creation and the Cosmic System: al-Ghazali & Avicenna* (Heidelberg: Carl Winter, 1992), p. 25; and my translation (note 7) pp. 42–3.

journey through the "worlds" which are invisible from the sensible world yet which regulate its activity:

> This servant, the pilgrim, returned and apologized for his questions and his censures, saying to the right hand, the pen, understanding, will, power, and the rest: "Accept my apologies, for I am a stranger only recently arrived in this land, and anyone who comes here is perplexed. I was resisting only because of my limitations and my ignorance. Now it is only right for me to apologize to you as it has been unveiled to me that the One who alone [possesses] the earthly world, the intelligible world, majesty and power, is the One, the Dominator.[10] And all of you are in His service, under His domination and His power, continually in His grasp – He is 'the First and the Last, the Manifest and the Hidden' (57:3)."[11] If anyone repeats that in the visible world people will consider it far-fetched and say to him: "How can something be first and last, for these two attributes are opposed to one another? For what is first is not last, and what is manifest is not hidden." To which he will respond: He is first with respect to existing things, for they all emanate from Him one after another in an ordered fashion; and He is last with respect to initiating undertakings, for they will only continue to progress from one stage to another in such as way as to arrive at their goal in His presence. So He is the last point on [their] journey, which makes Him the last in the visible world and the first in existence. Correlatively, He is hidden from those taken up with the visible world, seeking to perceive Him with their five senses, yet manifest to those who seek Him by the light which kindles in their hearts [269], by an inner vision which offers a hidden opening to the intelligible world. This is what faith in divine unity consists in for those actively journeying on the path of such faith; that is, those to whom it has been unveiled that there is but one agent.[12]

Ghazali then offers a description of the interrelation of willing and discerning which elicits the objection:

> Now you may say: this is sheer constraint [jabr] and constraint is in direct opposition to freedom of choice [ikhtiyâr]. And you do not deny freedom of choice, so how can those who are constrained also freely choose? To which I would respond: if the covering were unveiled, you would recognize that there is constraint in the course of freedom of choice, in such a way that it is itself constrained to choose. But how can you comprehend

---

[10] Divine names; cf. *Al-Ghazali The Ninety-Nine Beautiful Names of God*, trans. David Burrell and Nazih Daher (Cambridge: Islamic Texts Society, 1992), p. 74.

[11] Divine names; *Ghazali on Beautiful Names*, pp. 133–7 (note 10) which the following closely parallels.

[12] My translation (note 7), pp. 29–30.

this when you do not understand freedom of choice? So let us explain freedom of choice in the language of the theologians, but in a concise manner so as neither to intrude nor inconvenience, since the aim of this book is only the understanding of religious practice. I can say that the language of action is applied to human beings in three ways. Hence it is said: a man writes with fingers, breathes with lungs and his neck cleaves water when his body comes in to relation with it, in such a way that cleaving the water is attributed to him, as is breathing and writing. Yet these three are one in the essential reality of necessity and constraint, although they differ in ways other than that, which I shall clarify for you from three vantage points.

We call his cleaving water, insofar as it happens to him, in this respect a natural action; while we call his breathing a voluntary action [irâdîan], and his writing a freely chosen action [ikhtiyârîan]. Constraint is evident in natural action insofar as something happens to the surface of the water so that it overflows into the air, inevitably cleaving the air, so that the cleaving necessarily happens after the overflowing. It is similar with breathing, for the movement of the throat is related to wanting to breathe as the cleaving of the water is related to the weight of the body; since where there is weight there is cleaving in the wake of it, so where there is no willing there is no breathing. In a similar way, if one aims a pin at a person's eye, he will close his eyelids of necessity, and were he to want to hold them open he could not, even though this necessary shutting of the eyelids is an intentional action. Moreover, if the point of a pin were presented to one's perception, this necessary wanting to close [one's eyelids] would occur along with the movement; and were one to want to resist that, he would not be able to, even though it is an action of the power and the will. For the fact that this action is connected with natural action makes it necessary.

So for the third form of action, that of free choice, it is an ambiguous notion like writing and speaking. For of free choice it is said that one wills to do it or one wills not to do it, or sometimes, that one does not will at all; thereby imagining that one knows how matters lie, but in fact only manifesting one's ignorance of the meaning of freedom of choice. So let us remove the veil from it to explain it. Freedom of choice follows upon the understanding that judges whether a thing is appropriate for you, for things are divided into what your outer or inner perception judges, without confusion or uncertainty, to be right for you, notably regarding those things about which reason has hitherto been indecisive. For you determine without hesitation [what to do] when someone, for example, aims a pin at your eye or a sword at your body, nor have you any uncertainty realizing that you should repel them for your own good and benefit. And it is hardly wrong for the will to be aroused by reason or the power by the will, or for the eyelids to be put into motion by a thrust, or the hand moved by a sword thrust – yet without any deliberation or reflection. So it is with the will.

There are things, however, about which discrimination and reason remain undecided, without being able to discern whether they are appropriate or not, so that one needs to deliberate and reflect whether it is better to do them or to let them pass. [271] When after reflection and deliberation reason decides upon one of these courses of action, it prefers connecting that with what it determined without reflection or deliberation. At this point the will is aroused just as it is aroused by the thrust of a sword or the tip of a spear. So we call this will [irâda] which is aroused to action by what appears good to reason, "freedom of choice" [ikhtiyâr], as it craves the good [al-khaîr]. By that I mean that it is aroused by what appears to reason to be good for it, which is the source of this will. Nor does this will need to wait to be aroused by what it is expecting, for it is an evident good with respect to action, differing from the evident good in [resisting] the thrust of the sword only in that this took place spontaneously without any reflection while the other required reflection.

So freedom of choice consists in a specific willing which is aroused by a counsel of reason which also, once perceived, brings it to its term. It is said about this [process] that reason is required for it to distinguish which is the better of two goods or the lesser of two evils. We cannot conceive the will being aroused except by movement of the senses or the imagination, or by a decisive movement on the part of reason. As a result, if someone wanted, for example, to slit his own throat, he would not be able to do so – not for want of power in his hand nor for lack of a knife, but because the personal will to motivate the power is not present.[13] And the will is not present because it is not aroused by the movement of reason or the evident advantage of doing the appropriate action. Indeed, since killing himself is not an action appropriate for him, he remains unable to do it, despite the strength in his arms to kill himself – without bringing on a reaction so distressing that he could not bear it. In this case, reason withholds judgment and hesitates, because it is in doubt regarding which of the two evils is worse, yet if after reflection it thinks it better to refrain from killing, as the lesser evil, then it is not possible for him to kill himself. Yet if he should judge that killing is the lesser evil, and if his judgment is decisive – no longer simply inclining towards it nor turning away from it – then the will and the power will be aroused and he will destroy himself.

Such a person would then be like someone whom one was pursuing with a sword to kill him. Supposing that he threw himself from a roof and so met his end, [that action itself] would not have occurred to him nor would he have been able not to throw himself down. [On the other hand], if someone pursued him with light blows and he were to arrive at the edge

---

[13]   The expression here translated as "motivate" [dâ'iah] is treated extensively in Daniel Gimaret, *Théories de l'acte humain en théologie musulmane* (Paris: Vrin, 1980), *passim*, see Index des Termes Techniques, p. 407.

of the roof, reason would judge that the blows were of less significance than the prospect of jumping off, so his limbs would bring him to a stop and he would not be able to throw himself down. For no motivation to do so would be aroused, since the motivation of the will is subservient to the judgment of reason and the senses, while the power is subservient to the motivation, and movement to the power, and all of it is decreed necessarily to an extent to which one is quite unaware. A human being is but the locus and channel for these things, so it could not be the case that they would be from him.[14] So the meaning of his being constrained results from the fact that all of this is produced in him from outside him and not from himself, and the meaning of his being free to choose consists in his being the place in which the will originates in him what is constrained by the judgment of reason: that an action be unqualifiedly good and fitting; so the judgment which emerges is also constrained. As a result he is indeed constrained with regard to freedom of choice. Yet the action of fire in burning, for example, is unqualifiedly one of constraint, while the action of God the most high represents unqualified freedom of choice. So the action of a human being, while it may be constrained in freedom of choice, is on a level between these two.[15]

But how can we find a place between natural activity and divine action, between unqualified constraint and unqualified freedom of choice, and how ought we describe it if we can? Indeed, locating such a place will be consequent upon finding an appropriate description for it. Ghazali's response is to clarify the grammar of the matter, and then direct us to practice, as the title of this book from his magnum opus, the *Ihyâ 'Ulum ad-Din*, displays its two connected parts: "The Book of Faith in Divine Unity [*Tawhîd*] and Trust in Divine Providence [*Tawakkul*]."

Yet in the measure that the truth is revealed to those inquiring, they will know that things are quite the opposite, and they will say: O linguist, you have posited the term "agent" to signify the one who originates, but [in that sense] there is no agent but God, so the term belongs properly to Him and metaphorically to whatever is other than Him. That is, you must bear with the way in which linguists have determined it. When the authentic meaning happened to roll off the tongue of a certain Arab [Bedouin], whether intentionally or by chance, the messenger of God gave him his due, saying: "The most apt verse ever spoken by a poet is the saying of

---

[14]   Again, for an account of this "theory of action" involving such "motivations [*dâ'îah*]" see Gimaret (note 7) esp. pp. 143–8, and also Richard M. Frank, "The Autonomy of the Human Agent in the Teaching of 'Abd al-Jabbar," in *Le Muséon* 95 (1982), pp. 323–55, as well as his review of Gimaret in *Biblioteche Orientalis* 39 (1982), pp. 705–15.
[15]   My translation (note 7), pp. 34–8.

Labid: 'But for everything, what is without God is nothing'."[16] That is, everything which does not subsist in itself, but has its subsistence from another, from the point of view of itself, is nothing. For its truth and its reality comes from another and not from itself, so it is not true essentially [lâ haqq bihaqîqa] outside "the living and the subsisting [One]"(2:255, 3:2), to Whom "there is no likeness" (42:11), for He subsists essentially [bidhâtihi] while everything that is other than Him subsists by His power. So He is the truly real One [al-Haqq] and all that is other than Him is nothing.[17] As Sahl [al-Tustarî] said: "O poor man! He was and you were not, and He will be and you will not be. While you are today, you say: 'I, I'; be now as though you had not been, for He is today as He was."[18]

You may still object: it is now clear that all is coerced [jabr]. But if so, what can these mean: reward or punishment, anger or complete approval [ridâ']?[19] How can He be angry at His own deed? You should know that we have already indicated the meaning of that in the Book of Thanksgiving [Book 32 of the Ihyâ'], so we will not proceed to a long repetition here. For this has to do with the divine decree [qadar], intimations of which we saw with respect to the faith in divine unity which brings about the state of trust in divine providence, and is only perfected by faith in the benevolence and wisdom [of God]. And if faith in divine unity brings about insight into the effects of causes, abundant faith in benevolence is what brings about confidence in the effects of the causes, and the state of trust in divine providence will only be perfected, as I shall relate, by confidence in the guarantor [wakîl] and tranquillity of heart towards the benevolent oversight of the [divine] sponsor. For this faith is indeed an exalted chapter in the chapters of faith, and the stories about it from the path of those experiencing the unveiling go on at length. So let us simply mention it briefly: to wit, the conviction of the seeker in the station of faith in divine unity, a conviction held firmly and without any doubt. This is a faith deemed to be trustworthy and certain, with no weakness or doubt accompanying it, that when God – great and glorious – created all human beings according to a reason greater than reason and an understanding [275] greater than their understanding, that He also created for them an understanding that would sustain each one of them, and bestowed on them a wisdom that they would never cease describing.[20]

That wisdom is not available to those who merely speculate; it is reserved for the pilgrims who undertake the journey of trusting in divine

[16] Ibid. 2, 14, 16–19/3, 20.
[17] Divine name; cf. Ghazali on Beautiful Names (note 10), pp. 124–6.
[18] Story found in the collection of Qut al-qulûb 2, 6, 29–30/3, 9.
[19] For the sense of ridâ', see Marie Louis Siauve's translation of Kitab al-hubb of the Ihyâ': Livre de l'amour (Paris: Vrin, 1986), pp. 247–68.
[20] My translation (note 7), pp. 46–8.

providence. What sort of a practice is *tawakkul*: trust in divine providence? It entails accepting whatever happens as part of the inscrutable decree of a just and merciful God. Yet such an action cannot be reduced to mere resignation, and so caricatured as "Islamic fatalism." It rather entails aligning oneself with things as they really are: in Ghazali's terms, with the truth that there is no agent but God most high. This requires effort since we cannot formulate the relationship between this single divine agent and the other agents which we know, and also because things as we understand them to be are not *true*: human society lives under the sign of *jâhiliyya* or pervasive ignorance. Yet the effort cannot be solely an intellectual one; that is, I cannot learn "the truth" in such a way as to align myself with it, in the time-honored fashion in which speculative reason is supposed to illuminate practical judgment – for the all-important relationship between these disparate agents resists our formulation. Nevertheless, by trying our best to act according to the conviction that the divine decree expresses the truth in events as they unfold, we are *shown* how things truly lie. So faith [*tawhîd*] and practice [*tawakkul*] are reciprocal; neither is foundational. The understanding we can have is that of one journeying in faith, a *salîk*, which is the name which Sufis characteristically appropriated for themselves.

So there is a school of learning how to respond to what happens in such a way that we are shown how things are truly ordered. this school will involve learning from others more practiced in responding rightly: Ghazali's judicious use of stories is intended to intimate the Sufi practice of master/disciple wherein the novice is helped to discern how to act. There is no higher wisdom – philosophy; speculative reason is wholly subject to practical reason, but that is the inevitable implication of replacing the emanation scheme with an intentional creator![21] So the challenge of understanding the relation of the free creator to the universe becomes the task of rightly responding to events as they happen, in such a way that the true ordering of things – the divine decree – can be made manifest in one's actions-as-responses. Ghazali expresses this relationship between speculative and practical reason by noting that we need to call upon both *knowledge* and *state* in guiding our actions according to a wholehearted trust in God. What he wishes to convey by those terms in tandem is an awareness of the very structure of the book itself: the *knowledge* which faith in divine unity brings can, by dint of sustained practice, lead one to an habitual capacity to align one's otherwise errant responses to situation

---

[21] Cf. my "Why not Pursue the Metaphor of Artisan and View God's Knowledge as Practical?," included as chapter 3 in the present volume.

after situation according to that faith. In short, what Ghazali terms a *state*, relying here on a Sufi anthropology, would be more familiar to western readers as Aristotle's stable "second nature" of virtue. It is not, to be sure, tied to the Hellenic paradigm of "the magnanimous man," but to a Qur'anic faith. This is even more evident in his treatise on the names of God, for it is the ninety-nine names culled from the Qur'an, names by which God reveals the many "faces" of the divine, which offer a composite picture for human perfection. That book can be read, then, not only as a condensed summary of Islamic theology but also as an Islamic counterpart to Aristotle's *Ethics*. But enough said about Ghazali as an Islamic philosophical theologian. If he tends to resolve to mystical insight in places where philosophers would prefer conceptual schemes, we should recognize that he is gesturing thereby that certain domains quite outstrip human conceptualizing, so that what appears to be a weakness may indeed be the fruit of astute judgment. Even more significant, however, is that everything he says about practice can be carried out quite independently of such "mystical insight," as indeed it must be for the vast majority of faithful.

Implications of the Islamic Discussion

What can we gain from this debate and from Ghazali's manner of resolving it? We could begin to ask ourselves whether *choosing* should be allowed to present itself as the paradigm for free human actions. Or is there a more fundamental level of accepting or rejecting what one deems to be the case with oneself and with the world of which one is a part? On this model, such counsel or discernment would better explicate the freedom which we have, rather than invoking some autonomous agency within us unbeholden to history, embodiment, attractions or compulsions. Indeed these factors seem to represent the stuff of whatever capacity we do have to direct our own lives and be responsible for our actions.[22] Historical, in that freedom is not a mere on/off affair, but that we can be more or less free in the way we negotiate our lives; we can grow in freedom. Embodied, in that factors like gender and class contribute to our being more or less responsible in what we do. Compulsions and attractions, as we shall see, form the warp and woof of an account of progressive freedom, where awareness of the compulsions driving us allows us to negotiate them more

---

[22] I am indebted here to Joseph Incandela's doctoral dissertation: "Aquinas' Lost Legacy: God's Practical Knowledge and Situated Human Freedom" (Princeton University, 1986).

or less adequately, while we are called to discriminate among the attractions so as to order them fruitfully. Such a picture of freedom could be described as negotiating between constraint and sheer origination, between determinism, if you will, and utter autonomy; yet allowing us to take responsibility for our actions without thereby insisting that I am my own creation.

Moreover, such a picture of "situated freedom" would allow us to be grateful for all the help we receive, even from our creator! Note also that the creator's assistance will not be constraining, because the agencies involved are not competitive. Here Aquinas' serene remarks that God alone can move the will without constraining it[23] reinforce Ghazali from a more articulate perspective: "to be moved voluntarily is to be moved of one's own accord, i.e., from a resource within. That inner resource, however, may derive from some other, outward source. In this sense there is no contradiction between being moved of one's own accord and being moved by another" – so long as that "other" be the creator of all things.[24] For the creator of all, on Aquinas' metaphysical account, bestows the "act of being" [esse] which is "more intimately and profoundly interior to things than anything else,"[25] so such a One can only be called "external" to the creature in a unique sense determined by the original "distinction" of creature from the creator.[26] This observation parallels Ghazali's coupling his insistence that "there is no agent but God most high" with the reminder that we cannot hope to know – in the sense of being able speculatively to articulate – the relation between that originating and sustaining agency and our derived agency. Moreover, it is the counsel of both these thinkers that the only understanding available to us will be that acquired by the pilgrim: theory gives way to practice – a practice which can give each person intent upon the way a privileged access, but not of a Cartesian sort, and communicable to others only though their way of living.

Beyond these positioning remarks, what can we learn by considering Ghazali's efforts to articulate human freedom as they reflect a tradition

---

[23] ST 1.111.2.
[24] ST 1.105.4.2.
[25] ST 1.8.1.
[26] For this sense of "the distinction" see Robert Sokolowski, *The God of Faith and Reason* (Notre Dame IN: University of Notre Dame Press, 1982/Washington, DC: Catholic University of America Press, 1995), *passim*; Aquinas' treatment of these two freedoms is analyzed more closely in my *Freedom and Creation* (note 6), pp. 86–94, where I am expressly beholden to the now classic account of Bernard Lonergan, *Grace and Freedom* (London: Darton, Longman and Todd, 1971).

which takes as its initial premise the free creation of the universe by one God? First, that the impulse to secure human freedom by removing it from divine sovereignty is a nonstarter if we are to be faithful to the grounding insight of such traditions. Next, that we can avoid many a false conundrum by distinguishing among diverse senses of "agent," which should then allow us to become aware of any tendency to assimilate free and responsible agents to the creator by demanding that they be utterly "unmoved movers." Finally, that a positive articulation of human freedom in such a context will prove at once difficult and illuminating. Difficult, in that it seems to ask us to conceptualize the relation of the One creator to us creatures; illuminating, in that it opens us to an understanding of the trajectories of human freedom which gives full recognition to the real-ities of human action as we engage in it. If we think of those realities in the way just mentioned, as "pushes" or "pulls," we shall see that a full contextualization of created agents in relation to their creator will offer us ways of neutralizing the *pushes* and of ordering the *pulls* along a path which promises yet greater freedom.

For in an account which locates the origins of human freedom in humankind's free creation in the "image and likeness" of its creator, freedom (like existing) will not be a simple "on/off" property, but will rather demand to be treated as a capacity which we are called to exercise, yet which remains as much aspiration as achievement in us, given the obstacles – the "pushes" as well as our inveterate tendency to self-decep-tion – which bedevil it in practice.[27] The fresh perspective such traditions offer can also help us to see how purely "metaphysical" accounts, like that of early *Kalâm* or contemporary "could do otherwise" paradigms, show themselves to be too remote from the contextual realities to prove very illuminating. We need "thicker descriptions" of human action, as critics of "alternative possibility" accounts of human freedom have reminded us.[28] Reflection on literary sources, to take a salient example, can sensitize us to the more and less of human freedom; ideally, to the progressive real-ization of freedom through a person's life-journey, as exquisitely displayed in Dante's pilgrim. And these rich perspectives can remind us that a simple

---

[27] Christopher Hughes' *On a Complex Theory of a Simple God* (Ithaca NY: Cornell University Press, 1989) offers an illustration of how attempts to assimilate Aquinas' understanding of *existing* to a contemporary "on/off" notion lead one to miss his central point – cf. pp. 27–8, 83.
[28] See, among others, Eleonore Stump, "Intellect, Will, and the Principle of Alternate Possibilities," in John Martin Fischer, ed., *Perspectives on Moral Responsibility* (Ithaca NY: Cornell University Press, 1993), amplified in her recent *Aquinas* (New York: Routledge, 2002), Ch. 9: "Freedom: Action, Intellect and Will."

binary opposition of freedom/determinism will never capture the realities involved.

The perspective of created freedom – that is, free creatures freely created – can also alert us to infelicities in standard "libertarian" accounts, the nub of which can be found in the opening lines of Roderick Chisholm's Lindley lecture (1964), where the key issue of personal responsibility is parsed as demanding that "what was to happen at the time of the [action] was something that was entirely up to the man himself."[29] Responsibility – "the buck stops here" – is certainly the key, yet everything turns on what we deem that to require. If it entails being "prime movers unmoved," then I believe Chisholm is accurate in assimilating this requirement to a Mu'tazilite position: "if we are responsible . . . , then we have a prerogative which some would attribute only to God: each of us, when we act, is a prime mover unmoved."[30] Yet such an assertion ought to be off-putting to believer and unbeliever alike, albeit for opposite reasons: believers, for removing a considerable domain of creation from the sovereignty of its creator; and unbelievers, for postulating that utterly autonomous agents had managed to emerge from the surrounding landscape. Again, a glance at the efforts of those who have preceded us, and the dialectic among opposing positions on this elusive issue, may illuminate us. Chisholm's allusion to an *actus elicitus* of the will[31] is a legacy from John Duns Scotus' attempt to establish *will* as an agent in its own right, independent of the intellect whose counsel it needs.[32] Motivated, it seems, by the condemnations of 1277, and perhaps stimulated by Dominican–Franciscan rivalries, Scotus sought to enshrine human freedom in a self-moving faculty – the will – which could itself "elicit" acts. Effectively separated from "outside" influences, like discernment, human responsibility was secured by making the will a first mover. This perspective received new life in a fresh polemical context from Kant: virtue, if it really be virtue, must reside in the will alone; only wills can be good. This is the stream which has fostered "libertarian" accounts of human freedom.

It should help to focus our alternative by contrasting Scotus' account with that of Thomas Aquinas, whom he was often criticizing. Where Aquinas considers *will* in the line of nature, Scotus opposes the freedom

[29] "Human Freedom and the Self," in Gary Watson, ed., *Free Will* (New York: Oxford University Press, 1982), pp. 24–35, reference at p. 24.
[30] *Ibid.*, p. 32.
[31] *Ibid.*, p. 32.
[32] See Allan Wolter's selection of translations: *Duns Scotus on the Will and Morality* (Washington DC: Catholic University of America Press, 1986), pp. 178–205, esp. p. 183.

of will to the necessity of nature; where Aquinas expounds willing by analogy with reasoning and relies on the complementarity of these parallel intellectual faculties to construct the dynamics of willing as a moved movement, Scotus gives manifest priority to will as an unmoved (or "autonomous") mover. (This summary statement would be contested immediately by Scotus scholars, and I have tried to take their objections and nuances into consideration in what follows, as a way of signaling my gratitude for their helping us trace the subtleties of the "subtle doctor."[33]) It is true that one need not construe these considerable differences as polarizing these two thinkers on the subject of human freedom, for they do indeed "agree on the fundamental tenet that, ultimately, in a free choice it is an act of will that settles which alternative will be pursued," yet that characterization is so general that it can be misleading.[34] What separates them, it seems, is a diverse set of preoccupations, proximate among which must be counted the condemnations of 1277, which arose in part because some were not as careful as Aquinas in explicating the intellect's relation to willing.[35] Yet they divide even more on their way of conceiving the relation of creature to its creator.

With regard to our relation to God as our creator, Aquinas had found Aristotle's conception of natures with inbuilt aims to be a useful conceptual tool for elaborating the activity of intentional beings, now created in the image of their maker, whose natures would be oriented to that same One as their goal, yet that goal would only be realized through their free activity. (This activity will become a *response* in the light of divine grace.) Moreover, the Aristotelian principle, "whatever is in motion is moved by another," offered Aquinas a way of showing how the dependence of such beings on the One originating them could be incorporated into that very

---

[33] Three distinct views of human freedom can be gleaned from Scotus, represented by the work of (1) Lawrence Roberts, in "John Duns Scotus and the Concept of Human Freedom," in *Deus et Homo ad mentem I. Duns Scotus* (Romae: Societas Internationalis Scotistica, 1972), pp. 317–25; (2) Douglas Langston, *God's Willing Knowledge* (University Park PA: Pennsylvania State University Press, 1986), and (3) William Frank, "Duns Scotus' Concept of Willing Freely: What Divine Freedom beyond Choice Teaches Us," *Franciscan Studies* 42 (1982), pp. 68–89.

[34] The illuminating and irenic article by Patrick Lee, "The Relation between Intellect and Will in Free Choice according to Aquinas and Scotus," *Thomist* 49 (1985), pp. 321–40, concludes with these words. His laudable intent to reduce caricature and polarization need not extend, however, to asserting that "they agree on how intellect and will are related in the act of choice" (340), as Joseph Incandela's article ("Duns Scotus and the Experience of Human Freedom," in *Thomist* 56 [1992], pp. 229–56) demonstrates: what is intrinsic and constitutive for Aquinas is extrinsic or (at best) coordinate for Scotus (Lee, pp. 322–6).

[35] I am indebted to Joseph Incandela for this observation. On the condemnations of 1277, see Roland Hissette, *Enquête sur les 219 articles condamnés à Paris le 7 mars 1277* (Louvain: Publications Universitaires, 1977).

activity: the inbuilt orientation together with the initial "specification" of the will by that One to "the good" accounts for the will's ability to originate activity, without however determining the outcome of any choice. For the "comprehensive good" is not itself something chosen; whatever is chosen will be a means to this or lesser ends subordinate to it. And even in these choices, while the will may be specified (or "informed") by what one perceives to be best for one, the action itself flows from the action of the will: so "for Aquinas as well as for Scotus, there are no *sufficient* conditions of the choice antecedent to the choice itself."[36]

Yet that activity will always be conceived, for Aquinas, as the activity of a creature in the manner we have sketched; whereas for Scotus, it will be affirmed to be such, but conceived as the activity of a creature endowed with a capacity to originate activity, which enables it to "cooperate" with the divine will in a fully free act, which would direct it to its true end.[37] Indeed, the notion of cooperation (or "concurrence") represents Scotus' mature position on the relation of intellect and will in producing a free act, with the intellect (as a "natural agent") subordinated to the inherently free activity of the will "to elicit an act."[38] And once the created agent is deemed to be autonomous, precisely to guarantee its capacity of initiation, then creature and creator will be conceived in parallel, the divine activity will be termed "concursus," and the stage is set for a zero-sum game in which one protagonist's gain is the other's loss. Theologically, the polarities observed in Islamic *kalam* cannot help but emerge: either creatures freely initiate their actions absent divine influence or they "acquire" (or "perform") actions created by God. Metaphysically, one will find oneself drawn to a "possibilism" in which such "agents" will be conceivable "before" they are created, so that the creator can envisage which "ones" it is fitting to cooperate with. The affinity with such a metaphysical position stems from the initial propensity to conceive creator and creatures in parallel or by way of simple contrast – which turn out to be the same thing.[39] What such a perspective misses is the unique founding relation, creation, which seems best elucidated by a metaphysics which can understand *act* analogously, and so indicate how the originating activity of the creator continues to make the creature to be an agent in its own right.

---

[36] Patrick Lee (note 31), p. 341.
[37] William Frank, "Duns Scotus on Autonomous Freedom and Divine Co-causality," in *Medieval Philosophy and Theology* 2 (1992), pp. 142–64.
[38] Patrick Lee (note 31), pp. 322–6, citing C. Balic, "Une question inédite de J. Duns Scot sur la volonté," in *Récherches de Théologie Ancienne et Mediévale* 3 (1931), pp. 191–208, at p. 203; see Frank (note 34), where "co-causality" is distinguished from instrumentality.
[39] On this propensity and ways to counter it, see Kathryn Tanner, *God and Creation in Christian Theology* (Oxford: Basil Blackwell, 1988).

Aquinas puts this elegantly when he transforms the emanation scheme to schematize the providential care of a free creator: "divine providence works through intermediaries . . . , not through any impotence on [God's] part, but from the abundance of [divine] goodness imparting to creatures also the dignity of causing."[40]

From Philosophical to Literary Witnesses

The austere image of freedom quite separated from wider reaches of human motivation, initiated by Scotus and elaborated by Kant, also inspired Milton's image of the center of hell as a raging fire: passion overwhelming duty, the mainspring of Puritan morality. The completely opposite image at the center of Dante's *Inferno* offers a dramatic alternative: a lake of ice cutting off all possibility of responding to any solicitation at all. The literary structure of pilgrimage allows these images to be just that for us: images, warnings and contrastive illuminations of the authentic path. For the reaches of human freedom are displayed in sinners as well as in saints: abusing it can lead to its irrevocable loss, while exercising it can enhance our personal possession of it. Even to put things this way, however, reminds us how normative a conception of freedom is this alternative to Scotus. For if freedom is located simply in choosing, if our glory as free creatures consists in being total self-starters, then any discussion of it will focus on that fact alone. Whether the resulting actions lead to our demise or our flourishing will be a separate matter. But if such a unilateral elevation of choice is too much for us, if we believe that human freedom and ethics are more internally related, then the trajectory of our actions will be internal to understanding them. That, I take it, is what people tend to mean by "a normative view of freedom." Nietszche and Jean-Paul Sartre have helped us to clarify the polarities here: are we setting out to make ourselves or are we responding to a call?

Put this way, the position and role of a free creator enters as energizing our freedom rather then presenting itself as a dominating threat to it (even though it seems that Sartre could never rid himself of the latter image). For the action of such a creator terminates in natures whose inbuilt *telos* will be to return to their origin, while leaving open yet another level of interaction which can invite individuals so natured to respond to this call in such a way that these same human capacities are wondrously enhanced – the traditional distinction in Christian theology

[40] ST 1.22.3.

of *natural* from *supernatural*. While it was Aquinas, as we have seen, who fleshed out this picture of freedom, capitalizing on Aristotle's mean/ends analysis, and clarifying Augustine's understanding of *will* as a "moved mover," Dante's poetic assimilation of this detailed analysis offers our most humane access to it, while Gandhi's insistence that means must be related internally to the ends they subserve can help forestall many misunderstandings which the Aristotelian analysis may provoke.[41] We may also be in a position to see how distorting it can be to elevate *choice* to the paradigm of freedom. On an Aristotelian account, rooted in his conviction of the inherent *telos* of natures – an orientation grounded for Aquinas in those natures' deriving from their origination in the activity of a free creator, choosing regards means; ends are either consented to or refused, connected as they are with our very nature. Furthermore, means and ends are related Chinese-box style, so that most ends also become means in relation to further goals, with the result that there is a great deal of choosing to be done.

Yet that orienting activity which discerns proper ends and consents to them is not accurately called a "choice," as Jean-Paul Sartre's insistence that it must be displays, as he explicitly positions himself in opposition to this entire scheme of "natures." Yet while that activity is not fruitfully described as a "choice," the alternative of failing to consent to the recognized *telos* of one's nature, articulated in revelation perspectives as the creator's call, is always present for human beings. To this extent, Thomas Aquinas could be called a "libertarian": human beings can be utterly autonomous; the human will can be an unmoved mover, but only in *rejecting* one's destiny. Yet even that can only be accomplished, by human creatures, in a fashion so indirect that we allow ourselves to be distracted from our proper end by various forms of self-deception.[42] So Aquinas had no desire to make that self-destructive "activity" paradigmatic for human freedom. Nor is choosing paradigmatic on this account, for choice, properly speaking, regards means and not ends. These – when discerned as ends – are either consented to or refused. This insight, which seems to flow as a merely systematic result of an Aristotelian means/ends analysis, deserves pondering: are the most significant decisions in our life best described as "choices?" Do people *choose* their spouses – perhaps out of a field of contenders? Or even if one might see one's action this way,

---

[41] For a sustained analysis of Dante's scheme, see Christian Moevs' doctoral dissertation (note 2).

[42] Herbert Fingarette details the paradoxical feaures of this pervasive human activity in his *Self-Deception* (New York: Humanities Press, 1969).

especially in societies which have been described as "tyrannized by choice," is the decisive move completely "up to me?" Or is it rather that our significant life-decisions call for more discernment than choice, asking that we accept or reject what we have come to recognize about ourselves and about the situation in which we find ourselves?[43]

There are alternatives, certainly, but not *choices*; or perhaps better, choosing at such a point would be irrational. We tend rather to say: "I have no choice in it." Similar things could be said about "choosing" our path in life. In fact, we are imbedded in fields of force, some of which push and others of which pull us. We are, it seems, even phenomenologically, at best "moved movers," and we function at our best as we identify and compensate for the "pushes" or compulsions, and learn to respond – in an ordered fashion – to the "pulls" or goals. The ordering involves ranking these attractions as priorities, in such a way that the larger and more momentous ones encompass the lesser, in Chinese-box fashion, so that any deviation from such an ordering can fairly be defined as a seduction. On this account, an authentic human path becomes one which aligns itself with the relative worth of the goals it pursues, internalizing them as self-motivators through trial and error. In the presence of a free creator, our activity then aims to return all that we have received to the One from whom we have received it all – the operative sense of the term "islam" in Muslim life and teaching. Aquinas' understanding of our very existence as a free gift from God and also the source of all that I might do, for action follows upon being, delineates how the activity of sorting our goals and pursuing them constitutes human freedom as rooted more in discernment than choice, more in contemplation or vision than in "deciding."[44]

On such an account, while we humans may be a privileged part of the universe in being able to recognize, discriminate among, and order the goals presented to us as attractions, we nonetheless remain, in our natures, as goal-oriented as the rest of nature. This reality about us is most clearly demonstrated, tragically enough, in its absence: depression, where one can feel little or no motivation to do anything; or by its perversion: sin, where our endemic capacity for self-deception keeps us from calling things by their proper names and so inhibits our ordering prospective actions in a

---

[43] For a fascinating corroboration of human freedom as "interested, contextualized freedom," see M. Jamie Ferreira's *Tranforming Vision: Imagination and Will in Kierkegaardian Faith* (Oxford: Clarendon, 1991), chs 1–3; as well as her study of parallels with Newman in "Leaps and Circles: Kierkegaard and Newman on Faith and Reason," in *Religious Studies* 30 (1994), pp. 379–97, esp. p. 390.

[44] One may read John Paul IIs recent *Veritatis Splendor* [*The Splendor of Truth*] (Washington DC: United States Catholic Conference, 1993) as presenting the ethical life in this way.

scheme which bears any relation to how things really are. At root, then, such a scheme finds freedom exercised paradigmatically in accepting our God-given natures as part of the cosmos, rather than in choosing to stand out as an autonomous actor whose primary goal must lie in being one's own creator.

Summary Remarks

Perhaps the earlier controversy within *kalam* will have helped us to grasp differences not that dissimilar within the Christian medieval discussion regarding created human freedom. I have tried to indicate ways in which both discussions turn on the conception one has of God as creator and the way in which one then goes on to delineate our status as creatures. If initiating activity in such a way as to claim responsibility for that action must be identified with utter origination, then there would seem to be no place for a properly subordinate agent. Yet the doctrine of creation, as understood by Jews, Christians, and Muslims alike, certainly entails that creatures are subordinate to the creator in all that they are and do. So we need to discover the philosophical tools to craft such an agent. This is precisely what Aquinas' transformation of Aristotle's elucidation of human agency has done. If the means/ends analysis appears at first glance to be too complex, it must be compared to other analyses or mere assertions about human freedom, like "the capacity to do otherwise." Indeed, what commends Aquinas' account is the way we can employ it to help us understand the dynamics of our own action. In that sense, it can best be dubbed a "constructive analysis." Similarly, to be free and to exercise our inherent freedom does not require that we be autonomous, total initiator of our own actions, but rather that we respond discerningly to the attractions which beset us: responding at best to those which lead us expansively to that one good to which we cannot help but be attracted. A final word: if the foregoing arguments strike one as more rhetorical than probative, that is what they are meant to be. I have been persuaded by John Milbank, in his recent *Theology and Social Theory*, that arguments in favor of one perspective over another cannot, in principle, be probative, but must perforce be rhetorical in character.[45] Yet what such arguments can accomplish is to remind us of the *point* of our philosophical inquiries, and that may prove to have a usefulness well beyond argument.

[45] John Milbank, *Theology and Social Theory* (Oxford: Basil Blackwell, 1990). See my review article in *Modern Theology* 8 (1992), pp. 319–30, an issue devoted to responses to Milbank's formidable book.

Chapter 12

CREATION, WILL, AND KNOWLEDGE IN AQUINAS AND DUNS SCOTUS

While Thomas Aquinas (1225–74) and John Duns Scotus (1266–1308) were separated by little more than a generation, their use of reason as an instrument in elaborating an understanding of faith seems worlds apart. The standard descriptions of that difference – according to analogy/ univocity of *being*, and relative primacy of intellect or will – are useful enough as characterizations, but of little help in explaining why their approaches should be so much at variance one with another.[1] Nor do historical precedents *explain* the differences, although they can prove immensely helpful in delineating accurately the ways these respective thinkers use philosophical reason to elucidate their shared faith.[2] My own suspicions have to do with their relative proximity to twelfth century concerns with language.[3] While each was quite conversant with the speculative grammar of the day, which sought to establish critical links between language and logic, one might fairly say that Aquinas was more concerned to root logic in language, while Scotus ever sought to refine language in the service of logic.

Such a difference in *direction*, as it were, certainly sheds light on the analogy/univocity issue, as well as the ways in which philosophical analysis can be said to illumine faith positions. For again, it may fairly be said

[1] The wary reader should be forewarned that I have been accused of exaggerating the differences: Douglas Langston, "Burrell's Misconstruals of Scotus," in *New Scholasticism* 57 (1983), pp. 71–80. My reply follows: D. B. Burrell "Reply," in *New Scholasticism* 57 (1983), pp. 81–2. The fairness of this treatment will have to be judged from the text itself.
[2] Notably Etienne Gilson's magisterial articles: "Pourquoi S. Thomas a critiqué S. Augustin. *Archives d'histoire littéraire et doctrinale du moyen âge* 1 (1926), pp. 5–127 and *Avicenne et le point de départ de Scot. Archives d'histoire littéraire et doctrinale du moyen âge* 2 (1927), pp. 89–149.
[3] See chapter 1 in my *Aquinas: God and Action* (London: Routledge and Kegan Paul, 1979).

that Aquinas allows for the life of faith itself to contribute to a growth in understanding of key theological expressions, while Scotus presses for a conceptual clarity to be supplemented by a life of piety.[4] Here again, their different understandings of intellect and will, as well as the relations between them, come to the fore. As a test of these generic considerations, then, let us explore their respective treatments of creation, will and knowledge. Since Aquinas preceded Scotus, and since Scotus is betimes in dialogue with a position not unlike Aquinas', we shall tend to treat them in that order.

Creation

Both thinkers set themselves against an emanation scheme, to identify creation as the free act of a God who does not stand in need of creatures to enhance the perfection of the divine being. Where they will differ is in characterizing that relation to the first principle of all which *created* conveys. And their difference can best be located in the set of conceptual tools to which Aquinas will have recourse, while Scotus will not.

For Aquinas, "the effect proper to God's creating is that which is presupposed to everything else, namely the simple to-be [of things] (*esse absolute*)."[5] So "creation" applies primarily to the to-be (*esse*) of things; not to their being this sort of thing – since the act of creation is defined as the "emanation of all to-be (*totius esse*) from the universal being."[6] And it is precisely the nonunivocal character of being (*ens*), quintessentially displayed in the very act of being (*esse*), which allows Aquinas to characterize the relation of being-created as the resemblance of an effect to its cause, without having to identify a feature shared by both.[7]

It is no wonder, then, that creation can be regarded as the "hidden element in the philosophy of Aquinas" by so astute a commentator as

---

[4] Roger White, "Notes on analogical predication and speaking about God," in B. Hebblethwaite and S. Sutherland, eds, *Philosophical Frontiers of Christian Theology* (Cambridge: Cambridge University Press, 1982), pp. 197–226.

[5] ST 1.45.5.

[6] ST 1.45.4.1.

[7] "And this is how things receiving existence from God resemble him; for precisely as things possessing existence (*inquantum sunt entia*) they resemble the primary and universal source of all existence (*totius esse*)" (ST 1.4.3). All citations from *Summa Theologiae* (ST) are from the English translation, Blackfriars Edition (London: Eyre and Spottiswoode, 1967). I have offered one way of reading this "resemblance" in my *Aquinas: God and Action*, pp. 51–5 (note 3).

Josef Pieper.[8] For the act of existing, which he considers to be "more intimately and profoundly interior to things than anything else,"[9] is also the
proper effect of God creating each thing. So the same metaphysical *item*,
as it were, accounts for something's subsisting in its own right as well as
that same thing's depending upon the first principle for all that it is. The
ontological density as well as contingency of each thing resides in its
derived act of existing.

Not so for Scotus; and not because he would not agree that being-
created is a relation to the first principle of all, but because he would not
explicate that relation in terms of *esse*. The contingency of things, for
Scotus, resides not in their mode of being, but in the fact that they could
have been otherwise: something is contingent "whose opposite could have
occurred at the same time that this actually did."[10] Yet more precisely,
"that is why I do not say that something is contingent, but that something is *caused contingently*" (*ibid.*). This precision is crucial. It allows Scotus
to avoid speaking of "modes of being," and lets him locate the contingency of things not in their essences but in the free choice made by the
creator's will.[11]

We can trace this difference to that set of conceptual tools which
Aquinas had developed with great care, and which he employed so deftly
in treating creation: the distinction between essence and existence (*esse*),
and the proposal to under stand *esse* by analogy with *act*. Scotus forbears
any attempt to characterize the actual existence of things, treating that fact
(as did Aristotle) more like a presupposition than as something properly
to be understood. What can be understood are essences, and the relations
obtaining among them. Taken collectively, these may be regarded as
"possible worlds." That God would choose to make one such to be the
actual world turns on God's free choice. That fact is what is contingent
about our world; whatever else can be known to be the case about it has
to do with its essential properties.

Creation for Scotus, then, can be characterized as God's choosing among
possible configurations of being.[12] And since it is the configurations
(essences) and not the inscrutable choice which we can know, Scotus' world
combines a certain confidence regarding our capacity to grasp rational
connections, with a vertigo regarding why the course of events should

[8]   Josef Pieper, *Philosophia Negativa* (München: Kösel 1953), pp. 16–23.
[9]   ST 1.8.1.
[10]   J. Duns Scotus, *Ordinatio*, 1, d. 2, q. 1, a. 2 ad. 2; see A. Wolter, ed., *Duns Scotus: Philosophical Writings* (Edinburgh: Nelson, 1962), p. 55.
[11]   Etienne Gilson, *Jean Duns Scot* (= *JDS*) (Paris: J. Vrin 1952), pp. 306–8.
[12]   *Ibid.*, p. 323.

be this way rather than that. For Aquinas, God's will is involved, to be sure, yet the controlling image for the activity is the knowing proper to an artisan.[13] It is not as though God first knows (in a speculative manner) what might be, and then proceeds to actualize one such scenario; but rather that God knows how God wants things to be – as an artist does.[14]

There are, doubtless, other ways in which things could be configured, and every artist is peripherally aware of that. Moreover, it is convenient for us to construe freedom as a choice among alternatives, so the grounding conviction that creation is a gratuitous act of God seems well served by the picture of God's choosing among possible scenarios. Yet Aquinas is reluctant to espouse that picture, preferring the "hands on" image of an artisan at work. It is not as though the individual is determined at the level of knowledge, and simply chosen by the will; but rather that what is known to be thereby becomes.

Things are not said to be contingent, for Aquinas, because they might have been otherwise, but because they might not have been at all. The world as it is results from God's creative, practical knowing, which (as we shall see) includes the will.[15] This knowing (which is a *making*) operates together with "secondary causes," including freedom, so that God creatively knows (makes) things to be contingently. It is not as though contingency rests in God's choice of a pattern which could have been other, but rather that a world is brought into being which will only "for the most part" conform to given patterns.

This is especially true for human freedom, of course. So the artisan image which Aquinas proposes leads one to demand far more interaction between the creator and the human (or "intentional") dimension of creation than the causal model would suggest. Yet a moment's reflection allows one to see that God's creative knowing/making cannot be thought of as impersonally causal in character. In fact, the conviction of creation as free is better characterized by underscoring its intensely personal character than by having to see it as a choice among alternatives. (One's decision to marry this person may well presuppose a field of possibilities, or may not; in any case the decision is only superficially rendered as a selection.)

So Aquinas predilection for the language of "primary/secondary causality" must have one point to make: to relegate the causes we know to a

---

[13] ST 1.14.8.

[14] See James Ross, "Creation II" in A. Fredosso, ed., *Existence and Nature of God* (Notre Dame IN: University of Notre Dame Press, 1983), pp. 115–41.

[15] It is simple enough to recall Aristotle's division of knowing into *speculative* and *practical*, with the latter subdivided into *art* and *prudence* (making and doing), yet it takes considerable skill not to reduce *knowing* to an exclusively speculative paradigm, given the fact that practical knowings do not conform to the linguistic pattern: "A knows that-p."

secondary status vis-à-vis the "universal cause of all being." It would certainly be inappropriate, then, to seek to understand that "primary cause" by analogy with those familiar causes now relativized. What seems indicated, rather, is to let oneself be guided by the language he does use of God – "pure act" – to conceive of the first cause of all in thoroughly intentional terms.[16] And since knowing is a form of relating God's creative knowing/making, which is creating, will relate God to existing individuals from within, as it were, in causing them to be.

Since will is an intellectual appetite for Aquinas, it does not require a treatment separate from practical knowing, much as a distinct treatment of will is difficult to find in Aristotle. So it would not do for Aquinas to locate the contingency of this world in God's willing alone. Those conceptual parameters force him to conceive somewhat more closely than Scotus that mode of being we identify as *contingent*. For that work, as we saw, he employed the tools he had fashioned in response to Avicenna's observation that existence "comes to" essence: the distinction of essence from *esse*, together with the proposal to understand *esse* by analogy with act. Our suggested reading of "primary cause" confirms how central is the notion of *act* for Aquinas, and how crucial that it be understood analogously. Since his primary analogate for act becomes the act of understanding, let us next consider knowledge and will, treating them together.

Knowledge and Will

Knowing and willing represented, for medievals, two characteristic ways in which intentional beings were able to relate to what there is. What distinguished spiritual from nonspiritual creation was its capacity to relate to all that is: *capax omnia*. While the role of intellect is to unite the inquiring subject with the object known, the role of will is to unite the desiring subject with the object it wants. So a broadly realist view of knowledge, whereby the human intellect is capable of knowing what is the case, will not be inclined to bifurcate will from intellect, since what is known to be desirable will of course be desired. Since both Aquinas and Scotus can be said to be broadly realist in this sense, *will* is for each of them an "intellectual appetite."[17]

---

[16] Some preliminary ground-clearing can be found in my *Aquinas: God and Action*, pp. 131–4 (note 3).

[17] Etienne Gilson, *JDS* (note 11), p. 579 cites *Reportata Parisiensia* 2, d. 25, q. 1, n. 19; though the more usual phrase for Scotus is "rational appetite": J. Duns Scotus 1954, 3, d. 33, q. 1, n. 9. For Aquinas' treatment, see ST 2-1.6.1.

What, then, of their celebrated difference in ranking intellect and will?[18] It is true that for Scotus, "the will or faculty of love is more noble than either the active or possible intellect."[19] And the decisive reason for that primacy lies in the will's *freedom*, over against the intellect's necessary orientation to what is the case. When natural necessity is contrasted with freedom understood as the capacity to do otherwise, the very realism of Scotus' theory of knowledge makes him elevate will above intellect as one would extol what determines itself over what must conform to things as they are.[20] That contrast focuses on will as freedom (*libertas*), or auto-determination, rather than will as appetite for the good.

This feature of Scotus, more than any other, separates his consideration of intellect and will from Aquinas and from the entire classical world, linking him with a more modern conception of freedom as "capacity to do otherwise" – or self-determination of what otherwise remains undetermined. It is my contention, however, that this difference between Aquinas and Scotus is also rooted in their contrasting views of knowing, and specifically in their respective analyses of the possibility of our knowing individuals. For while Scotus apparently accords us a knowledge of the individual which Aquinas cannot, that knowing remains (in a sense to be determined) *abstract*. For "the subject must be fully constituted, i.e. be determined to individuality as a possible existent," to qualify as an individual – since "Scotus holds that the individual constituent is of the same order as the specific constituent."[21] This is Scotus' way of securing "that existence is of another order, its own, and that, consequently, existence does not confer individuality."[22]

This means of course, that knowledge terminates in the essence rather than in the existing thing, so the individual known will be an individual

---

[18] Etienne Gilson, *JDS*, pp. 594–602 has an illuminating discussion of this contrast.
[19] A. Wolter, p. 183, note 10.
[20] Etienne Gilson, *JDS*, pp. 599, 586. See his extended treatment of will as *libertas* rather than *appetitus* (pp. 578–93).
[21] William O'Meara, "Actual Existence and the Individual according to Duns Scotus," in *Monist* 49 (1965), pp. 659–69, especially pp. 664 ff.
[22] *Ibid.*, p. 665. So O'Meara must add: "Nevertheless, nothing exists but individuals and there *are* no individuals which do not exist." He concedes, however, that "in speaking this way it seems that we are talking about something already there to which existence is added. So it must be stated again that Duns Scotus' starting point is the given actually existing individual and the discussion is concerned with making analytic distinctions." Hegel reminded us, of course, that "starting point" is an inherently ambiguous notion. One wonders – with Gilson – whether Scotus' predilection for "absolute essences" did not in effect provide him with an alternative starting point to that of the existing individual.

essence – the famous *haecceitas*.[23] As a result, what unites us with the existing individual cannot be intellect but must be the will. This feature of
Scotus' epistemology conspires with his contrast of freedom with natural
necessity to give primacy to the will. For if we are related to reality via
both intellect and will, what relates us to that which actually exists will
certainly rank higher than what relates us with possible worlds. So once
again, Aquinas' and Scotus' concerns are cognate while their philosophical strategies diverge in a critical way. Let us examine those strategies (and
tools) in some detail to try to determine how and why they are at
variance.

Knowing as Relating Us to Reality

My contention regarding the contrasting epistemological strategies of
Aquinas and Scotus will be the more difficult to sustain the more one is
beholden to a pre-critical account of Aquinas on abstraction and concept
formation. That account, proposed by John of St Thomas and dissemi-
nated in Thomist circles for the first half of this century, views *abstraction*
as a refining process whereby the nature is extracted from the deliverances
of sense. Once extracted, it becomes the *species*: that which is known (*quae*)
as well as that whereby (*qua*) the existing thing is known to be one *such*
thing. This version of "conceptual realism" was effectively challenged by
Bernard J. F. Lonergan in his *Verbum: Word and Idea in Aquinas*, where his
careful analysis of Aquinas' central phrase, *conversio ad phantasmata*, led him
to propose "insight into image" as a more illuminating model for Aquinas'
account of concept formation by abstraction.[24]

So it remains possible to offer an account of concept formation mini-
mizing discrepancies between Aquinas and Scotus, but at the expense of

---

[23]   This teaching of Scotus inspired Gerard Manley Hopkins' poetry, especially his search
"for that 'individually-distinctive' form . . . which constitutes the rich and revealing
'oneness' of the natural object [for which Hopkins] coined the word *inscape*" (W. H.
Gardner, 1953, p. xx). For the manner in which Scotus' epistemology influenced Hopkins,
see Gardner's introduction (1953), pp. xxiii–xxv. The stress of Ignatius' *Exercises* on the will
reinforced Hopkins' fascination for Scotus.

[24]   The *Verbum* articles first appeared 1946, 1947, and 1949 and were subsequently
reprinted in 1967. See: Bernard Lonergan, "Verbum: Word and Idea in Aquinas," *Theological Studies* 7 (1946), pp. 349–92; 8 (1947), pp. 35–79, 404–44; 10 (1949), pp. 3–40, 359–93.
The emergent model – "insight into image" – provided the title for Lonergan's magisterial account of knowing, beholden to his study of Aquinas yet cast in contemporary idiom:
Bernard J. F. Lonergan, *Insight: A Study in Human Understanding*. London: Longman,1958).

overlooking Lonergan's provocative challenge.[25] Moreover, for me the differences are even more sharply drawn by the comparisons which Gilson drew between Avicenna and Duns Scotus, as he showed how Aquinas endeavored to distance himself from an Augustinianism which Gilson finds more beholden to Ibn Sina than to Augustine.[26] The issue turned on Avicenna's predilection for *absolute natures*, which are grasped directly by a mind illuminated by the heavenly intelligences. Hence the affinity between an "illumination theory" consonant with Augustine, and an epistemological scheme traceable to Ibn Sina. Aquinas, anxious to incorporate the agent intellect into the individual soul, and to underscore its *active* character as well, gave it a central role to play in discerning the "nature existing in corporeal matter" – the proper object of human understanding.[27] As we shall see, Scotus bears much more affinity with the current which Aquinas rejected; and these separate paths account for the vastly different *feeling* which attends the student of their respective epistemologies.

Both Aquinas and Scotus contend that the human intellect, in its present state "knows directly only the quiddities of material objects." Moreover, for both, "while the phantasm is the source for the derived potentially intelligible material [quiddities *in* material objects], it is the agent intellect that renders this material intelligible."[28] Yet everything turns on the way we characterize that role assigned to the agent intellect. For Aquinas, it functions as "the natural intellectual light by which we make abstract intelligible concepts from these images . . . derived from the sensible world (*cuius virtute intelligibiles conceptiones ab eis abstrahimus*)."[29] So Lonergan, explicitly avoiding the pictures long associated with the expression "abstraction," will speak of the agent intellect providing us with "insight into image."

For Scotus, however, it is the object itself, "the real singular known by the senses, which offers the intellect a quiddity, or nature, in itself as indifferent to existence as to nonexistence, to universality as to singularity."[30] Here we meet Avicenna's *absolute nature*, available for discernment by the

---

[25] See Douglas Langston's article cited in note 1 above. However, his criticisms regarding my use of "intuition" for Scotus are well taken, as we shall note.

[26] See references in note 2. For summary, Etienne Gilson, *JDS*, pp. 447–51.

[27] ST 1.84.7.

[28] Douglas Langston's article (note 1), pp. 79, 73. Etienne Gilson, *JDS*, p. 543.

[29] ST 1.12.13.

[30] Etienne Gilson, *JDS*, pp. 535ff. His treatment of "the cause of intellection" is as illuminating as it is careful (pp. 523–43).

intellect in the thing itself, yet as such neither universal nor singular. The role of the agent intellect, then, will be "to universalize the common nature, as the individual difference singularizes it [. . .] The intellect does not simply find the universal in the real things, to be sure, but it finds it there in immediate potency to be universalized" (ibid.). Such an activity hardly qualifies for what Aquinas calls "abstraction" – at least in the version I am presenting; yet it could certainly be assimilated to that of John of St Thomas.

The principal difference regards the manner in which what-is-known becomes intelligible: must it be made so? or is it available, as it were, to a mind, which has only to incorporate it into a system whereby it will be understood to be predicable of many? That difference is in turn displayed by the attitude one assumes towards verbal formulations of the essence. If one presumes Scotus' way of grasping the nature, the formula which accompanies that understanding will normally be presumed to have captured the essence as well. Or alternatively, one might be tolerant of diverse formulae, confident one has grasped the nature. In either case, closer attention to uses of language, or probing to settle nuances of interpretation, will be considered superfluous. For one either grasps the essence, offered to the intellect by the singular thing, or one does not. Since there is no process involved, there is no place for tentative coming-to-understand either.

In the version of abstraction which Lonergan presents, however, there is inevitably something tentative about the formulations proposed, since "insight into image" allows for differing degrees of penetration or understanding. So one will be forced to return to the examples offered – another meaning of "conversion to phantasm" – to confirm the adequacy of one's formulae. In this way, Aquinas' more active rendition of the agent intellect's role in "abstracting intelligible notions"[31] allows one to construe his account of concept formation in more hypothetical terms. It also forces us to attend more closely to uses of language, and consequently to historical contexts of expression. In short, Aquinas' realism is not of a conceptual sort, but one which demands an act of the intellect subsequent to understanding: judgment. At the level of understanding, his epistemology is compatible with the most far-reaching historical and hermeneutical criticism.

What, then, is the role which judgment plays in Aquinas? And how does that differ from Scotus? Here we return to their respective ways of handling our knowledge of individuals. We have seen how Scotus avers a

---

[31]   ST 1.12.13.

principle of individuality "of the same order as the specific constituent" – therefore expressible in essential terms *haecceity* – but we have not yet noted that this individual difference presently eludes our grasp. Since the principle of individuation is considered in the line of essential differences, yet cannot be identified with the form itself – though it is said to be the "ultimate actuality of form," well it might elude our grasp since it must escape formulation.[32] Nor does Scotus allow himself the easy way out of postulating "an intellectual intuition of the singular as such."[33]

What, then, can be said? That "Scotus had indeed a keen sense for the individual," but that he was unable to find coherent metaphysical expression for that sentiment.[34] For if the ultimate act is *form*, what can the "ultimate actuality of form" be? Aquinas has a response, of course, *esse*; but the proposal to understand being as act, and the act of existing as "the ultimate actuality of everything and even of every form"[35] involves so radical a break with the Avicennian tradition that one could hardly expect Scotus to be open to it. It was Ibn Sina, it is true, who had proffered a way of understanding existence distinct from essence, yet his tools for handling the distinction made it sound suspiciously like an *accident*.[36] What Aquinas did was to propose a level of understanding beyond our conceptual grasp identifying it with the act of judgment. And what is asserted by the act of judgment is that the situation is indeed as one understands it to be. That assertion reaches out to express, though not thereby to understand, the reality of the situation – its *esse*.[37]

So for Aquinas, too, what makes the individual to be *this* existing thing eludes our grasp, but it does not escape expression. We can locate the act of judgment, not in the form of our expressions, but in the ways we use them. Moreover, nothing can be an individual unless it exist; indeed, how else can one coherently speak of "this man"?[38] So Aquinas' identification

[32] Since the declarative sentence embodies the classical ontological discriminations of matter/form, one can only be pressed to the *uses* of language to express individuality. So Hopkins' translation of Scotus' metaphysical contentions into a deliberate poetic structure (see note 23) seem singularly right-headed. So Etienne Gilson, *JDS*, pp. 464 ff, 545 ff.

[33] Etienne Gilson, *JDS*, pp. 546 ff.

[34] See Gilson's extended treatment: *JDS*, pp. 454–66.

[35] ST 1.4.1.3.

[36] See the careful treatment of Ibn Sina by Fadlou Shehadi, *Metaphysics in Islamic Philosophy* (Delmar: Caravan 1982), pp. 71–118.

[37] See my comparative study of Lonergan on judgment, "C. S. Peirce: Pragmatism as a Theory of Judgment," in *International Philosophical Quarterly* 5 (1965), pp. 522–37.

[38] As O'Meara acknowledges on p. 664 in his "Actual Existence and the Individual according to Duns Scotus" (note 22): "We tend to assume that when we use such expressions as 'this man' we are presupposing that the man in question exists." The case moves

of the principle of individuation as the to-be (*esse*) proper to each existing thing, allows him coherent metaphysical expression for what cannot
properly be known: the individual. Yet the price he must pay for that step
is a notion of *being* which is irreducibly analogous, as well as an account
of the act of judgment which is ever open to misunderstanding by philosophers. And since the "analogy of being" itself cannot be grasped except
in an exercise of understanding which attends constantly to the proportional judgements relating diverse senses to one exemplary sense, the
potential for misunderstanding is concentrated into *existence* and *analogy*.[39]

By refusing to take either step, Scotus is less susceptible of misunderstanding by philosophers, who seem more at home with *essences*, yet his
"keen sense for the individual" remains an assertion without a proper
ontological home. Another way of putting the same point is to remind
ourselves how difficult it is to conceive of a "subject fully constituted"
this side of existing. For such a knowledge of "the individual" – however
we conspire to account for it – remains *abstract*. It was my contention that
Scotus' insistence on the primacy of will was motivated by this lacuna as
much as by his predilection for freedom over natural necessity. Since we
cannot be united with the existing individual by our intellect, which can
at best – and not even that in this life – attain the individual essence (*haecceitas*), it must be our will which effectively relates us with what is.

Willing as Fruition

Given the role judgment plays for Aquinas, in returning considerations to
the actual situation as their final measure, no further step is required to
incline towards what one judges to be one's genuine good. A distinct
faculty must be presumed, of course, for perceiving alone could not generate the wanting. But given that spontaneous tending towards one's
perceived good which we call *will*, the judgment suffices to elicit the

---

beyond presumptions when one proposes something called "middle knowledge" of *possible*
individuals. So Anthony Kenny states in his *God of the Philosophers* (Oxford: Clarendon
Press, 1979), p. 71: "Unactual states of affairs can no more be individuated, many philosophers claim, than non-existent persons can: there can be no individuation without
actualization."

[39]   The title of a treatise some have found useful for unraveling these misunderstandings,
by Eric Mascall in his *Existence and Analogy* (London: Longmans, 1949). For an elaboration of this account of analogical usage in Aquinas, see my *Analogy and Philosophical Language* (New Haven ST: Yale University Press, 1973).

inclination. Aquinas' analysis of the activity we call *willing* follows Aristotle's recursive treatment of means in relation to ends. We choose means in relation to ends, yet when our analysis comes at last to an end which cannot itself serve as means to a yet higher goal, we can no longer speak of choice. At this point we have no choice but to *consent*; and correlatively, the only goal or good which elicits consent with utter spontaneity is the ultimate end.[40]

The orientation of the intellect to what is true is matched, then, for Aquinas by the will's inclination to what is good. And since the good must be perceived as such, the mediating activity is that of judgment. In speculative knowing, we ascertain what is the case; in practical knowing, what is to be made or done. What moves us, in each case, are the "facts of the matter," calling for *assent* in the one case, and *consent* in the other. The power to act freely, and hence to move oneself, for Aquinas, then, becomes a function of a person's orientation and inclination to one's proper end.[41]

So freedom is less a question of self-determination of what otherwise remains undetermined, than it is one of attuning oneself to one's ultimate end. There are plenty of choices, of course, but these are to be made rationally, by taking counsel regarding the relation of perceived goods to that to which we have consented. Ends function like principles,[42] guiding the inquiry in which we must engage while taking counsel.[43] So Aquinas' model for free action remains one of inquiry, concluding this time, however, not in a proposition but in a performance: "just as the end functions like a principle, so whatever is done for the sake of the end functions like a conclusion."[44]

Aquinas finds no call to oppose freedom to natural necessity when that latter comprehends the intentional activity proper to understanding what is the case. Moreover, the engine of choice for him is not itself a choice, but a *consenting* to the orientation and inclination of one's nature.[45] And since that consent is spontaneous in the face of one's ultimate end,

[40] ST 2-1.15.3. This intentional dynamic is thoroughly delineated in Frederick Crowe's article: "Complacency and Concern in the Thought of St. Thomas Aquinas," in *Theological Studies* 20 (1959), pp. 1–39, 198–230, 343–95 (present volume: p. 74, note 34). I have chosen to translate both *consensus* and *complacentia* as "consent."
[41] ST 2-1.15.2.
[42] ST 2-1.14.2.
[43] ST 2-1.14.1.
[44] ST 2-1.14.6.
[45] I have tried to make this movement plausible in my *Aquinas: God and Action*, chapter 9 (note 3).

everything depends on the intellect's capacity to render that end present – though Aquinas' treatment of the virtues delineates how clarity regarding one's proper end involves more than speculative apprehension. In fact, the human self becomes itself by acting in the ways it does, and these ways come to stamp individuals with their particular character.[46]

Freedom for Aquinas, then, is lodged more in the act of consenting than in an overt power of self-determination. I have suggested that the existential realism of the act of judgment allows him to remain quite comfortable with Aristotle's version of willing as "rational appetite." For Scotus, however, will alone must complete the intentional circle, relating us to reality as it is, and especially to God as our fruition. For knowing remains (in Scotus) a matter of apprehending the natures of things even if at the limit one might hope to grasp an individual essence. If there is to be an ecstatic moment, then, when we can reach out to be united with what actually exists, that must be accomplished otherwise than by the intellect. And it must be negotiated in a spontaneous act of self-movement, since there will be no existential judgment to trigger it. Such an autonomous movement – at once *moved* (by what understanding can deliver to it) and *moving* (beyond the conceptual to the actual) – fairly defines *willing* for Scotus.[47]

The contrast between these two medieval and Christian thinkers on this crucial point also nicely delineates a divide among theologians regarding man's relation to God, as well as characterizing two tempers often contrasted as "classical" and "modern." It is characteristic of the modern temper to regard freedom as auto-determination, while the classical prefers to think of it as the capacity to attune oneself with the "true joints" of reality. Alasdair MacIntyre's recent work, *After Virtue*[48] suggests a postmodern way of retrieving the heart of the classical view, so rendering these terms more descriptive than evaluative. Yet it is worth recalling that contrast, as well as the more customary "intellectualist/voluntarist" one, to remind ourselves of the continuing fruitfulness of medieval inquiries into knowing and willing. So the figures named Aquinas and Scotus in our account may reappear in varying guises.

---

[46] Stanley Hauerwas' book *Character and the Christian Life: A Study in Theological Ethics* (San Antonio: Trinity University Press, 1975) shows how this "feedback" characteristically originates in Aristotle and is developed by Aquinas. See especially pp. 35–82.

[47] Walter Hoeres, *Der Wille als reine Vollkommenheit nach Duns Scotus* (München: Pustet, 1962), pp. 269–74.

[48] A. MacIntyre, *After Virtue* (Notre Dame IN: University of Notre Dame Press, 1981).

Concluding Remarks

If creation is the hidden element in the philosophy of Aquinas, his treatment of *esse* and of the act of judgment offers him a handle on characterizing "the distinction" of God from the world which creation demands.[49] Since Scotus "works with a notion of being which is common and univocal – in itself neither distinct nor determined – it could hardly function [for him] as the primary determinant of something else, that is, the immediate principle distinguishing it from everything else."[50] So what links the creator with creation will be what relates intentional creatures with their origin and goal: the will.

It is God's willing *this* universe which makes it to be the one it is, and that will remains inscrutable. It is this "voluntarist" sense of contingency which permeates Scouts' treatment of creation and of the relative ranking of intellect and will in us.[51] It also links him with a more "modern" temper, as we have noted. If my own preference for Aquinas' metaphysical strategies has been evident through this comparative treatment, the reasons for that preference should be clear as well.

---

[49] Robert Sokolowski in *The God of Faith and Reason*: (Notre Dame IN: University of Notre Dame Press, 1983/Washington, DC: Catholic University of America Press, 1995) develops "the distinction" with finesse and clarity.
[50] Etienne Gilson, *JDS*, p. 454.
[51] For a nice summary of the "intellectualist/voluntarist" contrast, see *ibid.*, p. 583.

Part III

INTERFAITH ENCOUNTER

Chapter 13

GOD, RELIGIOUS PLURALISM, AND DIALOGIC ENCOUNTER

A major question that can be posed among persons of diverse religious faiths is: Do we worship the same God? There are philosophical puzzles as well as theological problems built into the question, as we shall see, but we cannot escape asking it. What might have posed little difficulty at all from a tribal perspective, where the question would usually not even arise, becomes a major issue for us, for what has tended to separate one tribe from another is precisely the difference in their gods. Yet once the unity of the universe is seen as implying the oneness of God (and vice versa), then another argument can begin: Whose god is this one God? Since the major traditions that form the focus of this exploration – Judaism, Christianity, and Islam – share that perspective, the question arises sharply in our comparative study. We should note, however, how this question provokes precisely because it conflates perspectives: as though the one God could belong to a single group. Yet we must acknowledge that the history of religions insistent on God's uniqueness seems equally intent on confusing these perspectives, and fatally so. When conceptual confusion instills and fuels animosities, then political authorities have but one alternative: sever "religion" from the civil order; relegate it to personal preference and conviction, and urge civic tolerance. This is a history and a dynamic that Americans readily recognize and are accustomed to applauding. If a full-blown peace be impractical, we can at least hope for nonhostility.

The alternative has been all too clear since the seventeenth century: communal violence in defense of a group's identity, often reinforced by adherence to that group's God. We are inclined, then, to consider societies enlightened to the extent that they adopt a personalist view of religious faith. Yet the upshot of such a policy is to downgrade the Creator to one dimension of our lives and so in practice to subvert the sovereignty of the one God. The social strategy that exalts personal faith opens the doors to a practical polytheism: one god for the home, another for the workplace; one to be worshiped on the proper day of worship, another to be served during the rest of the week. In the wake of that initial bifurcation yet other divinities will assert their hegemony over further dimensions of our lives: physical fitness, erotic satisfaction, aesthetic enjoyment, intellectual improvement. Only time, opportunity, and energy will limit the list.

So the presumed consensus among philosophers and theologians regarding God's uniqueness is hardly limited to metaphysical concerns. In fact, it finds its psychological corollary in the human aspiration to wholeheartedness, a pull quite contrary to the inherent fragmentation of desire by many attractive objects. It is this attraction to unity of purpose that is addressed in Jesus' renditions of the "greatest and the first commandment: you must love the Lord your God with all your heart, with all your soul, and with all your mind" (Matt. 22:37, citing Deut. 6:5), as well as in rabbinic and Islamic teachings regarding the unity of God. While this insistence may have focused initially and polemically on there being one rather than many gods, the teaching itself soon took on a more substantive cast: God's being *one* intends to concentrate into one the diverse aspirations to which many gods had long answered. It is not difficult to see this dynamic operative across the three major religious traditions that affirm God to be one.

Jewish faith is expressed as a duty: for instance, a Jew is to recite Deut. 6:4 ("Hear, O Israel: the Lord our God is the one, the only Lord") twice daily. Whoever negates the truth stated in this text is said to deny the primary principle of the faith, so that " 'he who denies the root' (kofer ba-'Iqqar) is not therefore just one who denies God generally, but one who disavows God the Creator of the universe, the God who gave the Torah and the commandments."[1] So faith in one God entails trust in divine providence, in the One who creates and rules the universe. Meister Eckhart, a fourteenth-century Dominican, comments on John 14:8 ("Lord, show us the Father, and it is enough for us") by reminding us that "unity is attributed to the Father. But every desire and its fulfillment is to be united to God, and every union exists by reason of unity and it alone. . . . Therefore, when he says 'Show us the Father, and it is enough for us,' he asks us to be united to God and for this to be enough."[2] The first reason why Philip asks that the Father be shown to us is "that God,

---

[1] Ephraim Urbach, *The Sages* (Jerusalem: Magnes, 1979), p. 27.
[2] See *Meister Eckhart: Teacher and Preacher*, ed. Bernard McGinn (New York: Paulist, 1986), p. 182.

insofar as he is Lord and God, is the Principle of the creature, as the Father is Principle of the Son."[3] As the source of all, both begotten and created, the Father is preeminently one, and thus the One to whom all creatures aspire. Al-Ghazali, a twelfth-century Muslim religious thinker, offers a summary statement of Islamic *tawhid* (faith in divine unity):

> For whoever says: "There is no God but God" alone, and "there is no sharer with Him," and "to Him belong sovereignty and praise, and He is the Able to do all things" (64:1) – to that one belongs the faith which is the root of trust in God. That is, the force of this assertion induces a property inherent in the heart which rules over it. Now faith in divine unity is the source and much could be said about it: it is a knowledge of revelation, yet certain knowledges of revelation depend upon practices undertaken in the midst of mystical states, and knowledge of religious practices would not be complete without them. So we are only concerned with [in divine unity] to the extent that it pertains to practice, for otherwise, the teaching of divine unity is a vast sea which is not easy to negotiate.[4]

So each of these Abrahamic faiths insists that God's unity is not an attribute of divinity so much as a constitutive feature of the faith of those who believe in such a One and a formal feature of this God. (A formal feature does not describe an object but reminds us what sort of thing we are talking about.) So in this case insisting that the God whom Jews, Christians, and Muslims worship is one God does not correct a misapprehension regarding how many gods there are so much as it lets believers and nonbelievers know what it is to believe in such a One. So we are reminded, for example, that those for whom "their belly is their god" cannot be worshiping the God whom Jews, Christians, and Muslims have encountered.

Moreover, while we shall focus on these three Abrahamic traditions, since their shared faith in a free Creator makes our inquiry easier to follow, what will interest us throughout are the ways in which their *differences* enhance our understanding of the faith of each. Rather than seek for a common perspective, we will search for differences that help move us out of settled patterns of discourse into ways of understanding "the other" and a consequent fresh appreciation of our own traditions. The fact that all

---

[3] *Ibid.*, p. 189.
[4] Al-Ghazali, *Kitab at-Tawhid wa at-Tawakkul* (Book of faith in divine unity and trust in God), in *Ihya' 'Ulum ad-Din* (Beirut: al-Fikr, 1989), 4.261 (*Biyan haqiqah at-tawhid*), see my trans., *Faith in Divine Unity and Trust in Divine Providence* (Louisville KY: Fons Vitae, 2001), pp. 9–10.

religions make totalizing claims is a constituting feature of such faiths; it is not up to us to relativize them from some purportedly superior perspective. But we can come to understand one relative to another and so appreciate the ways in which traditions need to be poised to respond to challenges that their world is too small. When this is carried out not in the abstract but among believers, that mutual appreciation becomes an avenue to friendship as well. This is the tantalizing fruit of interreligious dialogue when it is presented as a new way of understanding ourselves along with the other.

Analysis of the Doctrine

Persistent challenge

If the affirmation of God as one is so pregnant an assertion, the doctrine of God must set itself the task of capturing the resonances of so radical a faith. The challenge has been to articulate God's unitary existence in terms that relate this One to our world and yet do not pretend to speak of God as though speaking of another item "alongside" the universe. For then God would be one in the sense of "single," and we would be misinterpreting the faith-assertion as giving information about how many gods there really are. So the spontaneous move has been to follow the lead of the Scriptures – Bible or Qur'an – and see God as the origin of all-that-is. That framework allows one to move either of two ways: that the One is such that all-that-is comes forth from it by "overflow" or emanation or by way of intentional activity. In the medieval period this polarity dominated discussions between philosophers and people of faith. Philosophers found the derivation of premises from principles to offer an elegant model for the coming forth of all-that-is from the One.[5] Religious thinkers in all three traditions resisted a formulation that seemed to compromise divine freedom in originating the universe and could even be construed to say that God needed the world so emanated to be fully divine.

Yet we may also be invited to think of originating freedom more as spontaneity than as choice, and especially in the case of the One who is the sole source of all, for there would as yet be nothing to "choose between." So other religious thinkers in these traditions could also be

---

[5] See my "Creation or Emanation: Two Paradigms of Reason," in *God and Creation: An Ecumenical Symposium*, ed. David Burrell and Bernard McGinn (Notre Dame IN.: University of Notre Dame Press, 1990), pp. 27–37.

enticed to explore the emanation model as a way of articulating the one God without postulating another item over against the universe that God creates.[6] For if the logical overtones of emanation lead to necessity, the anthropomorphic resonance of "making" leads one to think of a God poised over against the world, so that the totality of all-that-is would contain two items: God and the universe. We have already seen, however, that faith in God's unity does not assert that there is one God out there so much as it directs us to God as unitary source of all-that-is. Plotinus, the Neoplatonic philosopher, was compelled to say that this One was "beyond being," as a way of insisting on the unalloyed unity of the One, whereas Thomas Aquinas preferred to identify the divine essence with existing itself. That formula also met the needs of Moses Maimonides and of al-Ghazali (who adapted it from the thought of Ibn Sina [Avicenna]), so that all three religious traditions that aver the free creation of the universe also adapted the metaphysical wisdom of the Greeks to assert the connection of Creator with creation.

Yet they employed that metaphysics in such a way as to assert the "distinction" as well. Indeed, reconciling these dual requirements of *connection* and of *distinction* fairly defines the "doctrine of God." We can see this quite clearly if we think that there must be *something* in terms of which God and the universe can both be understood, yet if there were such a *thing*, then there would be something other than the source of all that links that source with all-that-is. So whatever the connection is between God and the universe, it must come from God's creating activity. That reminder runs usefully counter to our native propensity to conceive God as parallel to or over against the universe;[7] however, once we have insisted on God's being the sufficient source for all-that-is, then we need to assert "the distinction" of God from what God causes-to-be, since one might easily conclude that the world was but another appearance of the divine – or other crudely monistic articulations.[8] "Connection" and "distinction" here function parallel to theologians' use of "immanence" and "transcen-

---

[6] For the Christian tradition, see Bernard McGinn, "Do Christian Platonists Really Believe in Creation?," in *God and Creation*, pp. 197–219; for the Islamic tradition, we shall consider Ibn al-'Arabi; for the Jewish tradition, see Seymour Feldman, "The Theory of Eternal Creation in Hasdai Crescas and Some of His Predecessors," *Viator* 2 (1980), pp. 289–320, an article that presents with admirable clarity the complex logic of the debates.
[7] Kathryn Tanner's salutary warnings against this intellectual tendency are worked out in *God and Creation in Christian Theology* (Oxford: Blackwell, 1988).
[8] Robert Sokolowski's *The God of Faith and Reason* (Notre Dame IN.: University of Notre Dame Press, 1982/Washington DC: Catholic University of America Press, 1995) develops "the distinction" in clear and cogent detail.

dence": the One who creates all-that-is must by that very fact *transcend* the universe that it originates, yet since *all*-that-is comes from it, that same One must be present to all-that-is, and immediately so, hence *immanent* to creation.

When this unique relation was expressed by the image of *emanation*, the teaching of the three religious traditions on creation looked very much like a form of explanation, since the resolution of the multiplicity of beings in the universe into a unitary source showed the elegance of a deductive system. In this respect, the emanation scheme worked out by al-Farabi and adopted by Ibn Sina differed but little from that of Plotinus. Yet the Islamic philosophers at least intended to offer a model for the Qur'an's insistence on the origination of all things from a Creator, while Plotinus was not responding to the demands of a revelation but to the inner impulse of reason. Plotinus sought to secure the transcendence of the One, moreover, by removing from it all attributes whatsoever – indeed, by placing it "beyond being." In al-Farabi's hands, the simplicity of the One was secured by identifying essence (*dhat*) with existing (*wujud*) in it alone. On both of these schemes, however, it was inevitable that the relation of the One with all that emanates from it should be considered more natural than intentional. If creating the universe is a free act, it could only be seen as pure spontaneity, yet at such a remove from experience and ordinary grammar, "pure spontaneity" could be read either as a "necessary overflow" or as a free (or intentional) action. And when the language of emanation remains so ambiguous, what is in jeopardy is the "distinction" of the One from all that emanates from it.

In contrast, the image of *making* seemed quite anthropomorphic and was in fact tied to Plato's picture (in the *Timaeus*) of the Demiurge who crafts things out of preexisting matter according to heavenly archetypes. So a Creator who is a maker does not need to be the sole source from which all-that-is comes; there can be something already there for such a one to fashion. Nonetheless, religious thinkers beholden either to the Hebrew Scriptures or to the Qur'an found it more workable to remove the anthropomorphic residue from the Creator/maker picture than to accept the implication of "necessary outflow" that easily accompanied emanation. (There has always been a minority voice on the other side, however, and one often associated with the more mystical strains of each tradition – see note 6.) Aquinas' strategy is illuminating here: by removing any hint of pre-existent matter, he was able in one fell swoop to insist that creation is an action that does not involve change, since there is nothing that perdures through it, and that, hence, no process accompanies it. So the image of maker is radically transformed. All that is left is the intentional character, and that was the very reason for preferring *making* to *emanating*.

What is illustrative here is the way in which Scriptures and philosophical schemes interact to develop a virtual consensus in formulating a religious doctrine. No single statement of the Scriptures decides the issue, but a series of constraints offer cumulative criteria for preferring one formulation rather than another. Since no scheme can be expected to articulate matters adequately, however, alternative formulations remain possible, provided one can show that they too meet those same constraints. A further advantage of the image of making lies in its power to distance the doctrine of creation from expectations that it provide an explanation of origins. For asserting an intentional producer of all-that-is suffuses the universe with meaning without requiring that features of the world display their divine origin. If there is no natural (or necessary) connection between the source and what is originated, no specific traces need be found, and God is free to shape creation to meet divine concerns, as in giving the Torah or handing down the Qur'an. In fact, for both al-Ghazali and Maimonides, it is this fact that makes them decide against the model of speculative knowing embodied in emanation and in favor of the model of practical reason that *making* suggests.[9] So we can see how a community's experience with revelation tends to shape its teaching about creation, thereby reminding us that the doctrine of creation envisages far more than origins: the very meaning and destiny of the universe are at stake.

Doctrines of God in western contexts

This interrelation of explanatory schemes with religious traditions, including practices of worship and of formation in community, was interrupted by the pretensions of an enlightened West to a manner of doing theology more akin in meaning to that of the Greeks: rational reflection on the universe. Religious *differences* became a scandal to educated persons,

---

[9]   Sec al-Ghazali's discussion in his *Tahafut al-Falasifa*, best located in Averroës' refutation: *Tahafut al-Tahafut*, ed. and trans. Simon van den Bergh (Cambridge, MA: Gibb Memorial Trust, 1978), "Third Discussion," pp. 87–155; new trans. Michael Marmura: *The Incoherence of the Philosophers* (Provo UT: Brigham Young University, 1997), pp. 65–78; and Maimonides, *Guide of the Perplexed*, trans. Schlomo Pines (Chicago: University of Chicago Press, 1963), 3.21; see chapter 3 of this volume: "Why Not Pursue the Metaphor of Artisan and View God's Knowledge as Practical?"

who were at once repelled by the religious wars and attracted by Descartes's dream of a universal reason that would ground beliefs about God and the universe not in faith but in the very deliverances of reason. This confidence in "natural theology" took a different form in England than on the Continent, but for the history of theology the parallels are more telling than the differences.[10] The search for grounds for faith in a universal reason led to the reinvention of philosophy and even of metaphysics as disciplines independent of insights gained from faith, since they were to provide it the warrant of intellectual respectability. And if reason can discover the whence and the whither of the universe, "sciences of the human" will not be far behind. The next step, then, was into social theories, each of which offered such normative deliverances on the scope of human existence that they became virtual substitutes for theological discourse. A telling history of sociological theory cast in this mold has been written by John Milbank, where the argument reminds us that any pretension to articulate the aims and goals of human existence must perforce present itself as a *theology*; the names Durkheim, Weber, Hegel, and Kant stand paramount in the drama Milbank stages.[11]

In the case of the cosmologies offered in the name of pure reason, as well as the anthropologies undergirding a new practical reason, however, faith was disbarred from an initiating or intellectually validating role, so it became incumbent on theologians to align their discourse with that of social theory in order to gain legitimacy. Enter the phenomenon known as liberal theology, with the resulting polarities within the churches between those intent on preserving orthodoxy and those desirous of adapting to the modern world. Part of what today's postmodern optic brings to such matters is the legitimacy of a faith-perspective, so that the insights gained from participation in a particular community of faith once more become relevant to human discourse about God, the universe, and the destiny of human beings. One of the signal advantages of this shift in the intellectual valence of the knowledge that comes to us by faith has been an opening to worlds vastly more extensive than the presumptively superior European one in which the "enlightened" discussions took place. This setting leads us beyond familiar theological analyses of the discussion about God in the West to an appropriate reconstruction of the doctrine.

---

[10]   I am beholden to Michael Buckley's *At the Origins of Modern Atheism* (New Haven CT: Yale University Press, 1987) for much of this optic, although one should consult John Milbank's review of Buckley in *Modern Theology* 8 (1992), pp. 89–92.
[11]   John Milbank, *Theology and Social Theory: Beyond Secular Reason* (Oxford: Blackwell, 1990); for a set of critical appreciations, see *Modern Theology* (1992).

Reconstruction of the Doctrine

Christianity's presumptive hegemony

As Western Christianity made its peace with the Enlightenment, in one way or another, at an intellectual level, most of humanity continued to seek tangible symbols, and many of them alien to Christianity. Yet those who had made their peace with Enlightenment reason found themselves confronted with the threatening spectacle of other Gods — not just other "gods" — in the shape of YHWH and Allah. Threatening, since the God of reason owed its ethical superiority, at least ancestrally, to Christian revelation, so theologian and philosopher alike simply presumed Judaism to be *passé*, intellectually as well as theologically. (The "reformed" movement in Judaism was in large part motivated, in its search for an ethical core to Jewish teaching, by this pervasive judgment. If such a core were to be the substance of Judaism, then no unwelcome particularity would remain except in the residue of ritual.) Islam represented but the exotic fringe of the known world, once the "discoveries" had allowed Europe to bypass the Muslim heartland in search of the pleasures of life. A few hardy travelers composed haunting adventure tales, while "the Turk" became a feared yet fascinating figure. Yet none of this led to any desire to understand Islam, about which enlightened Europeans remained even less instructed than their medieval forebears, who had at least exploited Islamic scientific and philosophical culture.

Thus while the presumptive (even if now defunct) hegemony of Christianity in the West vitiated anything more than curiosity regarding the religious teaching of Jews or Muslims, the possible presence of other ways to God, and so in effect other Gods, offered a potential threat to religious believer and secular believer alike. Secular Westerners believed in the superiority of that ancestral Christian hegemony no less than their religious counterparts, and what proved threatening to each was both the fact that there might *be* another God (for secular thinkers respected the power of symbol even when they had evacuated the reality) and the "relativism" which that possibility entailed for them. Indeed relativism seems to be an even more powerful bugbear for secular than for religious thinkers since it threatens the intellectual counterpart of the presumptive Eurocentrism that shaped their shared convictions. Moreover, out beyond the respectable boundaries of monotheism, in the "Far East," lay Hindu and Buddhist worlds of belief and practices, which were regarded less as theological contenders than as cultural fascinations. So long as the Eurocentric presumptions of Enlightenment rationality were in league with Christian doctrinal superiority, the threat remained quite latent, since if one could still believe anything at all, one would certainly be a Christian believer. However, as the universality of Western reason became suspect, and some Christians began to wonder aloud about there possibly being other ways to God, perhaps even as part of God's own "dispensation," the specter of relativism would become more palpable.

The specter of relativism

Yet the specter of relativism gains in stature and threat as a function of Enlightenment presuppositions about reason and truth, for they presume a normative set of rational criteria available to all, over against which any claim to other sets of criteria is utterly unsettling. That is what we mean by relativism; that there are no longer any operative norms across human discourse; so power or even violence will have to arbitrate. However, like earlier debates over natural law, there may be other ways of thinking about those criteria that are not so laden with specific beliefs but that have to do with the fact that believers formed in quite diverse traditions can discourse with one another. Once the idol of pure reason has been shattered, and we can learn to accept diverse ways of arriving at conclusions, we will also find that we can employ the skills learned in our tradition to follow reasoning in another. Traditions, in other words, may indeed be *relative* to one another in ways that can prove mutually fruitful rather than isolating. Those traditions that prove to be so will be those that avail themselves of human reason in their development, and the patterns of stress and strain in their evolution will display their capacity for exploiting the resources of reason.[12] In short, relativism gives way before the fact that all inquiry takes place within a tradition, and the specter that it evoked turns out to be the shadow of our faith in pure reason, that is, in the possibility of human inquiry outside of any tradition.

So the discovery of reason that every inquiry employs presuppositions that cannot themselves be rationally justified opens the way to self-knowledge on the part of Enlightenment philosophy itself, which can then take its place among the traditions.[13] Once that has been accomplished, the specter of relativism dissolves in the face of developing the skills needed to negotiate among traditions, which can be accomplished because the

[12] Alasdair MacIntyre, *Whose Justice? Which Rationality?* (Notre Dame, IN.: University of Notre Dame Press, 1988), chs 18–19.
[13] *Ibid.*, ch. 17.

traditions can be seen to be related one to another. Because we have become accustomed to associating faith with tradition, we must then renounce the normative Enlightenment view that represented faith as an addendum to the human condition. For if that view itself reflects *a* tradition whose account can be rendered in historical terms (like a reaction to the devastating religious wars in Europe), then it too will have a recognizable convictional basis, and faith will once more emerge as part of a shared human legacy. Then the intellectual task, on the part of reason operative in any tradition that survives the test of time, becomes one of learning how such traditions develop and how one might learn from the other. *Reason*, in other words, becomes a functional notion, displayed in practices that cut across traditional boundaries, rather than expressing a set of substantive beliefs that must be adhered to *in those very terms* before discourse can be undertaken. *Rationality* will then show itself in practices that can be followed and understood by persons operating in similar fashion from different grounding convictions.[14]

What those persons have in common is the need to talk about what they believe. Here emerges the analogy with debates about natural law: what is so shared and common as to be dubbed "natural" are not necessarily substantive norms regarding human actions so much as the demand that any normative "law" must express itself in a coherent discourse. That very activity, which displays the fruitfulness of human ingenuity, also contains operative parameters whose function can be tracked by astute participant-observers who recognize analogies across traditions of inquiry, as Socrates' assembling linguistic reminders for Thrasymachus made him abandon his projected discourse without Socrates' having to exert any force at all.[15] Those reminders have to do with the possibility of any discourse at all and so governed the tradition Thrasymachus was defending as well as the totally opposed one that Socrates had set out to elaborate. Book 1 of the *Republic* does not defend Socrates' own position so much as display the terms for any debate. One may, of course, go on to imbed those terms in a much larger framework, as Plato does in the subsequent books of the *Republic*, but the exchange with Thrasymachus can stand on its own as displaying the coherence of the very practice that makes the rest possible. We will need to elaborate that coherence into a "philosophy" because practice alone seldom offers a persuasive display of its own

---

[14]   Here the reference is usually to the work of Ludwig Wittgenstein, notably the *Philosophical Investigations* (New York: Macmillan, 1956), and the extensive elaboration of reason as a human practice which that seminal work spawned.
[15]   *Republic* bk 1.

cogency. These reflections, however, should remind us that the elaboration is secondary, and there may even be many such, yet they will be able to be elucidated *relative* to one another. The fact and the possibility of dialogue begin to emerge as the shape that reason takes in our pluralistic age. We can gain perspective on that task by employing some salient examples from Christianity as it faced a pagan world as well as from the history of Islam.

God and the universe: Parsing a key relation

The primary opposition in the classical scenario was that between God and "the gods." It is originally a Hebrew opposition, so it was presumed among Christians, yet forcefully reiterated by Muslims. The opposition turns on what Robert Sokolowski has dubbed "the distinction" of God from the world: the insistence that God has no need of the universe to complete what it is to be God; that there is no way of moving by logic alone from divinity to world, and so *a fortiori*, the world cannot be conceived as a part of God.[16] These stipulations are taken to be grammatical reminders mirroring the metaphysical status of God, by contrast with "the gods," who represent a higher (and usually the highest) portion of the universe. It is usual to describe the relation between this God and the universe as free: that is, the universe cannot be said to derive from divinity as conclusions can be regarded as drawing out the virtualities of a logical premise. This need not imply an absolute beginning; such a spontaneous origination could well be everlasting and so (loosely speaking) "co-eternal" with God. Yet originated the universe must be, on this account of divinity, and in such a way as not to imply that it "completes" or "fills out" the divine Creator. So it is that the correlative terms "Creator," "creature," and "creation" have assumed the full-blooded sense that they have, especially for Jews, Christians, and Muslims.

Logically speaking, then, the very notions of *God* and *universe* must be parsed in terms of one another. The God who is Creator will differ from the One that necessarily emanates the universe as part of what it means to be that One. And the universes will differ as well, as Ibn Sina reminded us when he did not hesitate to suffuse the world with the same quality of necessity that realizes it: the logic of the emanation scheme, modeled

---

[16] Robert Sokolowski, *God of Faith and Reason* (Notre Dame IN: University of Notre Dame Press, 1983/Washington DC: Catholic University of America Press, 1995), chs 3–5.

on logical derivation, pervades his system, while a free Creator can have several kinds of relation to the universe spontaneously originated. The affirmation of creation, then, by contrast to an emanation scheme, will be compatible with diverse theologies or manners of elucidating that "distinction" of God from God's world. Some of these may even veer close to a kind of "monism" that eviscerates the distinction itself, but that will be for the respective traditions to discern. By a curious inverse logic, Hindu thought allows for "theologies" creationist in tone even when Hindu Scriptures are not so insistent on "the distinction." Hinduism seems to celebrate such diversity, softening the opposition between God and "the gods" as well, while tolerating "theologies" from monist to creationist. So this tradition will contain within itself the very debates that Jews, Christians, or Muslims would invariably strike up with Hindus. Monitoring those debates would help test our contention that the notions of God and universe must be parsed in terms of each other and would probably prove more fruitful than trading polemics about "logics" – Western and Eastern. Once again, the intellectual promise comes from understanding that such traditions are indeed *relative* one to another and that those who discover that fact have not thereby assumed a higher plane from which to peruse them all neutrally, but are rather reaching out from their own tradition to appreciate analogies with another, and thereby recognizing blind spots in their own as well.

It is a simple epistemological corollary of God's "distinction" from the world that such a One is unknowable: that is, *not* one of the items in the world. A sane epistemology will normally presuppose that our range of knowing is coextensive with the kinds of beings we are in such a way as to deflate pretensions to knowledge about things quite beyond us. That range cannot be equated with "our experience," however, and not simply because the term "experience" is notoriously protean. It is rather that our knowledge must extend to things presupposed to our experiencing anything at all, which might be called the "structures" of our experience. In fact, our greatest joys in discovery can come in domains like mathematics, where the elegance of an otherwise indiscernible "structure" is communicated to us. Yet the test of our grasp will certainly be our ability to communicate that discovery to others, so the limits of knowledge will reflect the kind of beings we are, in the sense of what can be communicated among us. Medievals like Thomas Aquinas used the scaffolding of the emanation scheme to depict our place in the universe as linking spiritual with material realms, thereby designating the "proper object" of human beings to be "the quiddity of material things," where our intellectual (spiritual) capacity to ask "What is that?" focused us on the "quiddity," while our bodily constitution linked us directly with "that" by *pointing* to it. Though little of that scaffolding may remain with us, the double orientation perdures in epistemology, however naturalist it may purport to be.

Free creation as the axis of a renewed doctrine of God

So the origin-of-all will be accessible only through the relation linking it with all-that-is, since it is not itself a member of that set – however paradoxical that may sound. Again, the philosophical attractiveness of the emanation scheme flows from its modeling that relation on logical deduction, thereby connecting the One with all the rest in a fashion otherwise available to us. But that also made it suspect to religious believers whose revelations accentuated "the distinction," for the first principle from which a set of conclusions may be derived is not itself adequately distinct from that deductive chain. So a Creator from whom all-that-is freely originates cannot be cast as the One from which all-that-is emanates in logical array. It is no less *one*, of course, yet such a One will have to *be* in a manner specifically distinct from the manner in which all-that-is exists. As noted above, Plotinus, in an effort to escape these logical constraints, insisted that the One was "beyond being," while subsuming the polarity *necessary/free* under the transcendent expression "spontaneous," so that it remains a nice question (as we shall see) whether his One is adequately distinct from the universe it spontaneously emanates. His phrase "beyond being," however, certainly intends to secure the semantic and epistemological distinction just noted. So the relation linking the origin-of-all to all-that-is will not be accessible to us; in fact, it must expressly be one that transcends relations among items in the world.

If the relation that relates God to the universe cannot itself be characterized, neither of course can God – at least in any way that might amount to a description. In that sense, then, in which God cannot be described as an object in our epistemological "world," God must be said to be unknowable. Yet that need not mean that we can know nothing at all about the *source-of-all*, for we do know that God answers to that formula. (It is, in fact, the "verbal definition" with which Aquinas begins his treatment of God in the *Summa Theologiae*.) This fact has led thinkers in Jewish, Christian, and Muslim traditions to insist that we may then attribute to God what we assess to be *perfections* in the world – with the proviso, however, that such attributions to divinity cannot be understood to be in God in the same *manner* in which they are in us, since this One must *be* in a unique fashion that sets it off from all-that-is. In fact, we may rightly attribute what we deem to be perfections to God only if we understand that their manner of being in divinity is quite unlike their manner of being among us. For that assures that we are attributing the perfection itself, as it were, bereft of the particular manner in which we encounter it. Astute readers will recognize immediately that we are hardly privy to the "perfection itself," so there is an unknowing in the very act by which we may be said to know anything about God! So be it; yet we can offer some clues: what can only be said *concretely* in our sphere ("Socrates is just") will be said of God both in that way ("God is just") and *abstractly* as well ("God is justice"). In fact, to be accurate in predicating such things of divinity, one must understand that they will only be said in one way if they can also be said in the other way as well. That semantic rule reminds us that God does not merely happen to be just but is just as the source of justice is just. It stands to reason that we cannot fully know what that would be like, as our very use of "just" demands that the norm outstrip our current conception, for we need to be able to ask whether justice as we conceive it is indeed just.

Yet such attributions can and must be said truly to be in God, if we are to consistently affirm that the Creator is the source of all being and of all worth. These attributions, however, will be in God not as something "added to" God but as part of what it means to be God. Their manner of being in God must cohere with God's own manner of being, which we saw had to be utterly different from that of all-else-that-is, lest God belong to what God creates. We have noted that Plotinus' way of expressing that difference was to insist that the One is "beyond being"; Aquinas' preferred way was to note that in God alone what-God-is is identical with God's existing – a formula already employed by Maimonides and al-Ghazali as well, and hence apposite for all three traditions. Here again we have a formula that could never be mistaken for a description of anything in our world but that can and must be said to be true of the God who is the origin-of-all. It is formulas like these that allow us to assert *of* God that God is unknowable: that is, we can know enough by what they state to insist that such a One cannot be located within the world of objects familiar to us, nor indeed as an object *in* any imaginable world. Yet we can make such statements only because of the link we have taken as our starting point, that God is the source-of-all, without thereby pretending to be able to characterize that link in terms familiar to us all this apparent contortion becomes germane to our topic – God and religious pluralism – precisely because there are limits to pluralism, and they are set by the demands shared by these religious traditions regarding the meaning of the term "God." God, here understood, is contrasted with "the gods," and if we wish to establish linkage with Hindu tradition, we are speaking of that One from which all-that-is emanates. If such a One, for Hindus, is not so radically opposed to "the gods" as it is for Jews, Christians, and Muslims, we will nonetheless be permitted to establish the analogies we can with that subset of Hindu assertions about divinity that reflects commonalities with our discourse. With Buddhists, however, who cannot subscribe to this metaphysics at all, the challenge is more radical, which pushes Christian theologians into a much starker form of the unknowability of God, one closer to Karl Barth's famous *totaliter aliter.*[17]

Interestingly enough, however, it is not "alien" religious traditions that threaten to undermine the distinction of God from the world so much as those Christian theologies that seek to reduce the distance between God and creatures, as they find the metaphysical corollaries we have seen associated with the source-of-all to present a quite inaccessible divinity. This presentation has tried to meet their concerns by highlighting a feature of Christian theology that has until recently been left all too implicit: creation. If creation is the spontaneous action of the One from whom all comes, then it is the primary "grace" or gift. Yet Christian theology has been content to treat it as a mere *given,* so adopting an effectively pagan stance toward the universe. (That stance, epitomized by Aristotle, treats the universe as the given context in which all else takes place and so one that need not itself require any explanation.) A concatenation of three reasons offers a plausible historical account of this situation, beginning with the liturgical replacement of the Sabbath by the day of the Lord, which in effect invited the community of believers to let redemption eclipse creation. A rabbinic understanding of the Sabbath, rooted in the Genesis account, had it that God created the world in a well-ordered fashion but left it to human beings to perfect. The point of the Sabbath rest, however, was our penchant to presume that we had made it as well, so long as we were busy perfecting it. So we were forbidden to take part in those sorts of activities that contribute to culture on the Sabbath, thus inviting us to recognize how the world went on without us and so offering us the opening to return praise to its Creator.

Much later, in the thirteenth century, Philip the Chancellor introduced a distinction that proved to be crucial to the assimilation of Aristotle: that of *natural/supernatural.* One of the corollaries of this distinction would identify "grace" with the "supernatural life" given in baptism, thus leaving

---

[17]   See David Tracy, *Dialogue with the Other: The Inter-Religious Dialogue* (Grand Rapids MI: Eerdmans, 1990), ch. 4.

people to surmise that whatever was *natural* must not be a gift but a *given*. This distinction became a bifurcation in the nineteenth century, when philosophers wrought a cleavage between *nature* and *history*, placing all redemption into history and leaving nature for science to explain. So it was, in fact, Christianity that impoverished its own self-understanding by a peculiar theological development. If recovering its roots in creation has become an ecological imperative, one of the side-effects of this movement has been to highlight Christian parallels with Judaism and with Islam regarding the free creation of the universe, as well as to recover classical modes of expressing "the distinction" of God from the world. Once we grasp the implications of the doctrine of free creation, we will not be tempted to conceive God over against the world, so that we will then be constrained to make such a one "more accessible;" rather, understanding God as the freely originating source of all-that-is, we will find in that gracious "transcendence" all the "immanence" we might need.[18] What must by its very nature not be an item in the world will nonetheless be known by its traces in a world originating from it. What remains crucial to such a scenario, however, is that the initiative rest with the free Creator, without whose self-revelation we could never have suspected ourselves to be so graced. Creation, by contrast with various theories of emanation, is itself a matter of revelation.

Testing the limits: Plotinus and Ibn al-'Arabi

We have so far been showing how a doctrine of God must attend to the distinction of God from the world, a position reflected most clearly in those religious traditions that avow free creation. We have also seen how that avowal of creation secures the distinction in a way that does not threaten to alienate God from creatures, as more simple-minded parallel constructions of God and world invariably tend to do. Yet the act of creation remains inaccessible to us, so diverse philosophical attempts to articulate it will inevitably emerge. Contrasting these with the stark assertions associated with "the distinction" may help us cast some light on the way

---

[18]   Tanner (*God and Creation*) traces the disastrous effects for Christian theology of neglecting the free relation of God to the world in creation. Her insistence that God not be construed "parallel to" or "by way of simple contrast to" the world may well be illuminated by certain Hindu discussions of "nonduality." See Sara Grant, RSCJ, *Toward an Alternative Theology*, edited and reissued by Bradley Malkovsky (Notre Dame, IN: University of Notre Dame Press, 2002).

in which one's understanding of God reflects one's understanding of the world and of the Creator's relation to it. As we shall see, much will turn on the contrast of *necessary* with *free*, which long characterized a debate between philosophers and religious thinkers. Asserting creation to be a free act of divinity seemed to allow divinity an arbitrary sovereignty over all things, so philosophers tended to adopt a relation they could understand: the necessity of logical derivation. Moreover, when explicating the manner in which God is free to create, religious thinkers often imported into divinity notions of *choosing* that seem quite anthropomorphic. So while the notion of creation as the primary gift of a gracious God is a precious legacy, especially of Jews, Christians, and Muslims, finding an idiom appropriate to explicate that relation remains a formidable intellectual task.

Two classical thinkers offer interesting test cases. One is ordinarily classified as a pagan; the other as a heterodox Muslim. Plotinus (205–70) lived in two environments inhabited by Jews and Christians – Alexandria and later Rome – but was never impressed with their "philosophy." Yet his way of casting the relation of the One to all-that-is has largely come down to us in its particular assimilation by Augustine (354–430) and Thomas Aquinas (1225–74). Here we shall consider how his expression of that relation might well have proved amenable to such a recasting, yet in itself offered a formidable alternative to faith in a Creator. Ibn al-'Arabi (1165–1240) was an Andalusian Sufi master who completed his immense corpus of writings in Damascus. His expressly mystical teaching, when separated from the context of spiritual discipline, has been read as a form of "existential monism" that focuses so intently on the sustaining presence of God to the world as to elide "the distinction."[19] Other readers are less critical,[20] however, and the contrast with "orthodox Islam"[21] appears less stark in more recent studies of this "greatest master."[22] While Ibn al-Arabi considered himself at the very heart of Islam, whatever his contemporary and posthumous critics might aver, Plotinus presented himself as a pagan, perhaps even as offering an alternative to Christianity. In any case, while Augustine found in his philosophy a serendipitous stepping-stone to faith, his friends who styled themselves "Platonists" presented their own lives as

[19] Louis Massignon, *The Passion of al-Hallaj*, trans. Herbert Mason (Princeton, NJ: Princeton University Press, 1982), 3:58.
[20] Annemarie Schimmel, *The Mystical Dimensions of Islam* (Chapel Hill NC: University of North Carolina Press, 1975), pp. 263–74.
[21] Fazlur Rahman, *Islam*, 2nd edn (Chicago: University of Chicago Press, 1979), p. 146.
[22] William C. Chittick, *The Sufi Path of Knowledge: Ibn al-Arabi's Metaphysics of Imagination* (Albany NY: State University of New York Press, 1989).

a viable alternative to Christianity. Yet in presenting Plotinus' thought to our era one writer will note how "in some respects his position was similar to Philo's."[23] So each of these figures will provide fruitful contrasts with the received forms of those traditions with which we shall place them in conversation.

From the perspective sketched here of free creation, Plotinus has long been seen as the prime proponent of "necessary emanation" and as the one who provided the intellectual base for the Islamic emanation scheme elaborated by al-Farabi and introduced into Western thought by Ibn Sina, often via Moses Maimonides' influential *Guide of the Perplexed*.[24] More recent studies, however, place him in the context of Platonic theologies of the time and show how he moved beyond them to a fresh synthesis of philosophy and theology, one ripe "for its subsequent absorption into the Abrahamic theological world . . . , providing it with a rich philosophical vocabulary and an account of divine primordiality."[25] As we have already noted, Plotinus was intent on articulating "the distinction": "[T]he One must be such that it depends on nothing distinct from itself and that everything distinct from itself is absolutely dependent upon the One." It is this primary constraint that dictates a simple ontological constitution for the One, and "the One must be said to be beyond 'being' in order to be represented as simple and ultimate." Moreover, since "what is most simple is also the productive source of all lower levels of reality,"[26] according to middle- and Neoplatonic axioms, the One will be productive of all-that-is. But how so: freely or necessarily?

That question is not so simple as it looks, for if our tendency to associate *necessity* with *need* seems to make that alternative unworthy of the One, so our propensity to link *freedom* with *choosing* makes that activity similarly beneath the dignity of the One, whose "will is in perfect conformity to its eternal activity."[27] So while the One may have no choice about the matter, it is hardly constrained to create by something like a need, so in that sense we would be tempted to call its action "free." A corollary to Plotinus' insistence that the One is beyond being, however,

[23] James Jordan, *Western Philosophy from Antiquity to the Middle Ages* (New York: Macmillan, 1987), p. 254.
[24] See my *Knowing the Unknowable God: Ibn Sina, Maimonides, Aquinas* (Notre Dame IN.: University of Notre Dame Press, 1986).
[25] John Peter Kenney, *Mystical Monotheism: A Study in Ancient Platonic Theology* (Providence: Brown University Press, 1991), p. 156.
[26] See *ibid.*, pp. 101, 102, 103.
[27] L. P. Gerson, *God and Greek Philosophy: Studies in the Early History of Natural Theology* (London: Routledge, 1990), p. 219.

may well be to place its action beyond our polarities of necessity or freedom. Yet what we know of all that comes from it makes us "confident that the *energeia* [activity] of the One does indeed result in production."[28] While the extent to which this production is "personal" and so can be said to be a "gift" remains quite implicit for Plotinus, one may argue that "the personal is in a way already constitutive of the One as an inferred cause of being."[29] Yet such a reading of Plotinus, which sees him as completing an explanation for the cosmos promised but never executed by Aristotle,[30] also suggests why Augustine will find this pagan scheme yearning for fulfillment in a more resolutely personal idiom: while "these books of the Platonists served to remind me to return to my own true self [and] prompted [me] to look for truth as something incorporeal, [nevertheless] their pages have not the *mien* of the true love of God."[31] That judgment summarizes a chapter wherein Augustine cites Paul's paean to "your grace [by which] he is enabled to walk upon the path that leads him closer to you, so that he may see you and hold you":[32] an idiom in which one could hardly speak of or to Plotinus' One. All this suggests that the *freedom* that Jews, Christians, and Muslims attribute to divine creation is not preoccupied with *choice* so much as with a particular divine initiative, reminding us once again that "free creation" is a matter of revelation rather than a philosophical inference and that each tradition's understanding of it will be modeled on the pattern of revelation proper to it. Here is where our insistence on the fact that inquiries reflect a tradition of faith allows us to learn from each without attempting to colonize others in the name of a "unique" Christianity.

Ibn al-'Arabi's thought, when summarized, seems to display those features of theosophy that attempt to *say* what cannot be said: "[F]rom the perspective of Unity and multiplicity, the Divine Presence appears as a circle whose center is the Essence and whose full deployment is the acts in their multiple degrees and kind."[33] Each of these acts is itself a manifestation of the activity of the One, according to the various perfections articulated in the "beautiful names of God." So the dialectic between reality and its manifestation, imaged as the interplay of light and darkness, attests to the evanescent character of created being – a kind of interme-

[28]   *Ibid.*, p. 216.
[29]   *Ibid.*, p. 217.
[30]   *Ibid.*, p. 140.
[31]   *Confessions* 7.10, 20, 21.
[32]   *Ibid.*, 7.21.
[33]   Chittick, *Sufi Path*, p. 25a (note 22).

diate reality "that separates a known from an unknown," a *barzakh*.[34] Light is the dominant image: the One is hidden from view in inaccessible light while whatever we can apprehend will be some admixture of light and darkness. The "distinction" between the One and all that depends on it for its existence, then, will be expressed as the difference between light that is pure and inaccessible and various adulterations of it. "Emanation" becomes a handy expression for the relation of the center to its successive peripheries, and the journey of all creatures during their lifetime reflects their inbuilt desire to return to the source from which they derive. This return is inscribed in every creature, but human beings are given the task of realizing their natures by free actions aimed at developing those character traits (*akhlaq*) that will manifest specific names of God.

What such summaries invariably miss is the movement where by this return to the source is also the realization of the virtualities implicit in existence bestowed, so that the difference between "unity of being" (*wahdat al-wujud*) and "unity of witnessing" (*wahdat al-shuhud*) is minimized in practice. In other words, one may be, at root, a manifestation of the divine and so *think* of oneself in terms that express a "unity of being," yet that very unity remains to be realized in such a person, whose path of realization will involve all of the actions and trials that shape those "friends of God" whose lives give witness to divine unity as their vibrant source. What seems to matter most is the manner in which Ibn al-'Arabi is read: whether as a metaphysician or as a master and guide. While his idiom is resolutely metaphysical, readers who are also potential novices (*murid*) will understand that they must supply the activities that the master's writings presume to be taking place. Indeed, such a reading is the only one congruent with the metaphysics itself, for the *manifestations* of the One are not presented as passive "appearances" so much as loci of the divine activity's emergence into existence. And "existence" here "defines our 'location' for all practical purposes: its most obvious characteristic is its ambiguous situation, half way between Being and non-existence, light and darkness, He and not-He."[35] The last characterization of the One and all-that-is as He (*huwa*) and not-He (*la-huwa*) does express starkly "the distinction," while "half-way between" seems to elide it.

Such is ever the expression of Ibn al-'Arabi, which seems as well suited to express the sense of participation in the divine light that guides novices on their path as it is ill-suited to secure the integrity of their strivings.

---

[34]   *Ibid.*, p. 118.
[35]   *Ibid.*, p. 7b.

Yet one who is expending considerable energy on the ascent is unlikely to read one's master in a "monistic" manner, so the difference in readers seems crucial to the task of interpretation here. A Western reader could be assisted by the ways in which Carl Jung is characteristically misread, perhaps most of all by those who call themselves Jungians. Jung himself is party to the misreading because he has such a penchant for flights of metaphysical expression, yet he also warns us that his writing is forged in the analytic encounter and ought to be heard always in reference to such a practice. In short, the key terms in his analyses find their focus in the interaction of analyst and client, and one unfamiliar with that "work" (which he explicitly likens to the "work" of alchemy) will be quite oblivious to the interior effort that any accurate use of such expressions involves.[36] So the theology and the metaphysics of Ibn al-'Arabi will be doomed to misunderstanding on the part of Western readers whose own religious studies have not characteristically required so interior a response from their inquirers. Like Jung, however, he seems to be party to obtaining for himself the label of "existential monism," for he cannot resist placing his directions in an idiom that will be read as a series of statements. Or put another way, his statements will not ordinarily be read as also embodying directions for seekers along the way precisely because of their declaratory mode of expression. Perhaps this explains why those engaged on the path salute him as "the greatest master" while other readers excoriate him as a danger to Islam. Again, it all turns on "the distinction" and how a tradition effectively secures it. The example of Ibn al-'Arabi shows how religious writers can be read in different ways within a tradition and by its onlookers and how one might discriminate between two very different readings.

Our attempt to understand each of these writers underscores the way in which we are always hard-pressed, as creatures, to formulate that relation with the Creator that we avow to be constitutive of our very selves. We need some sort of philosophical scheme to articulate it, but no scheme will be up to the task. For we are attempting to speak of the One from whom all-that-is derives, and no metaphysical scheme can pretend to encompass more that all-that-is! So our reading of various attempts will have to be tempered by our prior realization that such a task will have to stretch human conceptualities beyond their proper limits. As I have suggested, it will be our respective faith communities that will give us the

---

[36] See my *Exercises in Religious Understanding* (Notre Dame IN: University of Notre Dame Press, 1975), ch. 5.

tolerance necessary to see that endeavor through and to respect the stretching that will have to take place.

Praxis

I have tried to show how diverse religious traditions will exhibit in quite different fashion a fundamental feature of divinity, namely its "distinction" from the universe that is said to derive from it. This is clearest, of course, in those religious traditions that avow free creation of the world but will also manifest itself in others that do not. Indeed, theological variants that seem to elide the crucial difference of creature from Creator will emerge within those traditions that avow a free creation, but these may often be read as presupposing that "distinction" if we attend to the "depth grammar" of the statements made. This brief treatment also offers a way for theology today to exploit the diverse traditions that are becoming more relevant to its inquiries and capitalize on the fact that they can be read "relative to" one another. Yet this cannot be done in the abstract, as the American experience with Jewish-Christian dialogue has already taught us. We need to step outside our presumptive certainties – those of our own faith as well as those of a Western intellectual superiority that would minimize the truth claims of any religious tradition in the name of a radical pluralism. We must allow others the freedom to speak in their own voice, even when that voice threatens to eclipse our own. *All* religions will make totalizing claims; thence comes the sustaining passion of the convictions displayed. What the Enlightenment reacted against as fanaticism we can also recognize as sustaining human faiths. Genuine dialogue is a risky endeavor, for it requires that all participants forgo their own presumed superiority, yet the fruits appear abundantly worth the risks involved. Besides dissolving the abstract specter of relativism, a sustained practice of dialogue will invariably issue in an enhanced understanding of the reaches of our own faith – often reaches hitherto unexplored and even unsuspected. Moreover, what emerges through such practice in the faith of Christians is a fresh appreciation of the trinitarian dimensions of their faith, dimensions often less explicit in Christian self-understanding than in the classic professions of faith. What manifests itself in the confidence with which Christians can invite and undertake dialogue is indeed the presence of the Holy Spirit, a presence that animates the community of believers and that seems intimated in other religious faiths as well.

This reference to the Holy Spirit is far more than honorific, however, for the practice of dialogue is unnerving as well as enhancing. Indeed, it can expand the horizons of our faith only in the measure that it threatens the formulations with which we have become accustomed. This is especially true for North Americans, who can so easily presume themselves and their faith to offer the paradigm of what it is to be human. Where our predecessors had characteristically to contend with the challenge of atheism, we confront the lure of other faiths. This fact presents theology with what Karl Rahner has dubbed a *crisis*, for we lack categories appropriate to contending with conflicting claims that all articulate divinity in a way that calls for a wholehearted faith-commitment.[37] Yet this impasse, which might cripple a philosopher, need not debilitate a person of inquiring faith, for one can presume that the illumination worked in allowing the formulations of our faith to be stretched in encounter with the faith of others will also unveil gaps in our self-understanding and in our understanding of divinity, gaps that will let "the Other" reveal itself that much better than our categories have permitted thus far.[38] Such a confidence is the very stuff of faith in the revealing Spirit and hence sounds the most distinctive note of Christian faith. Its outworking in dialogue among partners in diverse religious traditions can effect that signal trace of the Holy Spirit among us: friendship. Those who have experienced the fruit of interfaith dialogue have done so in a context in which discussion fueled by mutual respect becomes an exchange carried out in enhanced esteem of the faith-traditions manifested in the life and practice of one's partners. And all that can take place because in the process people have become friends walking together in an inquiry that is as existential as it is intellectual and in which mutual needs and insights can be found strengthening one another.

[37] Karl Rahner, "Towards a Fundamental Interpretation of Vatican II," in *Theological Studies* 40 (1979), pp. 716–27.

[38] For an illuminating set of essays outlining this way of proceeding among religious traditions, see Gavin D'Costa, *Christian Uniqueness Reconsidered* (Maryknoll, NY: Orbis, 1990).

Chapter 14

THE CHRISTIAN DISTINCTION CELEBRATED AND EXPANDED

The author whom I discovered in *The God of Faith and Reason* displayed another face from the phenomenologist whose work I had come to rely upon to orient me in the often obscure world of Husserl. A bit of personal history will also help to show why I found the central argument of Sokolowski's work so utterly crucial not only to what I was doing but to the entire endeavor of philosophical theology in the current intellectual culture. The manuscript came to me in Jerusalem during the two years (1980–2) I was spending there, initially serving as rector of the Ecumenical Institute for Theological Research (Tantur), working to expanding their horizons from those of Christian ecumenism to a foyer for interfaith scholarship and understanding. The following year I spent in a personal project to gain sufficient Arabic to explore Islamic and Jewish philosophical theology, with the goal of putting the work of Thomas Aquinas into an interfaith perspective. For I had been persuaded by Karl Rahner's recent (1979) call to re-periodize the history of Christian theology, and come to suspect myself that Aquinas' classic synthesis of Christian understanding by way of Hellenic philosophy was in fact already an interfaith, intercultural achievement.[1]

One had only to note the plethora of references in Aquinas' mature work to Maimonides and to Avicenna to recognize that a powerful exchange was going on, and the burden of Rahner's seminal lecture had been to focus on a Christian tradition now placed vis-à-vis other major

---

[1] Karl Rahner, S.J., "Towards a Fundamental Interpretation of Vatican II," in *Theological Studies* 40 (1979), pp. 716–27.

religions, much as Jewish Christians of the first century had been faced with pagans wishing to affirm Jesus. That allowed him to offer 70 and 1970 as symbolic dates, so bracketing 19 centuries of Western European Christianity, and helping us to recognize that we stand on the threshold of a "world-church," as his proposal soon came to be called. I set myself initally to explore the conceptual interplay between Aquinas and the two whom he so often cites: Moses Maimonides and Ibn Sina.[2] What proved remarkable was the manner in which these thinkers – certainly Maimonides, and also al-Ghazali (whose works in philosophical theology had not been available to Aquinas) even more than Avicenna – coalesced in their concern to use Greek philosophy to offer an account of the origin and order of the universe in stark contrast to the acceptable philosophical versions of the day.[3] The source of their opposition was revelation, Bible or Qur'an, so the point of their contrast centered on a universe freely originated by the one God in such a way that it has an initial moment. And while the immediate philosophical obstacles turned on origination from nothing (ex nihilo) as well as the initial moment (de novo), the more significant difference had to do with the way one conceives the relation of the First or the One to the universe.[4] And while the emanation scheme tended to link the First too closely with all that emanates from it, on the model of axiom to premises in a logical deduction, the picture of a free creator tended to place God over against the universe in ways too anthropomorphic for philosophical taste or theological consistency.[5]

"The Distinction" in Philosophical Theology, with Some Consequences

Hence the crucial importance of what Sokolowski has tagged "the Christian distinction," which I would like to propose as a Jewish-Christian-Muslim distinction, presupposed to any account consonant with these

[2] See my Knowing the Unknowable God (Notre Dame IN: University of Notre Dame Press, 1986), "Aquinas' Debt to Maimonides" which is included as chapter 5 of this volume.

[3] See my Freedom and Creation in Three Traditions (Notre Dame IN: University of Notre Dame Press, 1993), and Richard Frank, Al-Ghazali and the Ash'arite School (Durham NC: Duke University Press, 1994).

[4] On the important difference between ex nihilo and de novo – often conflated – see William Dunphy, "Maimonides and Aquinas on Creation: A Critique of Their Historians," in Graceful Reason: Essays in Ancient and Medieval Philosophy Presented to Joseph Owens, CSSR, ed. Lloyd Gerson (Toronto: Pontifical Institute for Mediaeval Studies, 1983), pp. 361–79.

[5] For an example of the emanation scheme, see Richard Walzer, Al-Farabi on the Perfect State (New York: Clarendon Press, 1985).

three traditions' avowal of the free creation of the universe by one God, all-too often it has been egregiously overlooked by their philosophical theologians.[6] Yet this "distinction," as Sokolowski presents it, is intended to capture that singular relation of the created universe to its creator that preoccupied the medieval Jewish, Christian, and Muslim philosophical theologians whom we just identified. So while it is a bit of a conceit to speak of such an expressly ineffable relation as a "distinction," the conceit is deliberate here: "Distinctions make human life possible, and, more profoundly, the Christian distinction between God and the world makes possible the life of man with God that has been given to us in Christ."[7] So to make our extension viable, we shall have to show how a similar yet different such "distinction" makes possible the life of human beings with God given to Jews in the Torah, and to Muslims in the Qur'an. The "Christian distinction" has two sides: "as something for us to live and as an issue for reflection [it] is first lived and then theoretically formulated."[8] As something lived, it functions in the "illuminating, stabilizing, and liberating [way in which] distinctions [do] in life."[9] As an issue for reflection, "it opens the space within which the other Christian mysteries can be believed, [permitting them] to be thought as mysteries."[10] Again, if a similar distinction is to function for Jews or Muslims, it will have to effect something similar in their lives and in their reflection.

But what is it we are talking about? The fact, if you will, that avowing God to be the free creator of the universe means that one must thenceforth speak of things, indeed, of the entire universe, "as possibly not having been at all." So "the distinction" introduces a level of contingency unimaginable to Aristotle, for whom contingency meant that "things could have been very different from the way they are."[11] This entails that "God is understood as 'being' God entirely apart from any relation of otherness to the world or to the whole. God could and would be God even if there were no world."[12] Such a distinction must be contrasted with those which "occur normally within the setting of the world [in which] each term distinguished is what it is precisely by not being that which it is distinguishable from. [So] its being is established partially by its other-

---

[6]   See his *The God of Faith and Reason* (Notre Dame IN: University of Notre Dame Press, 1982; Washington DC: Catholic University of America Press, 1994), *passim,* notably chs 2–4.
[7]   *Ibid.*, p. 29.
[8]   *Ibid.*, pp. 23–4.
[9]   *Ibid.*, p. 29.
[10]   *Ibid.*, p. 37.
[11]   *Ibid.*, p. 32.
[12]   *Ibid.*, pp. 32–3.

ness, and therefore its being depends on its distinction from others."[13] Here is where the phenomenological infrastructure surfaces: sameness and otherness characterizes each item *in* the universe, each of which is and is known in virtue of that relation to its "world." God is not such an item; God is not *in* the universe. Indeed, "in Christian faith God is understood not only to have created the world, but to have permitted the distinction between himself and the world to occur. [And since] no distinction made within the horizon of the world is like this, . . . the act of creation cannot be understood in terms of any action or any relationship that exists in the world."[14]

In this work Sokolowski uses the celebrated distinction to offer a fresh interpretation of Anselm's *Proslogion*, where he identifies "an implicit premise [which] implies that God is to be so understood, and the world or creatures are to be so understood, that nothing greater, *maius*, is achieved if the world of creatures are added to God."[15] He insists that "Anselm had stated this understanding of God when he said he wished to establish that God is the highest good '*nullo alio indigens*; requiring nothing else', . . . for if the world or any creature were to contribute great-ness to God, then God would not be that than which nothing greater can be thought. God plus the creature or God plus the world would be think-able as greater than God alone."[16] This is an ingenious reading of Anselm, and far closer to the spirit of that author than contemporary efforts to enlist his support of something called "perfect being theology," in which Anselm's God is put forward as the prime "instantiation" of "great-making properties," in short, as the biggest thing around![17] It is such a presump-tion on the part of philosophers which Sokolowski is vigorously heading off with "the distinction" as it appears in *The God of Faith and Reason*, a work emerging from many years of teaching philosophy to students of divinity. His later *Eucharistic Presence* exploits the same "distinction" to develop "a theology of disclosure," where it is used to open the space within which "the other Christian mysteries can be thought as myster-ies."[18] Here again it is the presence and absence of such a God which

[13] *Ibid.*, p. 32.
[14] *Ibid.*, p. 33.
[15] *Ibid.*, p. 8.
[16] *Ibid.*, pp. 8–9.
[17] The prime promoter of this approach has been Tom Morris; for a sustained refutation, see Barry Miller's *A Most Unlikely God* (Notre Dame IN: University of Notre Dame Press, 1996).
[18] Sokolowski (note 6), p. 37.

informs his treatment, and gives a sufficiently distinctive edge to his treatment to deserve the title he proposes: "the theology of disclosure tries to spell out what this distinction between the world and God is, how it comes to light, and what it implies for our understanding of God, the world, and ourselves."[19]

Preachers and philosophers alike are tempted to speak as though God were resident among us; when the incarnation licenses Christian thinkers to speak so, it is all the more important that they be alert to the God who is so graciously present in Jesus: "the theology of disclosure is the attempt to formulate what occurs when the word of God changes the sense of the whole for us and allows us to see ourselves, and to live, in a new light."[20] Can the philosophical theology of other Abrahamic traditions be similarly understood, in the light of the God made known to them in the Torah or the Qur'an, so that something analogous to "the distinction" can be seen to be at work in their formulation of the relation of creator to creatures as well as evidenced in the structure of their religious thought? Recent work comparing these three traditions would incline one towards a positive answer, which can be bolstered by a few salient examples.[21] As mentioned earlier, al-Ghazali is a better representative of Islam in these matters than Ibn Sina, who seemed more anxious to establish the philosophical respectability of Islam in the face of the Neoplatonism of his time than he was to explore the unique features of the God revealed in the Qur'an.[22] Maimonides remains a key witness to Jewish thought, especially in that his stated aim in the *Guide of the Perplexed* is to reconcile Torah-faith with the Neoplatonism which he knew, notably that of Ibn Sina.[23]

---

[19] *Ibid.*, p. x.

[20] *Ibid.*, xi.

[21] Besides my own work (notes 2 and 3) see Avital Wohlman's twin volumes: *Thomas d'Aquin et Maimonide: Un dialogue exemplaire* (Paris: Cerf, 1988) and *Maimonide et Thomas d'Aquin: Un dialogue impossible* (Fribourg: Editions Universitaires, 1995), and Roger Arnaldez, *Trois messagers pour un seul Dieu* (Paris: Albin Michel, 1983), (English translation: *Three Messengers for One God*, trans. Gerald Schlabach (Notre Dame IN: University of Notre Dame Press, 1994).

[22] For a presentation of Ibn Sina both comprehensive and readable, see Lenn E. Goodman, *Avicenna* (New York: Routledge, 1992), especially ch. 2: "Metaphysics," for his contribution to Aquinas' metaphysics of *esse* – so important to Sokolowski's philosophical development of the God displayed in "the distinction," see my "Essence and Existence: Avicenna and Greek Philosophy," in *MIDEO* [=*Mélanges de l'Institut Dominicain des Etudes Orientales* (Cairo)] 17 (1986), pp. 53–66.

[23] The most literal rendition of the Arabic (in which Maimonides wrote the *Guide*, using Hebrew characters) is offered by the translation of Schlomo Pines (Chicago: University of

"The Distinction" in other Traditions

Before undertaking this exploration, a few orienting remarks about the endeavor. I have so far been careful to speak of a *distinction* analogous or similar to what Sokolowski has identified as "the Christian distinction." His astute observations about the role which early Christological contro-versy played in articulating the relation of creatures to creator suggest that a Christian faith and intellectual climate can be far more articulate regard-ing this "distinction," precisely by virtue of the challenge to relate divine to human *natures* in Jesus. Indeed, this observation ought to lead theolo-gians to a keen appreciation of the terms of those controversies for con-temporary theological inquiry.[24] The analogous vehicles of divine presence in Judaism and Islam, the Torah and the Qur'an, respectively, cannot be identified as "incarnations," of course, so these traditions will necessarily employ other terms for articulating what Sokolowski calls "the distinc-tion." Yet we shall see that their efforts to articulate the relation of creator to creatures will proceed along similar lines, noting at key places what must be said and what cannot be said, since all three traditions hold the relation to be, strictly speaking, ineffable. A final section on "nonduality" requires preliminary notice, since we have so far been concerned simply with Abrahamic faiths, and since I feel myself to be a very elementary student of Hindu traditions. Yet the affinities between Sokolowski's *dis-tinction* and a recent presentation of *nonduality* by a Christian writer are so startling as to merit at least extensive notice.[25] Among the Abrahamic traditions, however, let us begin with Islam as the first to articulate these issues philosophically, using al-Ghazali as our witness.[26]

Chicago Press, 1963) = P. An earlier, sometimes less reliable, rendition, yet employing more standard philosophical vocabulary, is the 1904 translation of M. Friedländer, *The Guide for the Perplexed* (New York: Dover Publcations, 1956). The Judaeo-Arabic text has been rendered into Arabic characters by Hüseyin Atay: *Delâletü'l-Hâirîn* (Ankara: Ankara Uni-versitesi Basivemi, 1974).

[24] A prime example of such an appreciation can be found in John McDade's "Creation and salvation: green faith and Christian themes," in *The Month* (November 1990), pp. 433–41.

[25] The work is entitled *Toward an Alternative Theology*, and comprises the Teape lectures given by Sara Grant, RSCJ, at Cambridge and Bristol in 1989, with the subtitle: "Con-fessions of a Non-dualist Christian" (Bangalore: Asia Trading Corporation, 1991), edited and reissued by Bradley Malkovsky (Notre Dame IN: University of Notre Dame Press, 2002).

[26] For an incisive overview of his thought, see Richard Frank, *Al-Ghazali and the Ash'arite School* (Durham NC: Duke University Press, 1994).

Al-Ghazali on "Faith in Divine Unity and Trust in Divine Providence"

Al-Ghazali is best known to philosophers as the author of the *Tahâfût al-falâsifâ*, usually translated as "The Incoherence of the Philosophers," in which he charges his philosophical predecessors in Islam, notably Ibn Sina, with formal heresy on five distinct counts.[27] This work was painstakingly refuted by Ibn Rushd [Averroës] in his celebrated *Tahâfût al-Tahâfût*, which incorporates Ghazali's entire text and so offers one English translation of both works.[28] Yet Ibn Rushd's refutation made little impact in the Islamic world, where Ghazali's charges succeeded in marginalizing later philosophical efforts, moving it from the sort of analysis which had characterized the work of early notables like al-Kindi, al-Farabi, and Ibn Sina, into the more "illuminationist" mode of Iranian philosophers.[29] There is another al-Ghazali, however, whose constructive work can be found in his *magnum opus*, *Ihya' Ulûm ad-Dîn*. Here he is concerned to bring philosophy to bear on explicating the sense and the consequences of Islamic faith, and so move beyond the antiphilosophical polemic of his earlier work. Indeed, his polemic against a certain way of incorporating philosophy into inquiries affecting Muslim faith might be compared to Kierkegaard's trenchant critiques of Hegelian attempts to recast Christian thought, which are no less philosophical for being directed against a certain way of doing philosophy and especially of bringing it to bear on religious faith.

The philosophical task of the *Tahâfût* had been to deflate the pretensions of the emanation scheme, which Islamic philosophers had adopted and elaborated in order to offer an intellectually respectable reading of the Qur'an's insistence that all-that-is comes forth from the One God. Ghazali objected to pretending that the scheme offered any interpretation of Qur'anic teaching, requiring as it did that the emanation follow necessarily, as premises from an single axiom, and so jeopardizing divine sufficiency as well as the intentionality of divine sovereignty. But if, despite its elegance, the necessary emanation scheme is inadequate to formulate

---

[27] These charges form the structure of Louis Gardet's perceptive *La Pensée Réligieuse d'Avicenne* (Paris: Vrin, 1951).

[28] Simon Van Den Bergh, *Averroês' Tahafut al-Tahafut* (Cambridge: Cambridge University Press, 1954); translation by Michael Marmura: *The Incoherence of the Philosophers* (Provo UT: Brigham Young University Press, 1997).

[29] See Seyyed Hossein Nasr's *Three Muslim Sages: Avicenna, Suhrawardî, Ibn 'Arabî* (Cambridge MA: Harvard University Press, 1964).

the relation of creator to creatures according to the Qur'an, how can reason be employed to help Muslims express that relation? This question sets the constructive goal of the remainder of Ghazali's work. Again, guided by the tenor of the Qur'an, he insists that the true relation cannot be modeled on logical deduction but must be intentional in character. So everything will turn on the *qudra*, the divine decree. Yet since the *qudra* must remain secret, as no one can claim to know the Most High's intentions, the relation must be unformulatable in principle.

It is here that I was once again reminded of "the distinction," and Sokolowski's observation that it is "glimpsed on the margin of faith and reason."[30] Ghazali concludes that philosophy cannot be foundational for such inquiries; faith must lead: in this case, "God says 'be' and it is" (Qur'an 19.35). Moreover, part of the faith in One God which marks Muslims is the believers' profound conviction "of the unalterable justice and excellence of things as they are [i.e., as they are created]: 'the perfect rightness of the actual.' " That is, of the *qudra* as the product and the reflection of divine wisdom: "the world in all its circumstances remains unimpeachable right and just, and it is unsurpassably excellent."[31] These remarks of Eric Ormsby point to a key book of the *Ihya'*, "The Book of Faith in Divine Unity and Trust in Divine Providence [*Kitab at-tawhîd wa tawakkul*]," where the total dependence of the universe on the One God becomes the ground for our trust in that same God's providential care.[32] In Ormsby's judgment this is the central conviction to which Ghazali's spiritual crisis brought him, and which he set himself to work out in his subsequent writings.

Yet it is not a naive Panglossian assertion that this is the best of all possible worlds, since there is none such for Ghazali. That is, there is no set of "possible worlds" such that there could be a best one; or even if there were, we would have no way of ascertaining which "one" was *best*. This conviction rather bespeaks the relation of *this* world to the creator as expressive of God's creating wisdom; *not* as possessing qualities which we would deem *best*.[33] So it is the actual order which proves instructive; not

---

[30] Sokolowski (note 6), p. 39.

[31] Eric Ormsby, "Creation in Time in Islamic Thought with Special Reference to al-Ghazali," in David Burrell and Bernard McGinn, eds, *God and Creation* (Notre Dame IN: University of Notre Dame Press, 1990), pp. 246–64, citation at 256–8.

[32] My translation appears under the title *Faith in Divine Unity and Trust in Divine Providence* (Louisville KY: Fons Vitae, 2001), with special thanks to Timothy Winter, Gray Henry, and my late colleague, Marie-Louise Siauve, translator of the companion book of the *Ihya': Le Livre de l'amour* (Paris: Vrin, 1986).

[33] This resolution to divine wisdom represents the conclusion of Eric Orsmby's *Theodicy In Islamic Thought* (Princeton NJ: Princeton University Press, 1984).

that order as embodying an abstract pattern. This is a key consequence of Ghazali's insistence that philosophy cannot be foundational in such matters, and sets the goal of his constructive efforts: not to attempt to formulate this unique relation ("the distinction") but to show us how to learn from it by removing obstacles which our customary habits of thought might throw up. So reason will function therapeutically at the service of faith, for the task is a properly theological one which outstrips reason but needs it critically: how to express a relation when that relation cannot be formulated. The source and the focus is faith, as the point of this book is *tawakkul*: trust in divine providence, while the means is *tawhîd*: faith in divine unity. Ghazali reads everything in the Qur'an regarding divine unity as counsel for a life of trust in that One God's providence. The is consonant with the paranetic thrust of the Qur'an as well as with the overall aim of the *Ihya'*, yet it also displays his way of putting reason at the service of faith, by allowing speculation to subserve practice. Let us see how this works, and how it supplies us with an Islamic analogue for "the Christian distinction."

What sort of activity is *tawakkul*, trusting in divine providence? As Ghazali elaborates it, it cannot be equated with mere resignation or "Islamic fatalism." It is rather the activity of aligning oneself with the way things really are, with the truth that "there is no agent but God most high," which is what *tawhîd*, or faith in One God, means for Ghazali. Now this alignment requires effort since we cannot formulate the relation between God and creatures, and so cannot see how the one divine agent relates to the other agents which we experience. Furthermore, things as we experience them are *not* things as they really are: human perception and understanding is shot through with *jahiliyya*, that pervasive *ignorance* (or waywardness) which characterizes humanity uninstructed by Torah, *Injil* [Gospel], or Qur'an. Yet for this reason the effort cannot be solely intellectual. It is not a matter of learning the truth so that one can align oneself with it – as though the first part of the book on faith in divine unity could be mastered in such a way that the second part would be its application. It is rather that by trying to act according to the conviction that the *qudra* [divine decree] is the truth we are shown how things truly are. Faith (*tawhîd*) and practice (*tawakkul*) are reciprocal; neither is foundational. Yet there it an understanding that we can experience, that of a pilgrim in faith [*salîk*]:

And if faith in divine unity brings about insight into the effects of causes, abundant faith in benevolence is what brings about confidence in the effects of the causes, and the state of trust in divine providence will only be perfected, as I shall relate, by confidence in the guarantor [*wakîl*] and tranquillity of heart towards the benevolent oversight of the [divine] sponsor. For this faith is indeed an exalted chapter in the chapters of faith, and the stories about it from the path of those experiencing the unveiling go on at length. So let us simply mention it briefly: to wit, the conviction of the seeker in the station of faith in divine unity, a conviction held firmly and without any doubt. This is a faith deemed to be trustworthy and certain, with no weakness or doubt accompanying it, that when God – great and glorious – created all human beings according to a reason greater than reason and an understanding greater than their understanding, that He also created for them an understanding that would sustain each one of them, and bestowed on them a wisdom that they would never cease describing.[34]

As has been mentioned, Ghazali will explicate this "faith which is an exalted chapter in the chapters of faith [tawhîd]" by:

showing that there is no agent but God the most high: of all that exists in creation – sustenance given or withheld, life or death, riches or poverty, and everything else that can be named, the sole one who initiated and orig-inated it all is God most high. And when this has been made clear to you, you will not see anything else, so that your fear will be of Him, your hope in Him, your trust in Him, and your security with Him, for He is the sole agent without any other. Everything else is in His service, for not even the smallest atom in the worlds of heaven and earth is independent of Him for its movement. If the gates of mystical insight were opened to you, this would be clear to you with a clarity more perfect than ordinary vision.[35]

Yet "for those who possess their heart and their vision, God will make every atom in heaven and earth speak to them of His decree [qudra]."[36] A Christian reader will be reminded of the vision which Augustine attained after "the light of confidence had flooded into his heart," when he could note how all things said – to those who could hear them – "God is he who made us."[37] In al-Ghazali's faith-world, things become signs [ayât] for those formed by the verses [ayât] of the Qur'an. Yet their speech, even if one were privileged to understand it, could not be communicated to others. (Here the echoes of Sufi teaching resonate.) For what things say

---

[34] See my translation: Book of Faith in Divine Unity and Trust in Divine Providence [Kitâb at-Tawhîd wa Tawakkul] from the Ihya' 'Ulum ad-Dîn (Louisville KY: Fons Vitae, 2001), pp. 47–8 [274–5]. Page numbers will be followed by pages in brackets from the Beirut edition of the Ihya', 1989.

[35] Ibid., pp. 15–16 [263].

[36] Ibid., p. 18 [264].

[37] Confessions 8,12; 10,6.

could only be grasped by those for whom God has "enhanced under-standing, wisdom, and reason . . . , unveiling for them the effects of things, apprising them of the secrets of the intelligible world, teaching them the subtleties of speech and the hidden springs of punishment, to the point there they were thus informed regarding what is good and evil, useful or harmful."[38]

Once again, a speculative understanding will be rigorously subordinated to practical counsel, as *causes* become conditions for the *sunnah Allah*, the ordering of the divine decree [*qudra*] as it can be perceived in nature. On such a perspective, human freedom will not be coherently understood as autonomous or proactive will, but always as a response – positive or neg-ative – to the good as a divine invitation.[39] One will distinguish different senses of "agent," to be sure, as Ghazali does with the example of an execution: both the emir and the executioner can be said to have put the condemned to death.[40] Yet the primacy always lies with the creator, and at this point Ghazali does not hesitate to use the pattern of necessary ema-nation to image the relation of the one agent with all the others: "in this way you may come to understand the emanation of things so ordained from the eternal omnipotence, even though the omnipotent One is eternal and the things temporal." Yet he stops short of endorsing the image as an accurate one by demurring immediately: "But this [train of thought] knocks on another door, to another world of the worlds of unveiling. So let us leave all that, since our aim is to offer counsel regarding the way to faith in divine unity in practice."[41] So the only understanding which

---

[38] See note 34, p. 48 [275].

[39] So far as this general statement is concerned I have argued that it parallels the authen-tic Christian tradition in *Freedom and Creation* (note 3) and "Aquinas and Scotus: Contrary Patterns for Philosophical Theology," in Bruce Marshall, ed., *Theology and Dialogue* (Notre Dame IN: University of Notre Dame Press, 1990), pp. 105–29.

[40] See note 34, pp. 42–6 [272–5].

[41] *Ibid.*, p. 42 [272]. See Richard Frank's *Creation and the Cosmic System: al Ghazali and Avicenna* (Abhandlungen der Heidelberger Akademie der Wissenschaften, philo.-hist. Kl., 1991/2; Heidelberg, 1992). Intent upon showing Ghazali's reliance upon Ibn Sina, Frank interprets *malakût* [intelligible world] as containing a plethora of "possibles" such that God selects one set to be the "actual world." These "possibles" (or "possible worlds") organized Ibn Sina's intellectual emanation scheme, which corresponds to the "necessity" of which Ghazali speaks obtaining in creation, so that the "created universe is the best possible." To my mind, al-Ghazali's use of the emanation scheme is one more inadequate image of the relation of creator to creatures, however rhetorically useful with philosophers. It does not – since nothing can – articulate the "secrets of the intelligible world," but merely offers a *façon de parler*. God can make use of such structured intelligible relations, much as guitarists rely on strings being in tune when they improvise. Moreover, their "necessity," inter-mediate as it is, results from divine wisdom.

Ghazali will countenance of this elusive relation between creator and creatures is associated with his Sufi image of *unveiling*, which is supposed to have the effect of convincing us that "all of it is unqualifiedly just" (Ormsby), leading us beyond sheer omnipotence [*jabr*] to divine generosity [*jûd*] – a form of the first of which is among the ninety-nine canonical "names of God."[42]

There is no other understanding possible, for we have come face-to-face with "the secret of the divine decree [which presents us with] another sea immensely deep, with vast extremities and chaotic swells, nearly as extensive as the sea of faith in divine unity, and the boats of those whose capacity is limited founder in it, for they do not know that this is something hidden, not to be grasped except by those who know."[43] And while for "those who know [*arafûn*]," these "understandings of unveiling [constitute] the basis of the [pilgrimage] station of trust in divine providence," Ghazali closes this speculative part of the book by insisting that we "return to the knowledge of practices," for that is where the vast majority of believers live and act. These practices are explored by a bevy of Sufi stories, all of which illustrate the guiding axiom that "there is no might and power but in God," whose practical consequences Ghazali explicitly distinguishes from trusting in *power* or *might* as attributes of God, reminding us that these are but names of God most High, the One in whom we put our trust. The stories of Sufi sheiks are offered to develop specific skills and virtues of trusting, habits of responding to different situations where one learns by acting how things are truly ordered, the truth of *qudra*. A large part of these skills is a discernment which turns on developing an eye for the manifest and hidden means offered to us by the divine wisdom [*sunnah Allah*].[44]

Ghazali's resolution of the vexing question how we should responsibly live within a relation which we cannot properly understand is to propose

---

[42] See *Al-Ghazali on the Ninety-Nine Beautiful Names of God*, trans. David Burrell and Nazih Daher (Cambridge: Islamic Texts Society, 1992), *jabbâr* (66–7).

[43] See Frank's *Cosmic System* (note 41), p. 41.

[44] A passage from our book of Ghazali's is relevant here: "So the renunciation of all means is contrary to His wisdom, and amounts to ignorance with respect to God most high, whereas acting according to the necessities of the practice [*sunna*] of God most high, while placing one's trust in God – great and glorious – and not in means, is not inconsistent with trusting in divine providence – as we emphasized earlier by the story of the attorney in the trial. Yet means are divided into manifest and hidden ones, and for the meaning of trust in divine providence, the hidden means will suffice without the manifest ones, while the soul finds its tranquillity in the cause which makes them to be means [i.e., the creator] rather than in the means [themselves]" (p. 283).

a school of learning how to respond to what happens in such a way that one is shown how things are truly ordered; this school will involve learning from others more practiced in responding rightly. Ghazali's judicious use of stories intimates Sufi practice of master/disciple apprenticeship (or spiritual direction) so that we can gradually learn the proper way to act in relation to circumstances. There is no higher wisdom than this; speculative reason is thoroughly subordinate to practical reason in these matters. Ghazali sees that as the logical implication of replacing the emanation scheme with an intentional creator. So the challenge of understanding the relation of creator to the universe becomes the task of rightly responding to events as they happen, in such a way that the true ordering of things [qudra] can be made manifest in one's actions, which are conceived as responses to invitations of the Most High.

One can easily read Ghazali's efforts here in the light of "the distinction." Where they take a peculiarly Muslim tack seems to be in insisting that key terms like "agent" must always properly be read – even when different related senses are explicitly acknowledged – with the divine agent as the primary analogate. Appreciating that terms like "act" and "agent" are paradigmatically analogous terms, as we use them properly in widely diverse contexts, why *must* the divine agent be seen as the only proper agent? Because all-that-is is always dependent upon the divine power, of course. Yet that same power empowers creatures to act in their own right; that is precisely how we distinguish a creator from agents acting within the universe. As Aquinas puts it, "God ordains [rational creatures] to act voluntarily and of themselves."[45] This is a key implication of "the Christian distinction" which Sokolowski has identified. It will also allow Aquinas to employ a standing distinction regarding the meaning a term carries [res signficata] and our use of the term [modus significandi] in a fresh way, to show how analogous terms can be used properly whether we think first of creatures or first of God. As he puts it:

> from the point of view of what the word means it is used primarily of God and derivatively of creatures, for what the words means – the perfection it signifies – flows from God to the creature. But from the point of view of our use of the word we apply it first to creatures because we know them first. That is why it has a way of signifying that is appropriate to creatures.[46]

We can see that creation is the linchpin in Aquinas' treatment, since the use of perfection terms of God depends on our familiarity with them in

45   ST 19.12.3.
46   ST 1.13.6.

creatures plus the fact that they "flow from God to creatures." This allows us to predicate "what they mean" of God, even though that meaning will remain beyond our ken. Yet we can know from our use of them with creatures that they are analogous, and so possessed of a transcendent dimension, as Socrates found out in pursuing the oracle regarding wisdom: only wise people realize they are not wise!

So Aquinas retains a strong note of God being beyond our ken, yet accessible to those who can realize that fact while they work with the peculiar subset of language whose terms carry the required inner differentiation to be used both knowingly and unknowingly of God. Yet there is certainly a different flavor here than in Ghazali, despite the overall similarity. To what can we attribute it? Sokolowski argues that "the Christian distinction between God and the world, the denial that God in his divinity is part of or dependent upon the world, was brought forward with greater clarity through the discussion of the way the Word became flesh,"[47] and I would concur. The elements are there in Ghazali, and ingeniously brought together, especially in relation to human freedom, but it seems that the struggle of the Christological controversies allowed Christian thinkers better to focus the mode of dependence so as to balance the competing uses of key terms like "agent" in a way more respectful of the reality of creatures.[48] So "the distinction" can be more perspicuous in Christian thinkers who attend to these realities. Yet it is also invoked and employed by Muslims like Ghazali, and so can be found analogously in their treatments of the relation of a free creator to all-that-is.

Maimonides and Free Creation

With the recent renewal in interest in Maimonides, much has been written regarding his views on creation, which are at once interesting in themselves and also telling for their influence on Aquinas, who faced the same questions, as well as their consonance with al-Ghazali.[49] At the heart of the debate is a hermeneutical controversy surrounding the *Guide*, and especially Leo Strauss' decision to read Maimonides' introductory remark that "in speaking about very obscure matters it is necessary to conceal

---

[47]   Sokolowski (note 6), p. 37.
[48]   See Thomas Weinandy's illuminating historical-conceptual account of the journey to a clear formulation in Chalcedon: *Does God Change?* (Still River MA: St. Bede's Publications, 1985).
[49]   For references to the *Guide* in translation, see note 23; see also my article at note 2.

some parts and to disclose others,"[50] as warning readers to be prepared for hidden meanings, especially in areas where Torah-faith and philosophical reason may come into conflict. On the strength of this license, of course, one could uncover a plethora of esoteric readings by following the fault line of deftly placed contradictions. Yet if the Rambam's [= Rabbi Moses ben Maimon] intent was to help his student Joseph to bring Torah-faith and current philosophical reasoning into a rapprochement, Strauss' working premise of an implacable conflict or unbridgeable chasm between Jerusalem and Athens hardly seems appropriate as a general hermeneutic tool. In any case, a recent response of William Dunphy to Herbert Davidson's exegesis of Maimonides on creation aptly illustrates the parameters of this discussion.[51]

Everything turns on God's freedom in creating the universe, by contrast with the prevailing philosophical picture of "necessary emanation" which (as we have seen in Ghazali) threatens "the distinction" of creator from all-that-is. The discussion is complicated for us, as Dunphy has shown, by a tendency of commentators to elide the distinction between *creatio ex nihilo* and *creatio de novo*: the first stipulating that the originating cause of the universe needed no coeternal (or "pre-existing") matter to work on, and the second linking the activity of creating with inaugurating an initial moment of time.[52] It is understandable that commentators could confuse these two notions, since neither Ghazali nor Maimonides distinguished them adequately. In fact, the Rambam felt that people who insist that "the world has always been and will always be like this" are not entitled to assert "that the world derives from the act of the deity or exists in virtue of His purpose, will, free choice and particularization, [for] that is not the meaning of purpose as we propose to conceive it. For we wish to signify by the term that it – I mean the world – does not necessarily proceed from Him, may He be exalted, as an effect necessarily proceeds from its cause."[53] So while the paramount issue is God's freedom in creating and so "particularizing" the universe, according to the divine wisdom and without having to conform to philosophical necessities, that concern is here seen to be *prima facie* incompatible with an eternal cre-

[50] *Ibid.*, Intro, p. 18.
[51] William Dunphy, "Maimonides' Not-So-Secret Position on Creation," in Eric Ormsby, ed., *Moses Maimonides and his Time* (Washington DC: Catholic University of America Press, 1989), pp. 151–72, responding to Herbert Davidson's "Maimonides' Secret Position on Creation," in *Studies in Medieval Jewish History and Literature* (Cambridge MA: Harvard University Press, 1979).
[52] See William Dunphy essay (note 4).
[53] See note 23, 2.21, pp. 314–15.

ation and so to incline one to accepting that creation entails an initial moment of time.

He insists that there can be no demonstration of this point, however, as the Muslim *kalâm* thinkers imagined, for we could never hope to *demonstrate* an action which turns on divine freedom. This sets up the tactical relation between faith and reason in which Aquinas will concur with "Rabbi Moses," as he called him. Yet Aquinas saw more clearly that divine freedom was the central issue, and while *creatio de novo* offered a more perspicuous *image* of the universe's free origin in God, that no contradiction followed from presuming its origination to have been without an initial moment, yet eminently free. A subtle yet telling distinction, for it reinforces our understanding of "the distinction" of God from the universe: not merely as prohibiting all anthropomorphism, but also calling attention to an agent *sui generis*: the creator of all. The Rambam was intent upon explicating all biblical anthropomorphism in a way which respected such philosophical limits, but apparently so taken with the power of the necessary emanation scheme that he failed to see how an everlasting universe could be compatible with the freedom in creating which he wished to defend as central to the Torah's treatment.

This offers us one more example of "the distinction" at work; here in Jewish thought. It is not so clearly present as it is for Aquinas, given the Rambam's apparent need to link divine freedom with the world's having an initial moment. Yet it is present throughout, in his treatment of the creator's relation to all-that-is, and his concern lest God's action be modeled on the role of a necessary premise in a logical deduction. Moreover, this is the difficult case for Maimonides, even though Aquinas clearly profited by his intellectual strategies to set up his own argumentation in *De aeternitate mundi*.[54] For the Rambam's treatment of divine attributes and language about God represents a radical "distinction" between the grammar of discourse *in divinis* and among creatures. Yet here again, the nuance with which Aquinas can accept Maimonides' axioms regarding "the distinction" as it governs the semantics of language about God, yet still find ordinary human expressions which will bear the freight, suggests once again that the incarnation offers a way of putting this *distinction* to which the Rambam had no access.[55] So a similar comparative judgment can be rendered as in the case of Ghazali: whereas something very like "the Christian distinction" is at work here, notably in securing the

---

[54] ET: *On the Eternity of the World* (Milwaukee WI; Marquette University Press, 1984).

[55] See my "Maimonides, Aquinas and Ghazali on Naming God," in Peter Ochs, ed., *The Return to Scripture in Judaism and Christianity* (New York: Paulist, 1993), pp. 233–55.

freedom of the creator, one feels that it lacks the nuance one can find in a thinker like Aquinas.

Concluding Remarks

Whereas I set out to show how Sokolowski's celebrated "Christian distinction" could just as well be a Jewish or a Muslim one, I have had to conclude that while we can speak of "the distinction" in the most notable examples of Jewish or Muslim philosophical theology – in this case, Moses Maimonides and al-Ghazali – that the paradigm instance of "the distinction" remains Christian. These reflections might also be read as another essay in the fertile area of "Christian philosophy," where one's faith commitments and tradition can allow conceptual moves less accessible to those who do not share the same faith. Once one has become sensitized to "the distinction" in its paradigmatic Christian mode, however, it can be seen to be operative in reflection inspired by these other Abrahamic faiths as well. A final observation, more in the form of a promissory note and an invitation to others to pursue, regards the celebrated "nonduality" of Sankara in the Hindu tradition. My source here is the slim volume of Teape lectures offered by Sara Grant, a religious of the Sacred Heart, in Cambridge in 1989.[56] They are subtitled, "Confessions of a Non-Dualist Christian," and present a powerful argument for reading texts from Aquinas on creation in such a way as to emphasize how creatures' very being consists in their *relation* to the creator. Read in conjunction with Kathryn Tanner's persuasive *God and Creation in Christian Theology*,[57] this argument offers an arresting set of images for the inexpressible relation of creator to creatures, or "the distinction" that we have been elucidating and expanding. For if this *distinction* is unlike those within the world, in that God cannot be conceived as another being over against the world, it may well be that our struggles to avoid malapropisms in theology could be mightily assisted by the conceptual endeavors of some Indian thinkers, notably Sankara.[58] That exercise remains beyond this chapter, however, so I leave it as a challenge for those who are better informed about these traditions, yet like me, find themselves ever informed by "the distinction" which Robert Sokolowski has so finely drawn.

---

[56] See note 25.
[57] Kathryn Tanner, *God and Creation in Christian Theology* (Oxford: Basil Blackwell, 1988).
[58] I am indebted to my colleague, Bradley Malkovsky, for these suggestions.

Chapter 15

INCARNATION AND CREATION: THE HIDDEN DIMENSION

To be fruitful, a paradigm shift must be inclusive rather than merely reactive. So if treatises on the sacraments focused on patterns of participation in the redemptive activity of Christ, as they characteristically did, it will not behoove a "creation-centered" account of the patterns of participation in the kingdom of God simply to bypass all of that, as though the "original peace" of creation could be appropriated (by Christians) other than through Christ.[1] Moreover, that would merely contribute to another myopia in theological inquiry parallel to the one we noted regarding creation, but this time attending the central second article of the creed: the drama of redemption. The proper strategy seems rather to be the inclusive one proposed and executed by Nicholas Lash in his recent *Believing Three Ways in One God*.[2] In order to show the inherently Trinitarian cast of Christian faith, Lash systematically comments on each of the three articles in the creed in the light of the other two. The implications for our inquiry are immediate: one restores the initial article on creation not by suppressing the others but by reading them in its light, and then reading it in the light of the other two. This strategy has been sketched out by John McDade in a recent article which shows how a fruitful dialectical rapport between creation and redemption must characterize a fully Christian theology.[3]

The first step in restoring the tension and rapport between creation and redemption, and so between the first two articles of the creed, is to recall briefly how it happened that the first was virtually suppressed in

[1] The phrase is John Milbank's, in his masterful *Theology and Social Theory* (Oxford: Blackwell, 1992); see *Modern Theology* 8 (1992), pp. 319–99 for a series of articles on it.
[2] Nicholas Lash, *Believing Three Ways in One God* (Notre Dame IN: University of Notre Dame Press, 1993; London: SCM Press, 1993).
[3] John McDade, "Creation and salvation: green faith and Christian themes," in *The Month* 23 (1990), pp. 433–41. I am indebted to Nicholas Lash for guiding me to this essay.

Christian theology. It was hardly a deliberate decision and certainly not the product of a conspiracy, but rather the result of a convergence of factors, three of which are quite sufficient to explain it. The first concerns the replacement of the sabbath with the day of the Lord. Rabbinic teaching on the sabbath had it that while God created the world well-ordered (Genesis 1), it needed to be perfected and that perfecting is precisely our work. Yet the periodic rest of the sabbath, most of whose regulations may be summarized under the injunction not to engage in the culture-creating work of lighting a fire, is psychologically required lest our involvement in perfecting the world lead us to presume that it is our work in its entirety. So foreswearing such activity one day out of seven reminds us forcibly, as the world continues, that we are not its originator. The second has to do with the extremely useful thirteenth-century distinction of supernatural from natural, which helped Aquinas immensely in his synthesis of Greek and Islamic philosophy with Christian faith. Yet an unintended connotation of that distinction, which identified grace with the supernatural order, was to imply that the natural order was not a grace, not a gift. And what is not a gift is a given. But taking the world as a *given* is precisely the pagan outlook which the revelation to Moses explicitly countered in the ancient world. Finally, the nineteenth-century distinction of history from nature tended to leave nature to scientific inquiry and locate the action of God firmly in history: salvation history. It is little wonder, then, that our belief in creation as a divine gift is largely "notional" in character (as Newman distinguished possible modes of assent in faith).

The following constructive step has to do with the way we present redemption: as a totally anthropological story, which then becomes the drama of "sin and redemption"; or within a cosmic story which presents the original order, so profoundly disturbed by humans, as the one that is to be "restored in Christ"? That original order (Milbank's "original peace") is, of course, the "order of the universe" which Aquinas identifies as the creator's primary intent in the free act of creating. In this way redemption becomes a "new creation" – a thoroughly patristic phrase – which then needs to be understood against the background of the initial gift of *creatio ex nihilo*, thereby giving fresh significance to that phrase. But the new significance is always reciprocal, since each of the traditions which avers free creation will speak about it in a language borrowed from their experience with revelation.[4] So the hermeneutical circle is operative and

[4] This is the burden of my *Freedom and Creation in Three Traditions* (Notre Dame IN: University of Notre Dame Press, 1993).

fruitful, as revelation requires creation as its background, and creation demands revelation to find its proper expression. (If "redemption" is replaced by "revelation" here, that is to offer a strategy which can include Judaism and Islam as well; for Christians, the primary content of revelation will be creation-cum-redemption.)

So the conceptual difficulty emerges immediately: we yearn for a single focus. Yet if the truth be told, rather than suppressed in the interest of tidiness, "the themes of creation and salvation act, within the [full] Christian tradition, as two poles corresponding to the broader context of God's relationship to the world and the particularity of the divine action in Jesus."[5] McDade acknowledges that these will give us "two dimensions of because of the difficulties of holding the range of connotations together within the one account." In other words, the difficulties are ours; they are conceptual, while the message of the tradition is clear: the two themes must be held together for an account faithful to the divine drama – not the merely human drama – of creation-*cum*-redemption. The reason they must be held together has to do with our understanding of each gracious act of God: the gift of creation and the incarnation. Taken by themselves, each will be misunderstood. So the conceptual difficulty of maintaining a dual focus actively reminds us that the very effort to do so is the price of getting a proper perspective on either one.

Let me illustrate this, beginning as the Christian tradition did, with Christ. Here is the singular point where God and God's creation meet, so clarifying the "ontological constitution" of Jesus will help us to articulate that ever-mysterious relationship of the creator to creation. Jesus is the "Word made flesh," and the Word in question is the very One "through whom the world is made." Again, for Aquinas, the emanation of all things from God in the Word is in strict continuity with the generation of the Word from the Father, even though the emanation which is creation is utterly free while the generation of the Word reflects the very nature of divinity.[6] What is significant here is that Aquinas does not

---

[5] McDade (note 3), p. 436.

[6] See the illuminating response to the question "whether the trinity of divine persons can be known by natural reason?" While he answers *no*, he goes on to add (in replying to the third objection) that "there are two reasons why the knowledge of divine persons was necessary [in Anselm's sense: serendipitous and most fitting] for us. [First,] for the right idea of creation. The fact of saying that God made all things by His Word excludes the error of those who say that God produced things by necessity. [Secondly,] when we say that in Him there is a procession of love, we show that God produced creatures not because He needed them, nor because of any other extrinsic reason, but on account of the love of His own goodness" (ST 1.32.1).

hesitate to use *emanation* as a metaphor for the free divine act of creating the universe, once he has shown how free creation renders the scheme of necessary emanation redundant.[7] Similarly, for Aquinas, the sending of the Word "for our salvation" is in strict continuity with the eternal generation of that same Word, so creation and incarnation follow a parallel logic for him.[8] It should follow that a better understanding of one will lead to a better grasp of the other.

But how? As often in theological matters, it is more a question of avoiding misunderstanding than of a positive grasp. And the misunderstandings occur on both sides, and readily so, as the history of theology testifies. It took more than four centuries of sustained reflection, replete with trial and error and often bitter conflict, to come to the balanced definitions of Chalcedon (451), for what was at stake was nothing short of the proper way of articulating the relation of God to God's creation – manifested and dramatized in this singular event.[9] Kathryn Tanner has reminded us of the semantic pitfalls of any discourse which "simply contrasts" God to the world.[10] Yet how can we talk of two things without contrasting them? When one of those "things" is the creator of all the others, however, then everything else is what it is *in relation to* that One. (As Aquinas puts it so succinctly and subtly: creation consists in a relation of the creature to the creator – that is, the very being of the creature is to-be-related.[11] So "non-divine being must be talked about as always and in every respect *constituted* by, and therefore *nothing apart from*, an immediate relation with the founding agency of God."[12] One thinks of Advaita "non-dualism" or the arresting image of the world as God's body suggested by Paul van Buren (among others), or other *panentheist* alternatives

---

[7] See my *Knowing the Unknowable God* (Notre Dame IN: University of Notre Dame Press), pp. 33, 49.

[8] As Timothy McDermott puts it so felicitously: "The life of Christ embeds in time the eternal issuing of the Word" (*Summa Theologiae; A Concise Translation*, ed. Timothy McDermott [Westminster MD: Christian Classics, 1989]). Aquinas' statement of this is in the final question which treats of God's triunity, immediately preceding those devoted to creation: "the Son proceeds eternally as God; but temporally, by becoming man, according to his visible mission, or likewise by dwelling in man according to his invisible mission" (ST 1.43.2).

[9] For an astute and readable account of the dramatic path to Chalcedon, see Thomas Weinandy's *Does God Change? The Word's Becoming in the Incarnation* (Still River MA: St. Bede's Press, 1985).

[10] Kathryn Tanner, *God and Creation in Christian Theology* (London: Blackwell, 1988), pp. 37–48.

[11] ST 1.45.3.

[12] Tanner (note 10), p. 84.

like that recently espoused by Elizabeth Johnson.[13] Yet the positive attempts to articulate this relationship, like those which call themselves "panentheist," seem to falter in offering more than they can deliver, inasmuch as they pretend to present more than a metaphorical expression of this grounding relationship to the creator. For me, the most adequate, as well as the most arresting, image is that of James Ross: the universe is to its creator as the song on the breath of a singer.[14] The ephemeral character of this image seems to remind us that it is an image, and cannot be more than an image.

In a similar vein, McDade suggests that "the adverbs of the Chalcedonian definition" are fashioned expressly to present this relationship of creator to creation in an appropriately negative fashion: "the natures of Christ are said to exist 'without confusion, without separation' [*inconfuse, indistincte*]: never confused — as though the divine and the human can be fused like wine and water in a pantheist mingling — and never separated, as though there is an autonomous creation which is outside God's action."[15] By reminding ourselves that the struggle to get straight about who Jesus is necessarily involved answering ontological questions (like *what* he is), we have already taken a significant initial step in our attempt to show how understanding one of these poles inevitably involves the other. For were it otherwise, Jesus could simply have been an adventitious visitor, an *avatar* with no other relation to the universe than his "coming." Yet our faith would resist any such reacting; Jesus could not be a mere visitor. So from the beginning, if Jesus was divine, he could be none other than the "Word through whom the world was made." As the history of the development of these matters makes clear, it was the struggle to define the reality of the person of Jesus which unveiled the revelation of God as triune.

Moreover, if the divine being which Jesus is were not the creator of the universe, then it could conceivably be that of *a* divine being, and the

---

[13]   For the Advaita suggestion, see the illuminating monograph by Sara Grant, RSCJ: *Toward an Alternative Theology: Confessions of a Non-dualist Christian* (Bangalore: Asian Trading Corp., 1991) with a new edition edited by Bradley Malkovsky (Notre Dame IN: University of Notre Dame Press, 2002); Paul Van Buren's suggestion, offered originally in *Discerning the Way* (New York, Seabury, 1980), pp. 109–19, has been taken up by Sallie McFague in *Models of God* (Philadelphia: Fortress, 1988) pp. 69–78; but see also Elizabeth Johnson on the relation of God to the world in her *She Who Is* (New York: Crossroad, 1993), pp. 224–45.

[14]   "The being of the cosmos is like *a song on the breath of a singer*" ("Creation II," in Alfred J. Freddoso, ed., *Existence and Nature of God* (Notre Dame IN: University of Notre Dame Press, 1983), p. 128).

[15]   McDade (note 3), p. 438.

plenitude of Gnostic interpretations would open up before us. So the affirmations so dearly won regarding divine and human natures in Christ only makes sense against the background implied by their use of the term *nature*: that one is creator and the other created. It could not simply be that two different *things* were so closely united in Christ as to constitute a *"hypostatic* union," whatever that might be! We are reminded of Kathryn Tanner's proscription, and reminded as well that the One who comes to us in Jesus is the same One through whom we are all created, and so is that One "in whom we live, move, and have our being." We are also reminded of the utter inability of liberal Christianity to make any sense of Jesus once it confessed its incapacity to negotiate Chalcedon. What appeared to them to be the opacity of Greek philosophy was in fact the original attempt of the Christian community to articulate the intrinsic connection of redemption with creation. And their failure to understand what was going on here relegated talk about Jesus to a thin veneer of anthropological discourse, to the point where discourse about redemption was undermined as well.[16]

There has to be a lesson here, and perhaps we are now in a position to articulate it more pointedly: *not* as an argument about the relevance of philosophy to Christian discourse so much as a matter of the integrity of the revelatory message which must include both creation and redemption as moments in God's undeserved self-giving. In responding to the question: what is the fundamental and basic conception within Christian theology, Karl Rahner responds with a phrase (endorsed by McDade): "the divinization of the world through the Spirit of God, within which incarnation and redemption arise as inner moments."[17] What that lapidary formula misses, on our account, is the crucial reminder that such "divinization" involves restoring the original order, the order bestowed "in the Word" as the creator's primary intent in offering the gift of creation. Nevertheless, the patristic expression "divinization" reminds us of something which the equally patristic term "restoring" could fail to connote: that this restoration is a transformation as well, promising an intimacy with God in friendship which beggars even the original "intimacy [of creation as] a relationship to divinity as its total ground," which already proscribed any contrastive modes of expression. Perhaps it is clear by now

---

[16]   Hence my critique of Schubert Ogden's version of "process theology" in *Aquinas: God and Action* (Notre Dame IN: University of Notre Dame Press, 1979), pp. 87–9.

[17]   McDade (note 3), p. 436; from P. Imhof and H. Biallawons, eds, *Karl Rahner in Dialogue: Conversations and Interviews 1965–1982* (New York: Crossroad, 1986), p. 126.

that, however difficult it may be to express their mutual relationship, one cannot speak of redemption without presuming creation, nor can one speak properly of creation without the idiom supplied by revelation. Indeed, the operative faith of Christians has always presumed this inner connection; the task of theologians is at best not to betray it.

We can show this from the viewpoint of creation as well, as Aquinas does in a revealing response to the question whether a proper under-standing of creation requires our recognition of God's triunity. It would seem not, since we have been presuming from the outset that Jews, Chris-tians, and Muslims concur in averring the free creation of the universe by God – indeed as the initial gift of a gracious God, while agreeing to differ on ways of expressing divine unity. Yet Aquinas replies that knowledge of God's triunity helps immensely in clarifying one's understanding of cre-ation. Indeed, using terms reminiscent of Anselm, he even regards such knowledge as "necessary," notably to "avoid the error of those who say that God produced things by necessity of nature" – the necessary emana-tion scheme, which philosophers of his time preferred for its conceptual elegance. That specific error, he contends, is excluded by "our saying that God makes all things in His Word," while the correlative misapprehen-sion that "God produces creatures out of some need to do so or because of some extrinsic cause" is precluded by "our placing in God a proces-sion of love," which makes it clear that God brings forth creatures "through love of His own goodness" (ST 1.32.1.3).[18] He is saying, then, that the doctrine of the triunity of God allows Christians to take the teaching they share with Jews and Muslims – that creation is God's free gift – and incorporate it into their doctrine of God, so bringing that teaching from the realm of insistent assertion to that of theological coher-ence. While this observation does not directly link creation with redemp-tion, it does remind us that the free creation of the universe cannot itself be the result of philosophical inference, but is always a matter of revela-tion. And linking creation with revelation makes it for Christians a mystery pertaining to the order of redemption.

Two recent theological aberrations can illustrate this point by what Lonergan has called an "inverse insight": seeing how and where they go wrong helps us to appreciate the need for the dual focus which we have been insisting upon. The first goes under the label of "process theology." After an early apprenticeship with Schubert Ogden (in the late sixties) I came to appreciate that my initial philosophical uneasiness with the

---

[18]   See note 6 above for the entire text.

program was less significant than my subsequent theological objections.[19] And those are cast in even sharper relief by this present inquiry: the initial impetus to have recourse to a version of Whitehead's philosophy to clarify the relation of God to the world stems from a liberal Christian view of God which had quite overlooked the Christian doctrine of divine triunity.[20] So God's "involvement with the world" could not be in the Word from whom all things were made, since that statement of the scriptures could only be taken metaphorically.[21] Moreover, the use of Whitehead's philosophy as an alternative to the caricature liberal Christians constructed of "classical theism" precluded any straightforward appropriation of the Christian doctrine of creation. That strategy – or lack of one – meant that everything had to be found "in Jesus" and specifically in the New Testament *logia* concerning him as interpreted by Bultmann. (While this last move seems conceptually distinct from the Whiteheadian "process" program, it cohered with the decidedly "anthropological" cast of their purportedly metaphysical inquiry.) Once it had been subjected in this way to a richer "analogy of faith," this curious concatenation of philosophical-cum-theological currents can easily be seen to be a Christian aberration, so the fact that it has virtually evaporated from the current theological scene should come as no surprise and indeed be welcomed as a heartening development in our collective sense for tradition which theology ought always to be engaged in recovering.

   The second is yet more contemporary and evidences a quite different philosophical inspiration: the preoccupation of recent "theologians of the cross" – notably Jurgen Moltmann and Eberhard Jüngel – to make "the death of Jesus mark a moment of division or separation within the Trinitarian life" of God.[22] This theology is robustly Trinitarian, by contrast with the "process" variety, yet equally oblivious of creation. Yet these thinkers do not lose sight of creation because it has been eclipsed by an alternate philosophical scheme (as in Whitehead's *creativity*), but rather because of a different combination of philosophical and religious emphases. One

---

[19]   These can be found in detail in my "Does Process Theology Rest on a Mistake" in *Theological Studies* 43 (1982), pp. 125–35. In brief, the response is *no*, four of them!

[20]   It has often been remarked that Schleiermacher, the father of liberal Christianity, relegated "the trinity" to an appendix in his *Glaubenslehre*.

[21]   For a "classical" response to the questions posed so trenchantly by "process theology," see Herbert McCabe, "The Involvement of God," in *God Matters* (London: Chapman, 1987), pp. 39–51 (originally published in *New Blackfriars*, November 1985).

[22]   The descriptive phrase is McDade's (note 3), p. 440 n. 13; the works in question are Moltmann's *The Trinity and the Kingdom of God* (London: SCM, 1981) and Jungel's *God as the Mystery of the World* (Edinburgh: T & T Clark, 1983).

suspects that a tradition influenced by Heidegger's critique of "onto-theology" could easily confuse classical reflections on the relation of crea-tures to the creator (as in Aquinas) with an independent philosophical "grounding," which proceeds in a manner quite indifferent to revelation.[23] Rather than accepting philosophical reflection as an indispensable moment in a larger theological inquiry, such thinkers invariably presume that phi-losophy must play a foundational role.[24] So by mistaking creation to be a preliminary (and hence virtually "philosophical") moment in Christian theology, rather than integral to its understanding of God's gracious activ-ity, "the centre of divine action becomes the event of the Cross and the subjectivity of the individual (the detached, introspective subject) who is faced with the dialectic of judgment and mercy"[25] – shades of Bultmann! The God in question is equally a subject yet quite detached from the world, it seems, except through the death of Jesus. So it is that death which must "make a difference" in God for there to be adequate contact between the two.

The poignant drama which results from this deracinated perspective has a fatal attraction for theological students, it seems, much as the series of objections which "process theology" leveled at its constructed foil of "clas-sical theism" caught the attention of a previous generation. Yet McDade's reminder of the roots of such affirmations in an "Augustinian Reformed tradition [which] manifests little appreciation of the mediating role of created reality in the individual's relationship with God"[26] can at least serve to orient a fascinated reader. We are thus forcibly returned to the need for a dual focus, since it seems inevitable that "those versions of the order-ing of Christian truth which treat salvation as the central Christian theme

---

[23]   This is a persistent theme in Chauvet's *Symbole et Sacrement* (Paris: Cerf, 1988), affect-ing his otherwise quite irenic attempts to incorporate classical modes of reflection in his hermeneutical perspective: see his citation of Claude Geffré's critique of Aquinas, where that author utterly misses the grammatical dimension of Aquinas' orienting remarks about divinity (p. 485), and his own preference of "mèontologie" over a "negative onto-theol-ogy," where the latter is simply presumed to employ univocal categories in its presentation of an *ens realissime* (p. 511).

[24]   Fergus Kerr's reading of "classical" tradition (as exemplified in Aquinas) in his *Theology after Wittgenstein* (New York: Blackwell, 1986) is instructive here, as can be my nonfoun-dational reading of the way in which the early questions of the *Summa Theologiae* employ the "speculative grammar" of the day to position the "divine object" without attempting to circumscribe its nature: *Aquinas: God and Action* (Notre Dame IN: University of Notre Dame Press, 1979), chs. 1 and 2. My own indebtedness is to M.-D. Chénu, *La Théologie au douzième siècle* (Paris: Cerf, 1957).

[25]   McDade (note 3), p. 437.

[26]   *Ibid.*, p. 437.

[will be] guilty . . . of being irreducibly anthropocentric."[27] Yet we can restore the focus of creation by recalling the relationship of creature to creator in the Word though whom all is created, a relationship which the Christian tradition has brought to its sharpest focus in the "Chalcedonian distinctions between the divine and created natures" in the person of Jesus.[28] In this way, we will be able to see the redemptive act as restoring that original order and indeed transforming it to an unimaginable intimacy. The redemptive act will not have to bear the burden of *establishing* a relationship, but rather of restoring one already embodied in an original order otherwise irremediably distorted by sin. At an epistemological level, however, the drama of such "dialectical theology" renders the indispensable service of reminding us that the "original order" of creation is hardly detectable without the illumination of revelation. And that reminder should keep us from the touted vagaries of an "onto-theology" which could pretend to establish that initial relationship of creator to creatures independent of revelation.

Where has all this brought us? To a challenging starting point. Everything we have done so far, with the able assistance of John McDade, has served simply to clear the ground. And if it has seemed cluttered, that is indeed the situation "on the ground." But we are now in a position to explore afresh diverse themes of the Christian life, showing how the actively dual focus which we have seen to be integral to a full Christian perspective can illuminate them: themes like justice, suffering, death, friendship; as well as the life shared by Christians and epitomized in the sacraments, which are usually considered solely as redemptive acts. While such exercises have been called "creation theology" or "creation spirituality," these reflections have suggested that such a description would be misleading because it is one-sided. For the intent cannot be to eclipse the drama of redemption with a more primordial one of creation, or even more outrageously, to presume that we might be able to recover that original order, for ourselves or our world, by our own efforts in "new age" fashion. The point is rather to begin to see how the redemptive drama, both in its goal (restoring the original order) and its means (suffering the effects of sin), is linked stereoscopically with the original order of creation, in a dual focus which will offer us a picture of our relationship with God as ennobling as it is humbling. In the context of Christian

---

[27] *Ibid.*, p. 437. See J. M. DiNoia, O.P., *The Diversity of Religions* (Washington DC: Catholic University of America Press, 1993) for a careful delineation of the way in which a focus on salvation can skew our discussion of "other religions."
[28] McDade (note 3), p. 437.

theological reflection, this might be dubbed a "Keplerian revolution," to remind us that it was Kepler's substitution of an ellipse (with twin foci) for a circle which allowed Copernicus' model of the solar system to meet the celestial observations in an elegant (and hence workable) fashion. The "revolution" involved replacing Aristotle's predilection for the "perfect motion" of the circle with an elliptical path.

Proceeding in this way, tensions between human and divine freedom will tend to dissolve before our eyes, as our own activities will become transfigured before us. Yet all this will take place in the Word through whom the universe was made, and the Spirit of Jesus in whom it has been and is being transformed. What we call that stereoscopic perspective remains to be seen; it cannot be called "creation-centered" except by a corrective mode of speech which reminds us that we are *adding* that other focus to our reflections. In that sense, it cannot simply be called "Christian" either, since much of what passes for Christian modes of reflection eclipses creation to showcase redemption. That is why an interfaith perspective will prove crucial to our efforts to attain this stereoscopic view.[29] It may also seem strange that we have focused principally on the first two articles of the Christian creed, apparently neglecting the third. Where does the Holy Spirit *fit* in all of this? Yet asking the question in that way already suggests an answer. Recalling Rahner's formula offering the focus of Christian theology – "the divinization of the world through the Spirit of God, within which incarnation and redemption arise as inner moments" – one could see that the entire process which our elliptical theological task seeks to articulate is carried on by the Spirit and in the Spirit. For the Spirit is ever the Spirit of Jesus, whose intent to restore God's original peace will be effected through the actions of his followers, that is, of those animated by the Spirit. So a theological effort which turns about the twin foci of creation and redemption does not for that reason overlook the Spirit; it is rather the Spirit who transforms such reflection into practice to give the theological inquiry its proper focus.

---

[29] See the concluding reflections in my *Freedom and Creation* (note 4), pp. 162–83, for some speculative suggestions along these lines.

Chapter 16

ASSESSING STATEMENTS OF FAITH: AUGUSTINE AND ETTY HILLESUM

In assessing the truth of statements of faith, we ought not to approach them as though they offer explanation, but rather for what they are: convictions. Convictions that there is a sense to it all; not that *we* can make sense of it all. What fuels that conviction is one's growing capacity to use a language which helps us progressively gain our bearings in the midst of a journey. (The image of *journey* comes quite naturally to Jews, Christians, or Muslims – where the exodus, Jesus' "setting his face towards Jerusalem" (Lk 9:51), or the *hegira* and the *hajj* offer ready paradigms for the faithful.) Unlike an "explanatory framework," this language is one into which we are called to enter if we would allow our life to become a journey. And the promise of undertaking such a journey is not only sense or direction for our lives, but sense for it all.

So the communal and cosmic dimensions are paramount, though accenting the first can threaten the scope of the promise by restricting it to a faith-community, while cosmic assertions tempt us to mistake faith-assertions for explanations. We can be helped to avoid both misreadings by focusing on the author who is called upon to make sense of his or her life, and the manner in which it must done, namely, to tell his or her story. So our guides will be two: one classical and the other contemporary, a man and a woman, a Christian and a Jew: Aurelius Augustine and Etty Hillesum. The first is a powerful figure of history, a prolific author and ecclesiastical leader, loved and maligned for the considerable influence his long life and manifold writings exerted. The second is known only to those whom her recently published diaries and letters have made privy to her truncated life: a victim of genocide yet the contributor of a vision that carries us well beyond "victimhood." It is in fact their similarities – as seekers and finders – which this essay shall explore; the differences in their faith communities only enhancing that project.

Augustine opens his *Confessions* asserting:

> Man is one of your creatures, Lord, and his instinct is to praise you. . . .
> The thought of you stirs him so deeply that he cannot be content unless
> he praises you, because you made us for yourself and our hearts find no
> peace until they rest in you.[1]

These words begin a reflective introduction of five short chapters to a
work which offered the West a paradigm for autobiography. Yet it differs
from more modern autobiographies in its form of address and its attribu-
tion of agency. It frequently shifts from first to second person, as its author
is moved to praise, since the narrative activity of remembering is less preoccupied with what happened to A. and how A. negotiated it than with
(1) identifying the sources of power and once located, (2) learning
how to receive from that source. If "autobiography," like "autonomy,"
suggests to us a self centered on itself, Augustine's journey delivers a self
related to its source and so ordered in itself – since to-be-related to
one's source and goal *is* to be properly ordered with oneself. Seeking and
receiving are reciprocally related, since recognizing *what* and *who* that
source is orients one to the proper ways to receive from it.

If the self Augustine articulates is not autonomous but related, the form
of his articulation is dialogic. How are the two – form and substance –
related? My interpretative hypothesis asks us to attend to three factors,
each features of the work. The first is a simple reminder that introduc-
tions are written once we have finished composing, for only then can we
confidently say where we wish to go. So the assertion which introduces
the narrative – a second-person assertion at that – is best thought of as
the fruit of the efforts required to articulate his journey of relating. And
those efforts – my second premise – comprise an experiment: that is, an
account of a life becomes an "experiment in truth," while the narrative
mode of accounting enhances the experiment by articulating it for us.
Finally, the response of God to Augustine's sustained yet fitful outreach is
exhibited in the life itself – that is, in what God accomplished in him by
way of right ordering. Book 10 offers a current "progress report" on that
transformation replete with Augustine's disappointment at its incomplete-
ness, yet the fact of what has been accomplished encourages him to move
beyond his own narrative to the cosmic commentary of Books 11–13
thereby offering the ground for his opening assertion: "Man is one of
your creatures, Lord, and his instinct is to praise you."

---

[1]   Saint Augustine, *Confessions*, trans. R. S. Pine-Coffin (Baltimore: Penguin, 1961), 1.1.

So the propriety of the dialogic form of the narrative-recollection which is the *Confessions* is corroborated as the reality of each partner comes more into evidence through exercises in dialogue: Augustine speaking, God working. What is more, each one is seen to be dialogic in nature: with God, the dialogue is reflected more in God's interaction with creation than within divinity itself (as in his *de Trinitate*); with Augustine, it is exhibited primarily in communal exchange with friends, with Monica, and with his son.[2] This feature of his narrative, notably evident after he leaves Africa for Italy, reminds us forcibly that this "autobiography" does not render an "autonomous individual" but a person-in-community.[3]

The character of that community proves to be the crucial middle term in the verification which Augustine seeks in trying to identify accurately the source of right order, capable of restoring himself and the world to its original ordering. For he comes to see how participating in such a community offers the most promising hope for attaining an ordered self, as its teachings offer a paradigm for assessing alternative accounts of world order. (Hence the apt observation of readers who have seen in this work the itinerary of a journey towards "joining the church.") To ask what kind of a community it is which he embraces (and by which he *is* embraced), however, is not to be directed to historical "proofs" but to be directed to ask: what sort of life does it exhibit? The response, especially of Book 8, is that it generates saints: exemplary individuals who exhibit an enviable ordering in their lives.[4] The community can be said to generate them, since we find this ordering in people who identify themselves as followers of Jesus. It is an ordering, moreover, which exemplifies the best of human nature, yet is all too seldom exemplified in individual human beings. So they testify to the presence and activity of the original orderer of the world, as well as to the further fact that individuals can relate to such a One: "You made us for yourself and our hearts find no peace until they rest in you."

---

[2] The relation with his long-term mistress is notoriously more problematic. His most inadvertent, and so most authentic, confession may be the indirect discourse he employs to relate how "the woman with whom I had been living was torn from my side as an obstacle to my marriage." Although he goes on to acknowledge that "this was a blow which crushed my heart to bleeding, because I loved her dearly" (6.15), does the initial "was torn" represent our usual ruse to avoid responsibility in the matter?

[3] I am indebted to an unpublished study by my colleague Frederick J. Crosson: "Cicero and Augustine," delivered at a colloquium at Notre Dame, 1985.

[4] One is reminded of the thesis developed by Patrick Sherry in *Spirits, Saints and Immortality* (London: Macmillan, 1984): "that the *absence* of such holy people over time could put a community's claims to question."

So much for the structure of the *Confessions*; how does it work? That, of course, is what the narrative is designed to show, in his case. What about us? What if our story – yours or mine – does not so conclude? Is that not the way with stories, in principle? They are not "universalizable." Or are there certain ones which are paradigmatic for the rest of us? Archetypal even, so that we cannot escape incorporation into their plot? These would be "everyman" stories, enlightening us regarding our origins and our destiny. And even if we would admit such stories, would Augustine's *Confessions* be among them? Can his story be archetypal, however much some of us would like it to be? Here it is useful to contrast the direction Augustine's journey took with a path it could have taken, at the penultimate milestone of the journey towards discovery. His is not an account, as the story of his Platonist guides would be, of the necessary ascent of a human soul to its inherent perfection, impeded only by willful inattention or blindness.[5] It rather spells out a free response to an invitation freely offered to each person and avowedly to all, yet the story unfolds into a willing response seen as contained within a dynamic initiated by the Other.

The narrative-recollection as Augustine offers it, then, may be paradigmatic but is not archetypal. That is, it can help to structure your story, but it cannot be said to structure it inescapably. So it is not only experimental in Augustine's case; it is inherently experimental: try it on, to see whether your story can be modeled upon it. The *promise* is that yours will be able so to be modeled, if you try. . . . The incentive lies in your observation that those who have, and are otherwise like you, exhibit an enviable ordering, so why not try? At least, those who participate in the same community as Augustine did hope that incentive is present.

If that is all we can glean from this exercise with Augustine, however, to what end? There seems to be little, if anything, new here. What has our study of the form and function of Augustine's *Confessions* succeeded in showing? Two things, I shall suggest, which may be more therapeutic than startling. The first regards the indispensability of narrative, especially first-person narrative, in framing an account of an invitation offered freely so that it elicits a willing response. Any other form of discourse, it seems, will tend to eclipse the free dynamic of invitation and response in favor of a mode of explanation. The second is a corollary of the first: the cen-

---

[5]   On the character of "the Platonists" whom Augustine mentions, and their role in his itinerary, see the chapter so titled in Peter Brown, *Augustine of Hippo* (Berkeley CA: University of California Press, 1968).

trality of friendship and of dialogue in human life, opening one up to the possibility, indeed the fact of such an exchange with the one source of all. The shorthand expression for such a relationship with God is "grace," and the contrast which Augustine finds between his Platonist guides and those who witness faith in Jesus as the word of God, epitomized in the tonal differences between Books 7 and 8 of the *Confessions*, displays the novelty which he discovers *grace* to be. And the fruit of that new power in his personal life is a transformed vision of the world itself, where all things have "the same message to tell, if only we can hear it, and their message is this: We did not make ourselves, but [the One] who abides forever made us."[6] Having negotiated the journey he recounts, Augustine is now able to hear this response from the things whose beauty he admires.[7]

A similar refrain, rooted more explicitly in her own feelings, yet no less cosmic in scope and import, punctuates the diaries and letters of Etty Hillesum.[8] Less structured than Augustine's self-conscious "confessions," these spontaneously reflective entries document a person seeking to center and order her life, who one day finds herself "forced to the ground by something stronger than myself. . . . I suddenly went down on my knees in the middle of this large room . . . almost automatically."[9] And the consequences of that action, in the context of her interaction with Julius Spier, her psychoanalyst and intimate friend, lead her inner life to unfold to the point where she can say – in the midst of the misery of Westerbork, a staging area for transport to Auschwitz – "time and again it soars straight from my heart – I can't help it, that's just the way it is, like some elementary force – the feeling that life is glorious and magnificent."[10] Nor is that feeling ephemeral, but a power making her over from within: "[As] the threat grows ever greater, and terror increases from day to day, I draw prayer round me like a dark protective wall, . . . and then step outside again, calmer and stronger . . ."[11] "It always spreads from the inside outwards with me . . ."[12] This courage is displayed by one who confesses: "I

---

[6]   *Confessions* (note 1), 9.10.
[7]   *Ibid.*, 10.6.
[8]   Etty Hillesum, *An Interrupted Life* (New York: Simon and Schuster, 1985) and more recently, *Letters from Westerbork* (New York: Pantheon, 1987); now combined in a single edition: New York: Henry Holt, 1996.
[9]   *Ibid.*, p. 76.
[10] *Ibid.*, p. 247.
[11] *Ibid.*, p. 147.
[12] *Ibid.*, p. 146.

have never been able to 'do' anything; I can only let things take their course and if need be suffer."[13] An apt remark from a woman who sought therapy shortly after her twenty-seventh birthday, sensing a void in herself and her relationships: "I am . . . just about seasoned enough I should think to be counted among the better lovers, and love does indeed suit me to perfection, and yet . . . deep inside me something is still locked away."[14]

So runs the opening paragraph of her diaries, plausibly the task given her by the man whom she had sought out, Julius Spier, as a catalyst to their inner work. What follows can usefully be divided into three roughly even parts: her discovery of herself through the relationship with Spier which ensues,[15] a period of preparation for serving others,[16] and the actual crafting of her life as gift.[17] The final phase begins at this point where all illusions are torn away: "What is at stake is our impending destruction and annihilation,"[18] and is focused by the death of the guide whom she had come to love: "You taught me to speak the name of God without embarrassment. You were the mediator . . . and now . . . my path leads straight to God. . . . And I shall be the mediator for any other soul I can reach."[19]

These remarks were written after she had volunteered to accompany the first group of Jews being sent to Westerbork. Yet they are rooted in the second, preparatory phase, as she discovers, encountering a former lover, that "everything is no longer pure chance . . . an exciting adventure. Instead I have the feeling that I have a destiny, in which the events are strung significantly together."[20] Less than two months later she will assert: "I have matured enough to assume my 'destiny,' to cease living an accidental life."[21] What happens in her happens in a scant two-and-a-half years as the restrictive legislation bars "Jews from the paths and the open country [yet] I find life beautiful and I feel free. The sky within me is as wide as the one stretching above my head. I believe in God and I believe in man and I can say so without embarrassment."[22]

It is at the end of this period that she begins to formulate expressly theological dicta, in the face of "the latest news . . . that all Jews will be transported out of Holland . . . to Poland:"

[13] *Ibid.*, p. 249.
[14] *Ibid.*, p. 1.
[15] *Ibid.*, pp. 1–82.
[16] *Ibid.*, pp. 82–160.
[17] *Ibid.*, pp. 160–243.
[18] *Ibid.*, p. 160.
[19] *Ibid.*, pp. 209–10.
[20] *Ibid.*, p. 91.
[21] *Ibid.*, p. 138.
[22] *Ibid.*, p. 151.

And yet I don't think life is meaningless. And God is not accountable to us for the senseless harm we cause one another. We are accountable to Him! I have already died a thousand deaths in a thousand concentration camps. . . . And yet I find life beautiful and meaningful. From minute to minute.[23]

This capacity for gratitude and praise which she finds within herself moves her in this period of formation beyond humiliation or hate to a newfound peace and freedom: "Despite all the suffering and injustice I cannot hate others."[24] "One day I shall surely be able to say to Ilse Blumenthal, 'Do not relieve your feelings through hatred, do not seek to be avenged on all German mothers. . . . Give your sorrow all the space and shelter in yourself that is its due . . . then you may truly say: 'Life is beautiful and so rich . . . that it makes you want to believe in God.'"[25]

Yet the God in whom Etty will come to believe is one to whom she introduces us in an entry which takes the form of a prayer:

Dear God, these are anxious times . . . but one thing is becoming increasingly clear to me: that you cannot help us, that we must help you to help ourselves . . . Alas, there doesn't seem to be much You Yourself can do about our circumstances, our lives. Neither do I hold you responsible. You cannot help us but we must help You and defend your dwelling place inside us to the last.[26]

The responsibility she feels is to what has happened within her, and so to the world to which she has come to relate with all that she has. As she writes from Westerbork, in the epilogue to the edition of her diaries: "I see more and more that love for all our neighbors . . . must take pride of place over love for one's nearest and dearest."[27] The reason is offered in a prayer from her diary which she shares with her friend Tide:

You have made me so rich, oh God, please let me share out Your beauty with open hands. My life has become an uninterrupted dialogue with You, oh God, one great dialogue.[28]

So the pattern of Augustine's *Confessions* is realized anew: the ability of each partner comes more into evidence through exercises in dialogue – Etty recording what God is accomplishing in her. In fact, what gives her

23 *Ibid.*, p. 157.
24 *Ibid.*, p. 89.
25 *Ibid.*, pp. 100–1.
26 *Ibid.*, pp. 186–7.
27 *Ibid.*, p. 251.
28 *Ibid.*, p. 255.

account its authenticity is not only what she finds herself able to do – in the midst of indescribable misery[29] – but that her capacities come as a continual surprise to herself. Just as Augustine's crafted narrative offered a confession of praise to the One who brought order out of his disorder, so Etty Hillesum's more spontaneous diaries celebrate the unlocking of "what is truly essential, and deep inside me,"[30] and the consequent transformation of a "miserable, frightened creature"[31] into a "soul . . . forged out of fire and rock crystal."[32] A soul, moreover, shaped by "an uninterrupted dialogue" which allowed her to make us the gift of her "interrupted life."

Some "hermeneutical" remarks would seem in order, for it is the life and deeds of someone like Etty which offer us a key to understanding what it is she says, as well as remarking on the authenticity of the relationships which she recounts. Her transformation is palpable to us as well as to herself, through the largely transparent medium of personal journals. Augustine, on the contrary, has acquired an immense *persona* over the course of fifteen centuries, and was already enough of a celebrity to need to craft his story with rhetorical skill. Yet *what* he confesses is what Etty celebrates: a real alteration testifying to a real power at work in the world. Each of them is able to identify that power as the source of all that is, Augustine explicitly and Etty by her transformed vision: "It still all comes down to the same thing: life is beautiful. And I believe in God – right in the thick of what people call 'horror.' "[33] And she addresses these words to her friend Jopie, by way of insisting that such a reality is accessible to her as well.

Indeed, what impresses one about Etty's diaries is the precise way in which they articulate a conviction shared by Jew and Christian alike: that life itself, indeed the universe, is a gift. A friend, Klaas, whom she introduces as a "dogged old class fighter" – that is, a confirmed Marxist – was indeed "dismayed and astonished at the same time," and challenged her: "But that – that is nothing but Christianity!" Her response is one we will by now have come to expect: "And I, amused by your confusion, retort quite cooly: 'Yes, Christianity, and why ever not?' "[34] For the historically pockmarked relations between Judaism and Christianity, I believe this

[29] *Ibid.*, p. 245.
[30] *Ibid.*, p. 1.
[31] *Ibid.*, p. 2.
[32] *Ibid.*, p. 241.
[33] *Ibid.*, p. 238.
[34] *Ibid.*, pp. 222–3.

response touches a profound nerve, but for present purposes, let us simply take it that she has hit upon a shared conviction: that life is a gift.[35] That will suffice to allow us some fruitful reflections on the way in which such convictions function in transforming lives.

If one focuses on "the experience itself" – whatever that might be – of transformation, then the accounts may be contingently related to what it is that we cannot help but remark in the person before us. But when we are privileged enough to have access to the narrative account, we come to appreciate how it is that these narratives are shaped by sets of convictions which can otherwise be expressed as doctrines of specific religious traditions. And correlatively, the fact that doctrines shape narratives reminds us that they do not play a theoretical but a *grammatical* role in the lives of the faithful.[36] They do not, in short, offer explanatory access to a reality behind the One to whom individuals like Etty or Augustine respond, but rather provide the manner in which their respective responses offer us access to the reality revealed in their transformations.

Doctrine, in other words, both comes to life and is embodied in the response of those whom we cannot but recognize to be saints. It is obvious enough how doctrine "comes to life" there; how can we say that it is *embodied* in such lives? The argument here is at once simple and subtle. It turns on the fact that we will always be forced to speak of religious matters in a language which is inherently analogous. The term "transformation" offers a handy example. Any formula we give for it will contain terms of a like quality – terms whose "open texture" or "systematic ambiguity" will demand that we offer an example to establish our "frame of reference" or "benchmark" usage.[37] And it is precisely individuals which provide the living examples to anchor our usage – a commonplace yet remarkable situation which accounts for the fact that we can recognize such exemplary individuals without always being able to *say* what it is that makes them such. Yet their narrative accounts, when available, can be found to be structured in such a way as to be shaped by what we other-

[35] It is illustrative to observe the use to which Marc Ellis puts these diaries in his *Toward a Jewish Theology of Liberation* (Maryknoll NY: Orbis, 1987), pp. 96–102. For an illuminating account of convictions, see James McClendon and James Smith, *Understanding Religious Convictions* (Notre Dame IN: University of Notre Dame Press, 1975).

[36] A synoptic exploration of this sense of doctrine has been fruitfully carried out by George Lindbeck in his *Nature of Doctrine* (Philadelphia PA: Westminster, 1985).

[37] See most recently James Ross, *Portraying Analogy* (Cambridge: Cambridge University Press, 1982), and for the history of these matters my *Analogy and Philosophical Language* (New Haven CT: Yale University Press, 1973), as well as my "Argument in Theology: Analogy and Narrative," in Carl A. Raschke, ed., *New Dimensions in Philosophical Theology* (JAAR Thematic Studies 49/1, 1982), pp. 37–52.

wise call doctrinal statements. That is the way in which their lives embody doctrine.

What, then, are we to do with the further fact that distinct lives may embody diverse doctrines, and yet each exhibit a comparable transformation? (We may even presume that their respective accounts can be shown to embody different doctrinal positions.) Celebrate it, I contend, for so far we have no way of placing ourselves in the position of comparing or ranking religious traditions. I am not pontificating, insisting that we cannot do so; in fact, I suspect that we must. I am only remarking that we are not *yet* in a position to do so. We must acquire a set of intellectual skills allowing us to compare cultural frameworks. In fact, nothing, so effectively displays the cultural particularity of Christianity as the emergence of a post-colonial world, in which Western Christians found themselves facing other religious traditions yet were no longer able to presume an accustomed superiority.

Karl Rahner, in a prescient lecture published in 1979, adduced cumulative evidence to propose 1970 as a threshold comparable to that marked by the destruction of the temple in Jerusalem in 70 – the date usually associated with the parting of the ways between Jews and Christians.[38] Rahner shows how these two symbolic dates each mark a theological threshold, in which questions arise which outstrip the resources of the theologies of the day to handle. Indeed, Paul's struggles to make room for an emerging Hellenic community of believers without forfeiting his own heritage underscores Rahner's thesis. Whenever subsequent writers sought to attenuate that struggle by offering a more plausible account, it turned out invariably that "new" covenant replaced the "old," betraying both Jews and Christians, since Jews were thereby denied any theological *lebensraum* and Christians deprived of their shaping heritage. So if we have been unable to offer an undialectical account of that relationship, how should we expect to be ready to confront the current radical religious and cultural diversity (or pluralism, if you will, but that is the benign term)? Yet Rahner's essay does offer both solace and direction: solace because we can appreciate ourselves to be standing in a liminal situation and realize that we will probably be posing the questions in an inadequate manner; direction, in that his periodization reminds us that the western European phase of Christianity is over.

Yet how are we to respond conceptually to such novelty? By reminding ourselves, I would suggest, that responses are structured by traditions

---

[38] Karl Rahner, "Towards a Fundamental Interpretation of Vatican II," in *Theological Studies* 40 (1979), pp. 716–27.

whose doctrinal patterns provide the grammar of the response. Insofar as those doctrinal patterns shape and give direction to a lived response so that it issues in an authentic transformation, then we must acknowledge them to be true: as the aim and correlative skills of an archer allow his arrow to find its mark. This strategy keeps us from directly comparing statements lifted out of different traditions, and reminds us that such statements — if they be religious statements — subserve that transforming relationship which we have noted in Etty and Augustine. Yet *within* each functioning tradition, there will be a set of such shaping beliefs or doctrines, the truth of which will (or will not) be exhibited in the life of the community, and especially in its notable exemplars. And where those exemplary individuals tell their story, as Augustine and Etty have, astute critics will be able to discern the doctrinal patterns which give their narratives a structure distinctive to the community in which they partake. Such is the grammar of this matter: lives are rendered in narratives which display a structure. We are compelled by the lives, inspired and illuminated by the narratives, and guided by what we can discover of their structure.

What have we given up, in trying to respond to the new situation of religious and cultural diversity? *Not* the "truth claims" of particular religious traditions, but rather a presumptive way of ranking them. *Not* the certainty which Newman attributes to faith, whereby we freely give "real assent" to what is offered us as liberating and life-giving, but a monocultural attitude of *certainty* in which we know that we are right.[39] What we have recovered is an attitude of critical modesty towards our modes of expression, which could help us recover a similar modesty displayed by medieval thinkers, and use it to profit from a situation which appears so unsettling. We have long overlooked just how intercultural and interreligious the medieval world really was.[40] I am referring to Aquinas' account of religious language, in which he used a sophisticated semantics to clarify and extend Moses Maimonides' views on attributing perfections to divinity. The portion of that account pertinent here is Aquinas' insistence that phrases like "God is just" can be said properly but imperfectly of divinity.[41] By exploring how expressions might "imperfectly signify" divinity,

[39] John Henry Newman, *An Essay in Aid of a Grammar of Assent* (Notre Dame IN: University of Notre Dame Press, 1979), with excellent introduction by Nicholas Lash.
[40] See my recent *Knowing the Unknowable God: Ibn Sina, Maimonides, and Aquinas* (Notre Dame IN: University of Notre Dame Press, 1986), as well as "Aquinas and Maimonides: A Conversation about Proper Speech," in *Immanuel* 16 (1983), pp. 70–83.
[41] See Herbert McCabe's appendix, "Signifying Imperfectly," in *Summa Theologiae* 1.12–13 (*Knowing and Naming God*) (New York: McGraw-Hill, 1964).

we could be led to see how one tradition can be complemented by another, and so use the encounter with alternative conceptualities to enrich its own. That is, I believe, the sense of Etty's cool retort: "Yes, Christianity, and why ever not?" Far from a call to syncretism, that response appreciates the particular power of the gospels and appropriates them to her situation. These complementarities work quite well in practice, as the faithful in distinct traditions find themselves drawn to incorporate prayer patterns from one another, much as Jung remarked (in 1948) in reference to a division within western European Christianity, that every cultured European he knew was either a Catholic Protestant or a Protestant Catholic.[42]

But what of that further assessment, to which we seem inevitably drawn, which would compare traditions by ranking them? I have already noted that we are not yet in a position to do that. I emphasize the "yet" not because I believe we may one day be able to, but to remind us how unskilled we are in comparing across cultural and conceptual frameworks. The immediate alternative of accepting the picture of religious traditions as several ways up one mountain is attractive but begs the central question by incorporating an answer. It is a useful antidote, of course, to the need for pre-emptive certainty, as is our strategy of locating doctrines in the grammar which structures narrative accounts of personal transformation. I find Wilfrid Cantwell Smith's programmatic suggestions in his *Towards a World Theology* helpful, as pointing to ways in which we could develop the skills required for fruitful comparative study: a seminar composed of articulate believers from distinct traditions, in which communication would be deemed to be achieved when each person could understand the other's account as one in which he or she could plausibly participate.[43] Such exercises, carried out regarding specific doctrines-cum-practices, might well be able to develop, in those participating, skills of comparative assessment. We might discover, for example, that the "distinction" of God from the world is more ably secured in a tradition which was also forced to articulate how two natures functioned in one person (Christ) than in the other two faiths which avow creation.[44] Short of such

[42]   C. G. Jung, *Psychology of the Transference* (Princeton NJ: Princeton University Press, 1966), p. 30.
[43]   Wilfred Cantwell Smith, *Towards a World Theology* (Philadelphia PA: Westminster, 1981), pp. 98–101.
[44]   Robert Sokolowski develops this point in his The *God of Faith and Reason* (Notre Dame IN: University of Notre Dame Press, 1982/Washington, DC: Catholic University of America Press, 1995), pp. 31–40.

live encounters, however, one fears especially that we in the West will not be sufficiently aware of the threshold on which we stand, inquiring into our own traditions (in the spirit of "faith seeking understanding") as they now face other major religious traditions with palpable histories of holiness.

INDEX